T0360744

MONEY AND EMPIRE

Charles Kindleberger ranks as one of the twentieth century's best known and most influential international economists. This book traces the evolution of his thinking in the context of a "key-currency" approach to the rise of the dollar system, here revealed as the indispensable framework for global economic development since World War II. Unlike most of his colleagues, Kindleberger was deeply interested in history, and his economics brimmed with real people and institutional details. His research at the New York Fed and BIS during the Great Depression, his wartime intelligence work, and his role in administering the Marshall Plan gave him deep insight into how the international financial system really operated. A biography of both the dollar and a man, this book is also the story of the development of ideas about how money works. It throws revealing light on the underlying economic forces and political obstacles shaping our globalized world.

Perry Mehrling is Professor of International Political Economy at Boston University.

STUDIES IN NEW ECONOMIC THINKING

The 2008 financial crisis pointed to problems in economic theory that require more than just big data to solve. INET's series in New Economic Thinking exists to ensure that innovative work that advances economics and better integrates it with other social sciences and the study of history and institutions can reach a broad audience in a timely way.

MONEY AND EMPIRE

Charles P. Kindleberger and the Dollar System

Perry Mehrling

Boston University

CAMBRIDGE
UNIVERSITY PRESS

CAMBRIDGE
UNIVERSITY PRESS

University Printing House, Cambridge CB2 8BS, United Kingdom

One Liberty Plaza, 20th Floor, New York, NY 10006, USA

477 Williamstown Road, Port Melbourne, VIC 3207, Australia

314–321, 3rd Floor, Plot 3, Splendor Forum, Jasola District Centre,
New Delhi – 110025, India

103 Penang Road, #05–06/07, Visioncrest Commercial, Singapore 238467

Cambridge University Press is part of the University of Cambridge.

It furthers the University's mission by disseminating knowledge in the pursuit of
education, learning, and research at the highest international levels of excellence.

www.cambridge.org
Information on this title: www.cambridge.org/9781009158572
DOI: 10.1017/9781009158589

First published 2022

A catalogue record for this publication is available from the British Library.

Library of Congress Cataloging-in-Publication Data
Names: Mehrling, Perry, author.
Title: Money and empire : Charles P. Kindleberger and the dollar system / Perry
Mehrling, Boston University.
Description: Cambridge, United Kingdom ; New York, NY : Cambridge University
Press, 2021. | Series: Studies in new economic thinking | Includes bibliographical
references and index.
Identifiers: LCCN 2021056132 (print) | LCCN 2021056133 (ebook) | ISBN
9781009158572 (hardback) | ISBN 9781009158589 (ebook)
Subjects: LCSH: Kindleberger, Charles P., 1910–2003. | Monetary policy – United
States. | United States. Federal Reserve Board. | Dollar.
Classification: LCC HG501 .M57 2021 (print) | LCC HG501 (ebook) | DDC 332.4/
973–dc23/eng/20211203
LC record available at https://lccn.loc.gov/2021056132
LC ebook record available at https://lccn.loc.gov/2021056133

ISBN 978-1-009-15857-2 Hardback

For my teachers and students
(from whom I also learned)

Contents

Preface

This book started out as a biography of the dollar, not of a man. It was intended to be an international version of the story I had told in *The New Lombard Street: How the Fed Became the Dealer of Last Resort* (2011). That book was a biography of the Fed, as seen through the analytical lens of the "money view," an approach to monetary theory that I had been developing in the classroom for the previous decade. The new project was supposed to extend the money view to a theory of foreign exchange and the international monetary system, and in doing so would enable the story of the emerging market-based credit system to encompass the story of financial globalization and the spreading dollar system. As in the previous book, I planned a story of institutional development as context for a story of economic thought development – this time international rather than domestic. Fortunately for me, my plan attracted support from the initial grant round of the fledgling Institute for New Economic Thinking (INET), which I gratefully acknowledge. However, in the first year the project began to change shape, and I decided not to request renewal.

As I reconstruct my process today, the shift in focus began with work I had been doing on the history of monetary economics at MIT.[1] Spending a few days in the Modigliani Papers at Duke University in January 2011, I found extensive correspondence with Charles P. Kindleberger about international monetary reform, and that is where the seed for the present book was planted. Subsequent discovery of the extensive Kindleberger Papers at MIT made me realize that there

---

[1] Mehrling (2014).

was enough material on which to hang an entire book, just as I had previously hung my history of financial economics on the life of Fischer Black.[2]

It should be noted for the record that I did not abandon the original project, but rather published its central chapters in individual papers rather than a full book, most importantly "Essential Hybridity: A Money View of FX."[3] With my previous commitment thus cleared, in the summer of 2013 I spent a month in the Kindleberger Papers at MIT and then, in January 2014, a week in the Kindleberger Papers at the Truman Library, with the result that by February 2014 I was able to construct a plausible chapter outline for the new book. By September 2015, this new conception of the project attracted renewed support from INET.

Still, it took me another six years to complete the book, which is quite a bit slower than my previous books, because of other projects I was working on. The launch of *New Lombard Street* (2011) brought unexpected demand for follow-ups of various kinds, which I felt obliged to supply. Then, in April 2012, INET asked me to organize a student gathering parallel to the INET Plenary in Berlin, which turned out to be the launch of what would become INET's Young Scholars Initiative. Even more, in Fall 2012, INET filmed my Money and Banking course, and over the next year I worked to edit the film into a MOOC (Massive Open Online Course) that launched on Coursera in Fall 2013. In January 2017, just as I was starting to fill in the outline of the new book, Boston University approached me about possibly shifting my academic base and I accepted, effective January 2018. The transition proved more disruptive than I anticipated. A thirty-year accumulation of files and books is not easy to shift, even less a thirty-year pattern of teaching and research, not to mention life. That accounts for the slow progress, but I wish to assert for the record that it was definitely worth it. I had hoped to find in The Pardee School of Global Studies the supportive academic home that I needed to complete the book, and so it proved to be, for which I am eternally grateful.

Starting in 2018, I began to make rapid progress, taking the opportunity to present each chapter for public feedback as it was completed. In

---

[2] Mehrling (2005).   [3] Mehrling (2013). Also Bernes et al. (2014) and Mehrling (2015).

this vein, my schedule included talks at the Kennedy School, Credit Suisse, the European Society for the History of Economic Thought, the Eastern Economic Association, Marist College, Duke University, and multiple presentations at my new academic home. For me this was a new way of working, since all my previous books had been produced essentially in isolation and under tremendous time pressure, with very little in the way of institutional support. A pleasant surprise, I found that I enjoyed this new way of working, and that is the final reason for my slow progress. For the first time in my life, I have had time to really enjoy the process of writing, and indeed even to indulge in some rewriting! I hope and trust that the result is a better book.

At INET, my main debt has been to Rob Johnson for his unwavering support over the last decade, his judgment perhaps distorted by lasting affection for Kindleberger, a key influence on his own early education as an economist. Tom Ferguson has been an invaluable reader and critic, especially of the later chapters, which have been immeasurably improved by my attempt to rise to his standard. I should also mention prominently Jay Pocklington, whose work to build the Young Scholars Initiative not only freed up my own time, but, even more important, created the intellectual community that I came to envision as the concrete audience for the words I was putting on paper. His periodic requests for progress reports on the book, starting in January 2015 with a talk to the YSI Economic History Workshop, provided much-needed stimulus to put words into PowerPoints, as preliminary to actual chapters. It was also Jay who arranged for YSI intern Mariam Tabatadze to serve as my research assistant for a while, gathering together the transcripts of Kindleberger's extensive Congressional testimony.

Second only to INET, I owe a debt to the Kindleberger family, especially Sally Kindleberger, nearby in Lincoln, Massachusetts, who opened the family archive to me, but also, farther afield, Charles P. Kindleberger III (now deceased) and Elizabeth Randall Kindleberger, who provided critical insight on the private life. I see in my notes that my first contact with Sally was July 2013, and I take this opportunity to apologize to the family for the long delay bringing this project to fruition. I don't work as fast as their father, obviously, perhaps suffering from a perfectionist streak of which he would definitely have disapproved.

Kindleberger wrote a lot for publication, but I have found the unpublished record invaluable for teasing out the underlying life story that brings the published work to life. In addition to MIT and the Truman Library, I thank archivists at the Kent School, the Jamestown Historical Society, the University of Pennsylvania, and Bucknell University. Special thanks are due to MIT archivist Myles Crowley who went beyond the call of duty when the pandemic closed the archive, providing Zoom access to critical documents needed to complete the book. Financial support from the Truman Library for my week there is gratefully acknowledged.

Along the way, I have accumulated additional debts to numerous individuals: Bob Solow, Stephen Magee, Ron Findlay, Hossein Askari, Bob McCauley, David Warsh, Deirdre McCloskey, Bob Pollin, and Peter Johns. Also, to the readers who saved me from error and helped me to sharpen my argument: Andre Burgstaller, Kevin Gallagher, Vivien Schmidt, Erik Goldstein, Maria Cecilia Schweinberger, Steffen Murau, Anush Kapadia, Michael Beall, Yakov Feygin, Frederick V. Hermann, Asgeir Torfason, Celine Tcheng, Eric Monnet, Muriel Dalpont, Bob Dimand, and Catherine Schenk. In the final stages of manuscript preparation, Andrew Grafton served as research assistant, checking quotes and references with a fresh eye.

Finally, as always, this book would not have been possible without the constant and patient support of my wife Judy. I've lost track of the number of times I assured her that there were only six months to go, though I insist that each time I believed it. In my defense, repeatedly I found that there was more to the story than I had anticipated, and repeatedly I was grateful that I was able to take the time to pursue the story where it led.

Introduction

HE TITLE OF THIS BOOK IS INTENDED AS HOMAGE TO MARCELLO DE Cecco's classic *Money and Empire, The International Gold Standard, 1890–1914* (1974). In de Cecco's story, the pound sterling is global money, managed by the Bank of England; borrowers and lenders from all over the world find each other in the money and capital markets of the City of London; and the British Empire is ruled, directly and indirectly, by elite graduates of Oxford and Cambridge operating out of Whitehall. As the dates of his book suggest, this sterling system came to an end with World War I, whereupon construction of the dollar system that would replace it began, bit by bit.

The present book tells the story of that construction. In my story, the dollar is global money managed by the Federal Reserve; borrowers and lenders find each other in the money and capital markets of New York; and global rule is outsourced to a variety of multilateral institutions and multinational corporations staffed by elite graduates of Harvard and Yale. For the dollar system, the myth of the United Nations plays the same role that the myth of the gold standard played for the sterling system, decorously veiling the political reality of dollar rule.

In a departure from de Cecco, the present book tells its story through the life and times of a single individual, Charles P. Kindleberger (1910–2003). It is in effect a Bildungsroman in which the development of the man parallels the development of the dollar system he devoted his life to understanding and advancing. As Professor of International Economics at MIT from 1948 to 1976, and author of the best-selling *International Economics* textbook (1953, 1958, 1963, 1968, 1973), he taught cosmopolitanism to

1

a world riven with primitive nationalist instinct, continuing with unflagging energy even after official retirement.

For Charlie, the historical task of the emerging dollar system was the economic development of what we now call the Global South, a task requiring long-term capital flow from the Global North. Channels of public capital flow, such as the World Bank that had been established at Bretton Woods, could get things started, but the big money would necessarily come through private channels such as Wall Street and the multinational corporation. And, for that, the crucial infrastructure was the international monetary system.

From H. Parker Willis, his teacher at Columbia University, Charlie learned about the long battle for domestic monetary reform in the United States that finally led to the creation of the Federal Reserve System in 1913, thereby unifying the previously disparate clearing regions into a single system. Here is the origin of Charlie's own lifelong battle for international monetary reform, specifically his ambition to do for the world system what Willis had done for the United States. For Charlie, the economic advantage of a unified international monetary system was clear, and so Darwinian evolution could be depended upon to tend in that direction. But politics was the ever-present obstacle – even more so in a world of separate nation-states than had been the case within a United States of separate economic regions.

Just so, depression and world war sidetracked the course of Darwinian evolution for a while, as individual nation-states retreated to autarky. For a long time, what capital flowed between nations flowed in public channels following political logic, not private channels following commercial logic: Lend-Lease during the War, the Anglo-American loan after the War, and then the Marshall Plan for reconstruction of war-torn Europe. The turning point came only in 1958 when European currencies returned to convertibility and private channels began to develop in earnest.

From the beginning, the emerging dollar system had its opponents, both outside the United States and inside. Nondollar countries resented what they saw as "exorbitant privilege," while US authorities resented the global responsibility that came with issue of the global money. The three bogeymen of American politics – big government, big finance, and the big wide world – came together in the idea of a global central bank, which US citizens therefore instinctively and viscerally resisted, even as business practice pushed ahead with the construction of the global dollar system as a concrete reality.

Having himself been a central banker from 1936 until 1942 – first at the Federal Reserve Bank of New York, then the Bank for International Settlements, then back at the Board of Governors – Charlie worked to assuage the fears of his fellow citizens, using education as his main weapon. If people understood how the dollar system actually worked, he thought, they would stop trying to destroy it. Having served in the Department of State from 1945 to 1948, first guiding the German reconstruction effort and then coordinating the legislative effort to launch the Marshall Plan, Charlie thought the key was to educate the junior staffers who, in his experience, actually made the policy that their superiors subsequently announced.

But education didn't work. One reason was that his fellow economists were feeding the fears of the politicians. Economists such as Robert Triffin wanted to replace the dollar with a nonnational world currency, and Harry Johnson wanted to replace the Bretton Woods fixed exchange rate system with a flexible exchange rate system. Even Charlie's MIT colleagues, ambitious Keynesians who found in President Kennedy an eager student, were swayed by the arguments of Triffin and Johnson. And educating them was an even harder task, since their professional economic discourse increasingly took the form of mathematical and statistical modelling, a language that Charlie did not speak.

In the end, politics won out and the opponents of the dollar system got their way. In August 1971, President Nixon took the dollar off gold, and in 1973 abandoned any attempt to stabilize the exchange rate. For Charlie, it was a devastating blow: not only the abdication of a crucial responsibility, but probably the end of the dollar system. Roosevelt's decision in 1933 to torpedo the central bankers' attempt to stabilize currencies had doomed the world to Depression. Nixon's decision in 1973 now doomed the world to stagflation, or worse.

Speaking at a colloquy on "The Global Economic Crisis" held at Bucknell University, February 27–March 1, 1975, Charlie took as his theme "The Lessons of 1929–1933 for 1975." His latest book *The World in Depression, 1929–1939* (1973) (hereafter *WID*) had argued that the Depression was fundamentally caused by a failure of world leadership, Britain no longer able to lead, and the United States not yet ready or willing to lead. From this point of view, the present crisis seemed also to be a failure of world leadership, the United States having abdicated in 1971 and no one else yet ready or willing to take its place.

The Bucknell students, however, were having none of it, and after the talk they peppered Charlie with questions about socialist alternatives instead. He should have expected it. The keynote speaker the previous evening had been Paul Sweezy, Charlie's wartime buddy in London when they both worked at the Office of Strategic Services, speaking on the topic "The Crisis of Capitalism." And radical economists from the New School for Social Research and the University of Massachusetts at Amherst had been well-represented in other sessions. Only six months earlier, President Nixon had resigned in order to avoid impeachment and been pardoned by his successor Gerald Ford. Suffice it to say that leadership was a problem within the United States, let alone worldwide.

The next year (1976) was Charlie's last of full-time employment at MIT, having reached the mandatory retirement age of sixty-five. He would continue teaching part-time at MIT for another five years, followed by stints at Brandeis and Middlebury. The point of all this teaching was partly to supplement his meager retirement income, but also, more importantly, to feed Charlie's new research focus – economic history – launched by *Depression* and culminating in the book he would consider his "chef d'oeuvre," *A Financial History of Western Europe* (1984). In retirement, Charlie largely stayed out of policy debate, and mainly just watched while, after the chastening experience with floating exchange rates, amazingly the dollar system got put back together, starting with Paul Volcker's appointment as Fed Chair in 1979 and continuing with the Plaza Accord of 1985.

Charlie did not live to see the Global Financial Crisis of 2007–9, which shook the dollar system to its core, but which resulted ultimately in stabilization of that core with a system of permanent central bank liquidity swaps, and which was then followed by expansion of the dollar system from core to periphery as national champions in the Global South found themselves able to tap global dollar capital markets. Nor did he live to see

4

the Covid Crisis of 2020, which the Fed met with rapid and massive intervention, acting now quite openly as central bank of the world, triple threat bogeyman no more apparently. In the end, Darwinian evolution thus seems to have got us where Charlie predicted after all, though of course it remains to be seen if the politics will hold.

The overall arc of this book follows the vicissitudes of the dollar system, as seen through the eyes of one of its keenest observers. But an important subtheme that also runs throughout concerns exactly why it was that Charlie could see things so clearly that were so opaque to others. A biography of the dollar, this book is also the biography of a man. Interestingly, Charlie wrote his own autobiography *The Life of an Economist* (1991), but it is a disappointingly unreflective and impersonal book, perhaps reflecting the WASP's ingrained reticence to talk about oneself. Most disappointing, there is very little discussion of his work or its larger context, just a chronology. Students and colleagues loved this man, for his wit and charm, for his integrity and responsibility, for his dedication and hard work, but more than one of them read his autobiography and came away disappointed. MIT colleagues admired his economic "intuition," but had no very good idea how he came up with what he did, since his process was so different from theirs.

Fortunately, I have found many other sources to fill in the gaps: a collection of papers at MIT, others at the Truman Library including Charlie's FBI file and the "Interim Biography" that he wrote in an attempt to regain his security clearance lost in the McCarthy witch hunt, family papers including a memoir "A 20th Century Family" put together by Charlie's sister, school records, and personal remembrances by colleagues and friends prepared for Charlie's eightieth birthday. And, of course, there is the work itself: thirty-one published books and hundreds of articles, but also unpublished memos he wrote at the Fed and BIS, speeches, and Congressional testimony. All that is more than enough to flesh out a three-dimensional picture of the man.

Born in 1910, Charlie came of age in the Roaring Twenties, the only son of a successful lawyer who wanted his son to follow him in the trade. Kent School formed his character, and he found economics at Pennsylvania University, but it was at Columbia University in the years of "hot money" (1933–6) that he became a scholar. Family finances having fallen apart in the Depression, he made his own way and chose his own intellectual fathers, all of them from within the tradition of American institutionalism. Not only Willis, but also James Angell and John H. Williams were critical intellectual influences, the latter mediated through Emile Despres, a student of Williams who became Charlie's lifelong friend and colleague. Williams' key-currency idea, first floated at the fateful 1933 World Economic Conference that Roosevelt torpedoed, was always core to Charlie's thinking. Later, it was Williams' Harvard colleague Alvin Hansen who drew Charlie's attention to the central importance of long-term capital flows to the Global South.

Equally important for his intellectual formation was Charlie's real world experience: as a practicing central banker starting at the New York Fed supporting the 1936 Tripartite Agreement, continuing at the BIS confronting the emerging challenges of war finance, and then back at the Board of Governors for contingency planning in the event of a German victory. But it was war service more than anything else that made Charlie into the mature economist he would be, pressing him to develop his analytical skills to the highest level, first as an intelligence analyst in the OSS and then in postwar service at the State Department. His Pantheon of heroes included the four great men he worked under in those years: Omar Bradley, William Clayton, George Marshall, and Allan Sproul. Closer to Charlie's own merely human condition, the demigods of his private religion were the economists with whom he worked: Emile Despres, Alvin Hansen, Edward Mason, and Willard Thorp. A self-diagnosed overachiever, Charlie never aspired to be one of the greats, but he could and did aspire to be an economist like these men.

It was only in 1948, at age 38, that Charlie landed his first academic appointment, at MIT, then as now primarily a school of engineering. Over the next decades, under the leadership of Paul Samuelson and Robert Solow, the department would pioneer the use of mathematical and statistical methods for economic modelling, and in so doing would transform itself into one of the leading departments in the world. Charlie himself, however, never retooled, and one reason is that he never felt the need. Twelve years in government service left him with a wealth of knowledge about how the system worked, and he had seen how the pragmatic empiricist method of the American institutionalists worked in practice to solve even the most difficult problems thrown up by the world. It was enough for him.

For Charlie, the bigger need to retool came when he lost his security clearance in 1951, as that meant he was unable to keep a foot in the world of practical policy as had been his plan. Subsequently, he came to rely instead on textbook writing as a more indirect means of influence, shepherding to publication multiple editions of both *International Economics* (1953) and *Economic Development* (1958) before his swan song *Power and Money: The Politics of International Economics and the Economics of International Politics* (1970). It was his students – in person at MIT, but also the readers of his books – who would have to solve the problems thrown up by the world, problems in which economics and politics were inextricably intertwined.

For the international money story, particular interest attaches to two of those students, Egon Sohmen and Robert Mundell, the former an early advocate of flexible exchange rates and the latter the originator of what became the standard model of open economy macroeconomics, for which he would be awarded the Nobel Memorial Prize in Economic Sciences in 1999. Charlie wrangled with them both, favoring fixed exchange rates against Sohmen and seeing Mundell's advocacy for a common European currency as an incorrect extension of Williams' key-currency approach. For Charlie, the optimal currency area was always the world as a whole, and the central problem was making the dollar system work, not finding alternatives to it.

After twenty years of this, as the MIT department changed along with the rest of the economics profession, Charlie came to see that it was time for a change himself, and that's when he embraced a new identity as economic historian. Most historians spend their days digging in the archives for new facts; Charlie instead used his intelligence analyst skills to spin stories about what the facts mean. Having mounted his first major effort in this vein, the *Depression* book, while still on the MIT payroll, he was ready to hit the ground running when mandatory retirement required him to step down, starting with *Manias, Panics, and Crashes* (1978), which became a best-seller and remains in print to this day.

In biographical context, we can read Charlie's self-identified 1984 masterpiece *Financial History* as a synthesis of the multiple strands of his life work. The first three Parts – titled respectively "Money," "Banking," and "Finance" – can be read as an attempt inductively to sketch for the reader his own analytical framework for understanding the international monetary system, building on his earlier nonhistorical works *The Dollar Shortage* (1950), *Europe and the Dollar* (1966), and *International Money* (1981). Here, in effect, we find his treatise on money. The second two parts – "The Interwar Period" and "After World War II" – use this analytical framework to make sense of the dramatic monetary events of his own life. In effect, *Financial History* is Charlie's own *Money and Empire*, a Bildungsroman of both the dollar and himself.

In all of this postretirement work, we see Charlie not so much turning himself into an economic historian, but rather using the material of economic history finally to do the kind of comparative political economics that he had intended to do when he left government service for the academy. Indeed, Charlie signals as much himself in the title of his final collection of favorite papers: *Comparative Political Economy, A Retrospective* (2000). Resilient in the face of multiple obstacles, Charlie ultimately achieved what he had set out to way back in 1933 when he found himself confronting the reality of global economic collapse and the necessity of making some kind of life for himself.

I

INTELLECTUAL
FORMATION, 1910–1948

CHAPTER 1

Golden Boy

My father used to tell me, as I tell my journalist son about news-
work, that lawyers don't know anything, but have to be quick
learners in a case in a new field.[1]

Born October 12, 1910, Charles "Charlie" Poor Kindleberger II was the
third child but first son born to up-and-coming New York City lawyer
Evertson Crosby Kindleberger (1875–1950) and his socially ambitious wife
Elizabeth Randall (née McIlvaine) (1879–1959).[2] Elizabeth had been raised
to be a "lady," and Crosby had been raised to marry one, and so the marital
bargain was struck while both were vacationing in North Hatley, Quebec.
Married in June 1906, she, at twenty-seven years the oldest of four sisters, felt
herself lucky to have avoided dreaded spinsterhood. He, lame from childhood polio, felt himself lucky to have attracted such a beautiful wife.
Episcopalians and "rock-ribbed Republicans" both, they made an attractive
couple in local social and political circles, which they were careful to
cultivate. Crosby worked long hours at his law practice and Elizabeth kept
herself busy with social calls, while the help kept the household running.

After Charlie, two more daughters would follow, but no more sons.
Charlie thus grew up sandwiched between pairs of sisters – Katharine Wirt
(1907) and Mattie Lindsay (1908), and Elizabeth Randall (1911) and Mary
Bolling (1914) – but he was always closest to Elizabeth (Betty), only eleven
months younger and so almost a twin. All five children were born at home,

---

[1] Kindleberger (1991a, 71).

[2] The family history here recounted draws on "A 20th Century Family" (1994), an
unpublished collection of essays about the Kindleberger family put together by
Charlie's sister Betty Stone. KPMD, Box 40.

which was 11 West 8th Street in New York City, just a block from Washington Square Park. There they lived in an increasingly crowded fourth floor apartment shared with two servants, an Austrian cook who lived in the back room, and a succession of nursemaids who came and went during the day. Child-rearing practice was informed by Mother's Emersonian ideas – "self-reliance, plain living, and high thinking" – plus a strong dose of the newly fashionable and purportedly scientific Watson behaviorism, which warned of the danger of excessive mother-dependence and thumb-sucking.[3] Because of Father's irregular income, family finances operated almost entirely on store credit, repaid in part whenever a big fee came in. As Betty remembers: "Being in debt never seemed to bother her or Daddy in the least."[4]

In his autobiography, *The Life of an Economist* (1991), Charlie opens the narrative by telling the reader, "Mine is an Eastern seaboard family."[5] This I take to be characteristic circumlocution. Not to put too fine a point on it, Charlie was a WASP of the generation chronicled by Tad Friend in his memoir *Cheerful Money: Me, My Family, and the Last Days of Wasp Splendor* (2009). In Charlie's case, the ancestral WASP splendor was naval, specifically three admirals, two of them doctors. His grandfather, Admiral David M. Kindleberger (1834–1921), had married Mattie Lindsay Poor, herself the daughter of Admiral Charles Henry Poor (1808–82), and they named their first son Charles Poor Kindleberger (1870–1957) in honor of her father. That first CPK dutifully made his career in the Navy and rose to admiral rank, but without producing progeny.[6] It was left therefore to the second son, Charlie's father, to continue the name with his own first son, Charlie himself. In due course, Charlie would continue the name with his own first son, Charles Poor Kindleberger III. Thus did ancestral splendor live on in memory, even as successive generations turned to other things.

---

[3] 20th Century Family, 36–37.
[4] 20th Century Family, 6.
[5] Kindleberger (1991a, 4).
[6] Biographies of these admirals, useful for our purposes mainly for the names and dates of their progeny, can be found at MOLLUS, Military Order of the Loyal Legion of the United States, www.suvcw.org/mollus/mollus.htm.

Charlie continues his narrative: "It was a middle-class family, comfortable until the depression of the 1930s deepened, but far from rich."[7] Again, a certain degree of circumlocution. Most important, "comfortable" meant summers at the sea. Only a year after Charlie's birth, the Kindlebergers bought property at the top of Shoreby Hill in Jamestown on Conanicut Island in Narragansett Bay, Rhode Island, and began construction of "June Cottage" (now 13 Standish Road). Betty remembers: "away from the dark and constricted life of the city into a place of light and freedom, blue sea to swim in, wild flowers you could pick, great bunches of wild strawberries and blackberries and raspberries you could stuff yourself with, half-starved as you were, in that pre-vitamins age, for vitamin C." For his part, Charlie remembered tennis and golf, crabbing in the tidal marsh, and rocks and surf on overnight camping trips to Beavertail, the southernmost tip of the island and so most exposed to the open ocean.[8]

Father had himself spent summers in Jamestown as a boy, in the big house "Beachhaven" that Grandfather had built in 1886 right on the shore at 141 Conanicus Avenue.[9] The naval base on the mainland in Newport had made it a natural choice for the Admiral, and in his retirement Grandfather had shifted with his third wife to a smaller house up the hill at 45 Calvert Place, where he devoted himself to painting. But the record makes clear that the driving force for the Kindlebergers' purchase was not Father or Grandfather, but rather Mother and Grandmother. The very day of the purchase, the Kindlebergers subdivided the land and sold the part with an existing house (now 3 Standish Road) to Fannie McIlvaine, Elizabeth's mother, who would spend summers there for the next two decades, along with the growing families of her other daughters.[10]

Grandma Fannie's husband, Henry Clay McIlvaine, a naval engineer who then became owner of a wholesale drug company, had died young of diabetes and Fannie never remarried, preferring instead to remain in

---

[7] Kindleberger (1991a, 4).

[8] 20th Century Family, 9, 15–18.

[9] Rhode Island Historical Preservation and Heritage Commission. 1995. *Historic and Architectural Resources of Jamestown, Rhode Island.* Available at https://preservation.ri.gov /sites/g/files/xkgbur406/files/pdfs_zips_downloads/survey_pdfs/jamestown.pdf.

[10] In 1912, the Kindlebergers bought an additional 15 feet of abutting land, and in 1915 transferred an additional 15 feet to Grandma Fannie.

mourning clothes, attended in summer by her four beautiful daughters and in winter by her sole surviving son, Henry Clay Jr., the youngest.[11] At peak capacity, Grandma Fannie's house held twenty-two beds, including space on the third floor for nursemaids and cribs. Suffice it to say that Charlie grew up with his mother's family, and lots of cousins, absorbing Grandma Fannie's tales of her Grand Tour of Europe in 1869, as well as the tragic loss not only of her husband but also of her brother in childhood, and of her first-born son Randall at only 18 – lots to mourn. The hopes of both sides of the family thus rested on Charlie's shoulders, but his mother's side was the more influential. Charlie might have been talking about himself (notoriously a difficult thing for WASPs) when he wrote, "A man with a strong mother and weak father tends to have a stronger need for achievement than one with parents in the converse situation."[12]

Today Jamestown is linked to the mainland by a bridge, but that is a modern perversion.[13] Until 1922 when they acquired a car (a Dodge, *not* a Ford or Chevrolet), the Kindlebergers got to Jamestown by boat, starting with an overnight ferry that traveled from New York City up the East River and Long Island Sound to Fall River, then a train to Newport, and another short ferry to Jamestown. Once there, Mother and children stayed for the entire summer, May to September, joined by Father on occasional weekends and for an extended two-week vacation when Charlie would earn pocket money by "caddying for Daddy" at the local golf course. Social life revolved around the nearby casino, a kind of beach club with daily swimming and dances on Monday, Wednesday, and Saturday nights. After Prohibition in 1920, there was no more alcohol, but there were still lots of boisterous tea parties. Moral instruction was Sunday School at St. Matthew's Episcopal Church, where Charlie and his siblings were confirmed.

It was during those long summers that Charlie became a sailor, racing without distinction with family friend Bill Hodges at the Yacht Club in the

---

[11] Biographical details again usefully available at MOLLUS, www.suvcw.org/mollus/m ollus.htm.

[12] Kindleberger (2000a, 183).

[13] The books of Rosemary Enright and Sue Maden (2010, 2014, 2016) provide a vivid picture of Jamestown life in the early days, sources usefully supplemented by material on the website of the Jamestown Historical Society.

Kindlebergers' boat *Spider* (a gift from Morton Otis, the elevator tycoon), and cruising in *Wham* with Bill Wetherill (who would eventually marry Charlie's oldest sister, Katharine). Essentially unsupervised, the boys sailed all around Narragansett Bay to "Fall River, Bristol, Hope Island, Prudence, West Greenwich, Warwick and Point Judith," and once even to Block Island. It was also during those long summers that Charlie became a reader, raiding the cottage bookshelves for "E. Phillips Oppenheim, Gertrude Atherton, A. S. M Hutchison (*If Winter Comes*), Henry Sydnor Harrison (*V. V.'s Eyes* and *Queed*), *Beau Geste, The Prisoner of Zenda, Rupert of Hentzau.*"[14] Left to their own devices by adults on extended vacation, Charlie, along with his siblings and cousins, learned to make their own fun.

The taste for the sea formed at Jamestown stayed with Charlie for the rest of his life, even as he eventually settled into academic life as an economist. In retirement, he wrote a small book, *Mariners and Markets* (1992), that in effect joined his two lifetime interests – the sea and economics – including on the back cover a picture of himself in 1930 as deckboy on the SS *Bird City*, about which episode there is more later.[15] For present purposes, the important point to emphasize is how the "halcyon days" of Jamestown remained always a place of security and comfort, an unshakably solid emotional foundation to which Charlie could repair in times of need simply by taking the helm of a small boat. That's what lies underneath the surface when Charlie writes, "I prefer for vacations above all else, to go sailing in Maine."[16]

Having acquired a summer house, the Kindlebergers' next logical move was for more space during the winter, but that move was delayed first by the birth of Mary and then by World War I. Thus, it was not until September 1919 when, flush with "superpatriot" wartime savings in the form of Liberty bonds and just in time to avoid capital loss from the interest rate rise later that year, the family was finally able to move to 81 Maple Avenue (now 134–28) in Flushing, Queens, a Long Island suburb,

---

[14] 20th Century Family, 17. I have corrected minor misspellings and misrememberings.
[15] Charlie dedicated the book to "W. H. S.," which refers to William H. Sands, his best friend in his college fraternity and a lifelong sailing enthusiast.
[16] Kindleberger (1991a, 4).

on a block inhabited by "nice people" whose children became Charlie's playmates and schoolmates at PS 20. Charlie remembers:

> I sang in the choir at St. George's for 5 years. There is a picture of me in my working regalia, at some point in this career. I worked up from 15 cents per service to 45 cents, and 75 cents for funerals and weddings. In my last years I sang solos.
>
> During these years I belonged to scouts, built the usual number of cabins, huts, tree houses, etc., proved very inept at the telegraphy schemes of my friends; got my last spanking when I chose to absent myself from dancing class on Washington's Birthday – it was a holiday, wasn't it – which happened to be the day that my father chose to see what he was getting for his money.[17]

A central institution of family life in Flushing was Sunday lunch, the only meal of the week when the children joined the adults. It was a dress-up affair, the four girls in identical dresses each in their own designated color – blue, pink, yellow, lavender – and Charlie in knickers. Regular male guests, Dr. Charles Camac and Colonel Crosby, livened on occasion by a visiting Episcopalian dignitary, made adult conversation while the cook passed the roast leg of lamb, candied sweet potatoes, and spinach with slices of hard-boiled egg – a culinary treat for children more accustomed to the bland and frugal weekday children's fare.[18] As Father was an avid reader of multiple daily newspapers, the content of these adult conversations can readily be imagined in those years right after World War I: the Paris Peace Conference of 1919, the controversy over Woodrow Wilson's proposed League of Nations, the Washington Naval

---

[17] This passage is taken from "Security Report – An Interim Biography," which Kindleberger wrote in 1956 in an attempt to get cleared for government service. This unpublished document, though referenced in the published autobiography (1991a, 127) and clearly a source close at hand in the writing of that book, provides considerably greater personal detail as well as subtly different accounts of several key life episodes. Writing for an imagined inquisitor seems to have loosened Charlie's tongue, which was noticeably more circumspect for an imagined public audience: "Because of its limited purpose, the document will be long on opinions and on relations with 'controversial persons,' brief on other aspects of my life" (1). KPTL, Box 8.

[18] 20th Century Family, 27.

Conference of 1921–2 that settled the global balance of naval forces, and maybe even the Genoa Economic and Financial Conference of 1922 that agreed the postwar gold-exchange standard. All seeds planted in the developing young Charlie, just beginning to be aware of the larger world outside.

But these seeds would have to grow to fruition elsewhere, as "it was decided after one and a half years at the Flushing High School that I be sent away."[19] Roger Williams Jr., the son of Mother's younger sister Frances, attended the Kent School, and so it was decided Charlie should too. He passed the entrance exam, but began at Kent in the third form, receiving no credit for the years he had skipped in public school. At age 13, Charlie left home for boarding school and did not return for any extended period until after college.

Today the town of Kent, Connecticut, lies at the end of the Harlem line of the Metro-North Railroad and is commutable to New York City in about two hours. Back then, in the age of the steam locomotive, it took twice that long and there were only two trains a day. Kent School was thus an isolated community, not unlike a ship on a transatlantic crossing, self-contained and untouched by either the comforts or the stresses of life on land. Founded in 1906, the School was in 1924 still very much a work in progress: a collection of drafty repurposed wooden farmhouse structures and not at all the well-endowed brick campus of modern day.

From its founding, Headmaster Frederick H. Sill, a celibate monk in the Episcopalian Order of the Holy Cross, made virtue of what we might today consider deficiencies, promoting "Simplicity of Life, Self-Reliance and Directness of Purpose" as the guiding trinity of the school: "The standard of life I had in mind was that to be found in the average country rectory."[20] Self-reliance meant that students, not teachers or employees, took charge of supervising study halls and dormitories, serving food, filling the coal bin and even serving on work gangs for the neighboring farms that supplied the school. "Directness of Purpose" references

---

[19] Kindleberger (1991a, 6).
[20] Frederick H. Sill. "Address on the Subject of Simplicity of Life, Self-Reliance and Directness of Purpose," Feb. 27, 1926. Kent School Archives.

preparation for college: students were to come out of Kent with a clear sense of direction toward a future vocation.

Sill himself made sure that the daily life of the school reflected its founding values, enforcing strict discipline, including compulsory daily chapel. Remembers Maitland Edey, a classmate of Charlie's and also a neighbor from Queens: "Father Sill had a mesmerizing personality and appearance, unique in the secondary-school world. Short, stout and with a big head, he nevertheless cut a commanding figure in his long white robe with its knotted cord girdling his stomach and a large black cross dangling from his neck."[21] Charlie recalls: "Sill would rant and rave when something went wrong, and send a form, or the whole school, out to do penance, sometimes running around the big pond several times, occasionally working on a job such as cleaning up a construction site."[22]

Having himself rowed crew (actually coxswain) at Columbia and perhaps having in mind the pitiful state of the school library, Sill put great emphasis on sports and less on intellectual achievement. His crowning glory was the crew team in the class ahead of Charlie, which competed in the Henley Royal Regatta in 1927. Charlie's own class, however, was "more intellectual than sporting," as was Charlie himself: "I played second-team football, class hockey – unable to make either the first or second team – and became manager of the tennis team," but became "number two on the Kent School News and number one on the chess team," as well as the winner of two essay contests and the Latin Prize. "Some of my classmates hated school. I happened to love it, whether from lack of imagination or merely a good digestive tract that predisposes one to like whatever happens along."[23]

What did he like about it? Simplicity of life and self-reliance, certainly – these could have been the motto for Jamestown summers as well – but also directness of purpose. It is perhaps telling that, after graduation, Charlie chose to spend the summer of 1928 at Kent rather than Jamestown, undertaking "a job surveying Kent School, learning to use the tape, stadia rod, transit, and triangulation."[24] But his autobiographical chapter on Kent

---

[21] Edey (1983).
[22] Kindleberger (1991a, 7).
[23] Kindleberger (1991a, 6–7).
[24] Kindleberger (1991a, 18).

reveals an additional dimension: the appeal of being part of a team of men organized around a common purpose; if one is not good enough to play, one can always manage. Kent was above all about building character. Charlie thought enough of the experience that he would send both of his own sons, though only the oldest would stick it out to graduation.

Some flavor of life at Kent can be gleaned from Charlie's letter to his father, dated January 10, 1926, a Sunday:

To-day I learned what the life of an assistant manager is really like. As it had snowed after chapel the IV form needed my services in helping clean off a place on the pond for the form team and I worked on that from 11–12:30. Then on the way to my room I was accosted by Snyder the hockey manager who asked me to eat early and wait on the New Haven Boy's Club whom we played against. By eating early I got lots of food but waiting is a tedious job especially if you have just waited the meal before. Then I set 7 tables for supper and hasted down to the rink to work some more after the game which we won 7–0, Ding Palmer scoring 6 goals and being partly responsible for the other. We swept the rink and proceeded to flood it. Then we flooded a small adjoining rink which we had built betimes and piled snow up to prop the side board. Then there was still a piece of bad ice on the big rink we had to fix and to do this we mixed snow and water and sort of cemented it. Meanwhile it was after supper and cold and wet. Then we wandered up to the school and went to the kitchen and cooked 3 eggs apiece with fried onions and potatoes and had the best meal Kent has ever furnished me with ... Please send a check for about $30 to my account soon as I only have $4 left and I haven't gotten the crew pants yet. Give my love to mother and the family please. Yours filially, Chas.[25]

"My account" in this passage refers to the school's internal payment system. Students paid for incidentals, including chapel offering, by writing checks, and there was no cash allowed on campus. Students ran the bank, as they ran everything else, clearing

---

[25] KPMD, Box 20.

checks and reconciling balances. Edey tells the story of one remarkable transaction:

> One Easter morning [Ernie] Jacoby went from chapel to the athletic store where he worked. A few minutes later the Sacristan, DeWolf Perry of the Class of 1927, came in to count up the receipts. Among the checks was one: "Pay to Jesus Christ for Easter Offering (signed) Herbert Barnum Seeley." "What do I do about this?" asked Perry in some agitation. "Just endorse it Jesus Christ," replied Ernie calmly, "and then sign your own name underneath."[26]

At that time, Charlie's interest in banking had yet to emerge. Instead, the prize essays that he wrote testify to Charlie's interest in mastering the essay form, a skill that would stand him in good stead later in life. ("Essays by Charlie Kindleberger! They are a treat for all who read them," writes Peter Temin in the foreword to Charlie's last book.[27]) The subject matter of the school essays is also relevant, testifying to Charlie's developing intellectual interests, "stimulated first by Cuthbert Wright, unhappy at school but incapable through various weaknesses of finishing his advanced degree in history; Gordon Haight who stayed only a short time and then left to end up in the English department at Yale; and Everett Gleason, also in English, who was too high powered for such a school and left."[28] Essays on Cardinal Wolsey and Oliver Cromwell evince a schoolboy's fascination with men of action and power. Essays on world disarmament and the future of relations between the United States and Britain identify the field of action open to such men today. In the latter essay, young Charlie enthuses about the results of the 1921 Washington Naval Conference, but presses for more: "Toward a warless world, of disarmament, free trade, a strong League of Nations, and a strong World Court."[29] So much for Directness of Purpose, but we may well imagine that Father was not fully pleased with what he was getting for his money.

---

[26] Edey (1983, 7).
[27] Kindleberger (1999, ix).
[28] Interim Biography, 8.
[29] Kent School Archives, "Kindleberger Term Papers."

Charlie recalls: "When I was born it was decided I would be named after my uncle, that I would go to Penn, and that I would be a lawyer."[30] Charlie's classmates went to Harvard, Yale, and Princeton, and likely he could have as well. But Father insisted, and so Charlie went to the University of Pennsylvania, where Father and also Uncle Charlie had gone as undergraduates, and also for graduate study in law and medicine, respectively. One good thing about Penn: it had a 150-pound crew for lightweights like Charlie, which Kent had not. He seized the chance, working himself up to alternate for second seat in the eight-man boat; Father Sill would have approved. On the other hand, encouraged by Father Kindleberger, Charlie joined the fraternity Delta Psi (St. Anthony's Hall) and began to travel in Philadelphia society circles, turning his back for a while on simplicity and acquiring a taste instead for the good life: "For a while I got in this social circuit, and stayed down in Philadelphia, rather than go home at Thanksgiving, to attend debutante parties. For a while, I was sleeping all day and dancing all night, and it took some time to get straightened out again."[31]

Having thus outwardly satisfied both of his fathers, Charlie apparently felt free to pursue his own developing intellectual interests independently. In his freshman year, he joined the Philomathean Society, a literary society and the oldest student group at the university, and also the school newspaper, *The Daily Pennsylvanian*. Most important, however, was a friendship he struck up with Andrew J. Biemiller, a graduate student and "convinced Socialist" who happened to live across the hall.

Biemiller represented intellectual sophistication to a boy from the backwoods of Kent. I do not want to suggest that he converted me to Socialism. Primarily, he built on the foundations laid at Kent ... to make me intensely interested in intellectuality. The seed was already there ... but I then became intensely involved in the world about me. One aspect of this was that when every Sunday evening I went to take supper with my grandmother [Fannie], we used to argue violently about Woodrow Wilson, she against, I for. She belonged to that group of unreconstructed

---

[30] Kindleberger (1991a, 12).
[31] Interim Biography, 14.

Republicans who thought Wilson represented the devil. I differed. She was in her 80s. I was 18.[32]

Having excelled at Greek and Latin at Kent, Charlie entered Penn as a classics major but, after the brush with Biemiller, switched to economics and never looked back: "My real interest in economics was of a kind that matures only after about twenty years of age ... Children grow up in homogeneous environments, and are unaware of the complexity of the typical social situation until they have been exposed to a series of them in the city, the university, or both."[33]

Though Charlie turned away from classics in favor of economics, his classical training left a permanent mark. Not only did it leave him with a lifelong facility for languages, it also gifted him with a distinctive appreciation for the human condition. In later life, when he spoke of the "human condition" as "a world full of ambiguity, paradox, uncertainty and problems,"[34] we hear him approaching economics as a classicist. The rational maximizing agent of whom economists are so fond is nowhere to be found in Kindleberger's own economics. Instead, there are real people:

> Man in his elemental state is a peasant with a possessive love of his own turf; a mercantilist who favors exports over imports; a Populist who distrusts banks, especially foreign banks; a monopolist, who abhors competition; a xenophobe, who feels threatened by strangers and foreigners, and above all, a child who wants to have his cake and eat it too.[35]

Such is the poor stuff of which we are made, but which our better nature may aspire to overcome.

"International economics began in 1929,"[36] Charlie tells us, and immediately we think of the stock market crash in October 1929 that ushered in a widening global collapse that did not find its bottom until 1933. Certainly that is part of Charlie's story, if only because of the consequences for his family's income. After 1929, the upper-middle or lower-upper class life into

---

[32] Interim Biography, 10.
[33] Kindleberger (1991a, 15–16).
[34] Kindleberger (1987a, 62).
[35] Kindleberger (1984b, 39).
[36] Kindleberger (1991a, 19).

which Charlie had been born was effectively over, though money was found to keep him in college to completion, and his sister Betty at Bryn Mawr as well. But of course in 1929 no one knew that future. The actual contemporary importance of 1929 for Charlie was not the Depression but rather his summer job as cadet on the SS *California*, a passenger ship traveling between New York and San Francisco with stops in Cuba, Panama, and Los Angeles. His uncle, Roger Williams, arranged the matter. For Charlie, it was about seeing the world and engaging the range of people who choose the seafaring life.

He liked it so much that he did it again the next year, signing on in summer 1930 with a job as ordinary seaman on the oil tanker MV *Australia* and then, again thanks to Uncle Roger, as deck boy on the SS *Bird City*, which traveled to Copenhagen, Gdynia, Helsinki, and Leningrad. His unpublished account of the latter journey, "A Seaman Visits Leningrad," dwells equally on his impressions of Leningrad, then in the throes of its first five-year plan under Joseph Stalin, and his impressions of his shipmates, two of them Russians. For our purposes, special interest attaches to Charlie's account of a four-hour argument with an agitator sent from the Soviet of Seamen while their boat was docked in Leningrad:

> [The agitator's argument that] there is no unemployment in Russia, while there is a lot in the United States, ergo Russia had a better government than the United States, was easily disproved. A country under construction obviously has more work to be done, than one already built up. However, when Russia finally is industrialized, she too will be subject to business depressions. – She will not. The people will work less hours. – But for the same amount of money? – That is Socialism (Marxian). – Explain it then. He was unable to. That was my biggest score, and another point on which he was unable to be evasive, was what was the difference between the present depression and all the others from which we had recovered. He replied that this was an international crisis and the others had been local. Well then the nations of the world will recover together, with one or two exceptions, and the depression will be over, I offered. No. Why not? It won't.[37]

---

[37] Part III, 3–4. KPMD, Box 14.

Here we see Charlie, after only a year of economics, testing what he had learned against the world events unrolling in front of his eyes. For him, international economics was about seafaring adventure, but it was also about expanding the horizon of his own sight to encompass the larger world, even as most everyone else – whether in business, banking, or politics – adopted more limited "decision horizons."[38]

Returning to school after the Leningrad adventure, Charlie signed up for classes in money and banking. Then, in spring 1931, he took part in a model League of Nations held at Princeton and competed successfully for a place in the two-month summer school operated by the Students International Union in Geneva, Switzerland, along with about twenty other Americans. It was during the crossing to Europe, this time as passenger rather than crew, that Charlie fatefully made the acquaintance of one Francis T. Miles, who was traveling to Munich for a summer school in nuclear chemistry. On the return journey, Francis was met on the dock by his sister Sarah, and that's how Charlie met the woman who would eventually become his wife.

In a second stroke of fate, Francis' roommate at Princeton was Robert T. Miller, who had been a class ahead of Charlie at Kent and editor of the *Kent School News*. Continuing connection with Francis thus led to continuing connection with Miller, who was subsequently denounced as a Communist by Elizabeth Bentley in her testimony to the House Un-American Activities Committee. Charlie's connection to Miller would be one of three counts against him that caused him to lose his security clearance in 1951: guilt by association. In his autobiography, Charlie makes a point of proudly stating his continuing association with Miller. Notwithstanding one relative who turned his back on Miller, "none of the rest of us did, including my brother-in-law Francis T. Miles ... My wife and I see him from time to time and find him and his wife delightful friends."[39]

Of course, in summer 1931, both marriage and security trouble lay far ahead in the unknowable future. More immediately important, the

---

[38] On business, this would be the whole point of his extensive work on multinational corporations (see Chapter 5). On speculators and politicians, see Kindleberger (1966, 119 and 146).

[39] Kindleberger (1991a, 10).

summer school lost its planned director at the last minute, and so the undergraduates were enrolled instead in a more advanced summer school operated by the Graduate School of International Studies, a training arm of the League of Nations, along with 200 more advanced students. The SIU students remained a separate unit for meals and housing, but during the day they were essentially treated like graduate students, with lectures in the morning, afternoon, and evening, for seven long weeks. This was Charlie's first exposure to first-rate economists, teachers and students alike, and he realized for the first time the second-rate education he had been receiving at Penn. One fellow undergraduate, F. Tyler Ostrander, "who was writing an honors thesis in economics at Williams ... knew about such things as the Keynes-Ohlin controversy [concerning war reparations], of which I had never heard."[40]

Summer 1931 also turned out to be a momentous time in international money matters: the failure of Credit Anstalt in May, Hoover's moratorium on war debt payments in June, the British Macmillan report (penned largely by Keynes), and the German banking crisis in July, all leading up to Britain's abandonment of the gold standard in September. All of these were matters that Charlie would treat in detail forty years later in *The World in Depression* (1973), but of which he remained "sublimely unconscious" contemporaneously. In summer 1931 his attention was elsewhere: "The social life – swimming, climbing, partying in the cafes – was delightful." For him, the experience "did perhaps what good teachers can best do, which is to stimulate appetite and create enthusiasm. Students teach themselves (and each other). The role of experience and teachers is to encourage and to motivate. The summer of 1931 did that for me."[41]

The summer of 1931 was also the origin of Charlie's misbegotten infatuation with one Caroline Thompson, a student from Bryn Mawr whom he had met at the model League of Nations and who had introduced him to Francis Miles during the crossing. One thing led to another and "in the fall of 1931 I thought I was in love, despite receiving no encouragement, and decided to graduate from the University of

---

[40] Interim Biography, p. 18. Charlie's notebook from the summer survives in his papers, but Ostrander (2009) provides a fuller account.
[41] Kindleberger (1991a, 25–26).

Pennsylvania at the earliest opportunity – February 1932 – to get a job, and prepare myself to support a family."[42] In the event, Miss Thompson had other ideas, and so did the world of work.

At that time, Charlie's dream job was in foreign exchange at some New York bank, ideally the Federal Reserve Bank of New York. Father's connections got him an interview with George Harrison, president of the Bank, but not the job: "The Fed had no use for the likes of me, with a simple bachelor's degree and no experience. And besides, there was a depression."[43] In fact, though Charlie did not know it at the time, his future friend and colleague Emile Despres had successfully managed to move directly from a bachelor's degree at Harvard into a position at the New York Fed as a foreign exchange analyst. But Penn was not Harvard, and perhaps it could be said that Charlie was not Emile, a "brilliant, perfectionist, [with] a recorded IQ of 192."[44]

Rejected by the Fed, Charlie settled instead for lowly office work at the conservative National Economy League until July, when Uncle Roger came through with a job at Johnson and Higgins, a marine insurance brokerage. Maybe this was the answer – a career combining the seafaring life with economics? Charlie started at the bottom as a messenger boy and began to learn the business: "I enrolled in a course on marine insurance in some insurance institute with classes in Wall Street and read a book by a distant cousin of mine, Wharton Poor, an admiralty lawyer, with the enticing title *Charter Parties and Bills of Lading*. I did well in the course, too."[45]

Summer 1932 thus found Charlie living at home, depressed by the failure of his grand life plans, and picking fights with his parents over politics as the Depression deepened. Come November he would cast his first presidential ballot for Norman Thomas, seeing no essential difference between Hoover and Roosevelt, "balancing the budget, only better. I was not a Socialist in any doctrinaire sense, although the influence of Biemiller et al may still have been there. I did not agree with my father at whose house I lived. His defence of the Republican principle moved me

---

[42] Kindleberger (1991a, 27). He kept track of her sufficiently to note her marriage to John Farr Simmons, US Ambassador, in Interim Biography, p. 19.
[43] Interim Biography, p. 27.
[44] Kindleberger (1991a, 48).
[45] Kindleberger (1991a, 28).

not; his detailing law cases in progress or prospect at the dinner table found me unamused."[46]

Betty followed her big brother in supporting Norman Thomas and more besides as she recollects:

> New York City during the thirties was thick with communists as well as socialists. A friend and I attended a meeting of New York City Trotsky communists in the apartment of the attractive young woman who was the group's leader ... there were a few communists at Bank Street College and some at the New School for Social Research where Henry and I took a course by the psychiatrist Fritz Wittels ... A couple of communists worked with Henry and me in the welfare department ... I felt about communists what I now feel about radical right Christians; these are hostile people who want permission to feel good about themselves while doing violent and hurtful things.[47]

Suffice it to say that in summer 1932, the world was in turmoil, and so was Charlie. For the first time in his life, he faced squarely the prospect of making his own way in the world. In a contemporary fragment titled "Stock-taking," he reflects:

> How am I fitted for existence, for happiness, for social relations, for this economic system, for any other, for the marine insurance world, for marriage, for parenthood? Where have the mistakes been made in my upbringing and by whom? Am I any different from anybody else, from the great mass, from my class, the upper middle class mentally, morally, spiritually? What difference does it make to anyone beside myself? In what measure do I embody the virtues I have been trained to admire – intellectual honesty, integrity, personal, social and commercial, and paradoxically enough courage and moderation?

The choice confronting him, as he saw it, was between three possible directions: foreign banking, law, or economics. Having tried with no success to get into foreign banking, the very real danger was that he would wind up in law, the direction his father favored but mere "fence walking" as Charlie then saw: "I admired my father, but was turned off law

---

[46] Interim Biography, p. 21.
[47] 20th Century Family, p. 147.

on the ground that most of it was fighting over spilled milk, so to speak, rather than dealing with current problems."[48] Economics offered escape from that fate, but also more positively a kind of engagement with the world that he thought might actually suit him: "summation of personal characteristics, economic views world and personal, political."[49] But how to do it? Here, not for the last time, fortune took a hand.

As it happened, the Columbia College chapter of his fraternity, looking to rebuild its Alpha chapter, "proposed that I be given money to undertake graduate work, provided I would live in the Chapter House, 434 Riverside Drive, and work with the undergraduate chapter. The suggestion was made to me that I might like to study law. I said I would be delighted to accept, but that I wanted to study economics."[50] In February 1933, all the while continuing to live at home and to work at Johnson and Higgins, Charlie dipped his toe into the water by taking an evening class in banking with Ralph W. Robey, Financial Editor for the *New York Evening Post*, which turned out to be a ringside seat from which to watch the collapse of the US banking system that spring. Charlie's choice of topic for his term paper, "The Discount Rate in Federal Reserve Policy, 1927–1933," reveals his continuing interest not just in banking, but more specifically in central banking.[51]

Of course, the ringside seat that Charlie really wanted was at the Fed, where his future colleague Emile Despres spent "perhaps a week, sleeping in the infirmary, as the bank staff tried to solve the problem of reopening the banks, which had been closed in Roosevelt's bank holiday of March 3, and at the same time to avoid the reporters that were circling the building like piranhas."[52] That's the life Charlie had sought, and he still wanted it, even if it meant more school and delayed entry into adult life. Years later, when he was a professor himself, Charlie would sympathize with the plight of his graduate students: "A graduate student is by definition unhappy; he has the appetites of a man and the income of a child."[53] Starting Fall 1933,

---

[48] Kindleberger (1991a, 16).

[49] KPMD, Box 40, "Stock-taking" (July 30, 1932).

[50] Interim Biography, p. 23.

[51] KPMD, Box 4.

[52] Kindleberger (1991a, 29).

[53] Charles Staley, in "Reminiscences of Charles P. Kindleberger on his Eightieth Birthday." KPMD, Box 24. See also Kindleberger (1988a, 144).

that would be his own plight, as he resigned from Johnson and Higgins and hunkered down to full-time graduate study.

But first, a visit to Jamestown for a sailing trip with friends out on the Sound, in a Friendship sloop named the Sea Fox. Capsized when the mainsheet jammed during a sudden squall, Charlie was injured and rescued from "almost certain death," according to the local newspaper.[54] Returning to New York, he moved out of his parents' house and into St. Anthony Hall, keeping a personal diary for the first and last time in his life. Herbert Keith Fitzroy ("Fitz"), a friend from Penn days now working on a doctorate in legal history at Columbia, and Eileen O'Daniel, an acquaintance made at the Geneva Summer School now living at home in nearby Englewood, were his best male and female friends in that first year, providing ample social diversion. But Charlie was clearly serious about becoming an economist, recording not only what he was reading for class (Hawtrey, Keynes, Ohlin, and Hayek), but also his thoughts about his eventual dissertation topic.

November 2, 1933:

> I have become interested in the possibilities of selecting 'capital flights' for a doctorate dissertation, attempting to measure them, fit them in adequately to the gold standard, gold exchange standard and managed currencies, and the evolution of a sound doctrine for their control, whether through the discount rate or foreign exchange . . . by governments.

December 8, 1933:

> I still feel strongly that international economic theory, in regard to the balance of payments mechanism . . . comparative cost and gold standard theory, does not fit the facts and wonder concerning the possibility of deducing a new – and probably more complicated theory – from *la situation actuelle*. Given time, this is the field in which I hope to contribute to the so-called science.[55]

---

[54] Interim Biography, p. 16. The accident happened Sept. 10, 1933, in Fishers Island Sound off Stonington Point. First entry in the Personal Journal is Sept. 16, 1933. KPMD, Box 40.

[55] KPMD, Box 40, "Personal Journal."

CHAPTER 2

Columbia

I have a strong impression that economics is a countercyclical industry that attracts adherents when times are troubled. Some are drawn
to the subject by the opportunity to do good, to save the world so to
speak by curing depression. The stronger drive in my view is curiosity. How does the economy work, and what has gone wrong?[1]

In his autobiography, Charlie dispenses with his graduate study at Columbia
in a single chapter. The first paragraph sets the tone: "Economics education
at Columbia in the 1930s was not terribly exciting. In the first place there
were too many students ... Secondly, the faculty spent a great deal of time
off campus ... Thirdly, banking was taught in the business school, not the
economics department which made for reduced interaction." Of Wesley
Clair Mitchell, the most famous and widely published economist at
Columbia, whose institutionalist brand of empiricism gave distinctive flavor
to the entire program, Charlie writes: "Mitchell taught the history of economic thought in a manner that the students liked – connecting theory with
economic history – but his lectures were later regarded as pedestrian when
he gave them in England." Similarly, of H. Parker Willis, his professor of
banking in the business school: "memorable less for his ideas ... than for his
polished lectures." Similarly, of his eventual thesis supervisor in the economics department: "Our course in money had been taught by James
W. Angell, whose work in the field has not survived."[2] Nothing to see

---

[1] Kindleberger (1991a, 179).
[2] Kindleberger (1991a, 31, 32, 34). I read these passages as a retrospective view distorted
by the lens of thirty years at MIT, where there were fewer students, faculty spent time in
their offices, and banking was taught in the economics department.

here, Charlie seems to be saying, impatient in retrospect to move on to life after graduate school, as no doubt he was contemporaneously.

But, in fact, there is quite a bit to see here, specifically the intellectual formation of the mature economist, and in multiple dimensions. Most fundamental, Charlie's first-year diary charts his evolution from socialite party boy, for whom the crowning event of the year was the repeal of Prohibition on December 5th, to the budding economist who would write only a month later: "To the Hall and reading, cold and alone, the lectures of Wesley C. Mitchell on the development of English economic theory. They are delightful bespeaking his wide background in learning, his knowledge of all phases of the period, and clear, sometimes brilliant exposition of the relation of economists and economics to the changing historical landscape. They are charming."[3] Pedestrian in England and in retrospect perhaps, but clearly a significant influence on Charlie at the time, and also a lasting influence, as we will see. His retrospective dismissal of Willis and Angell needs similarly to be understood against contrary contemporaneous evidence. Writing on September 26, 1933, Charlie tells his diary what courses he is taking: "H. Parker Willis' seminar, a theory course with W. C. Mitchell, a course in central reserve banking with Beckhart, and international trade, and currency and credit with Angell. The Willis seminar will deal with 'inflation' and should prove the best."

The Willis seminar was part of a large-scale research project, funded originally by the Social Science Research Council, continuing now in its second year with support from the Columbia University Council for Research in the Social Sciences. The first year of the project had produced a comprehensive survey of *The Banking Situation: American Post-war Problems and Developments*, with one-third of the 924 pages written by Willis himself and the rest by seminar participants.[4] The second year was to focus more narrowly on the problem of "inflation," defined by Willis as the expansion of bank balance sheets by the purchase of long-dated and hence illiquid

---

[3] KPMD, Box 40, Personal Journal, Jan. 14, 1934. Probably the lectures he references are the mimeographed student notes later published as *Types of Economic Theory* (Mitchell 1967). Rutherford (2011) is the best source on the institutionalist movement more generally.

[4] Willis and Chapman (1934).

assets, especially noncommercial government debt. It also would produce a book, *The Economics of Inflation: The Basis of Contemporary Monetary Policy*, including a few pages on "The Theory of Inflation and Foreign Trade" by one Chas. P. Kindleberger, essentially a verbal summary of his largely empirical Master's thesis which stemmed from work he did in the seminar that first year.[5] In later years, Charlie would be at pains to distance himself from Willis as an advocate of the erroneous real bills doctrine, and he would view the banking problem of 1933 as a problem of deflation not of inflation.[6] But in his first year at Columbia, Charlie described himself as an "intelligent deflationist," more concerned with disequilibrium in the structure of prices than with price levels and willing to scale down debts directly, which was more or less the position of Willis.[7]

Indeed, it is not going too far to say that Charlie was, for several years, a kind of protégé of Willis. In his first year, he became friends with and tutored Willis' son Parker B. Willis in monetary economics and was invited to the Willis home on Staten Island for dinner, over which Father Willis memorably presided as an old-fashioned father figure, "dominating the dinner-table conversation. He was by no means tyrannical or malevolent, merely what I understood to be Victorian."[8] In his second year, Charlie served as teaching assistant in Willis' class, and Willis arranged for him to make extra money by teaching at the American Institute of Banking. And in his third year, Charlie financed his studies with a fellowship from the Business School – which is to say from Willis. During that year, in partnership with others from the Willis circle, Charlie produced three chapters – "The United States Treasury and Banking," "Balance of Payments," and "The Government and the Foreign Exchanges" – for a banking textbook that never got published because others did not deliver their chapters.[9]

In the two summers between his three years at Columbia, Charlie worked at a small New York firm called Economic Statistics: in summer

---

[5] Willis and Chapman (1935).
[6] Kindleberger (1991a, 34).
[7] KPMD, Box 40, "Personal Journal," Jan 3, 1934.
[8] Kindleberger (1991a, 35).
[9] KPMD, Box 4. The others were John Chapman, Anatol Murad, Vladimir Kazekevitch, and Eric Kjellstrom. Interim Biography, p. 26.

1934 selling their economic forecasting service, and in summer 1935 coauthoring with his boss, G. O. Trenchard, an article for the practitioner's weekly *Barron's* titled "Bank Credit and Business Demands" (July 29, 1935) in which he concerned himself with the condition of banks in the anticipated economic recovery when the Fed would presumably be raising interest rates.[10] What caught his attention were the very large bank holdings of government securities, which would have to be liquidated to make room for rising business credit:

> The government debt does not represent the invested savings of the country, but rather credit created by the banks. This credit is liquid only in the limited sense that it is shiftable, or that the asset can be transferred to another holder (the Federal Reserve Banks), while it cannot be paid off out of current income on the part of the debtor, the United States Government.

Here he expresses his concern that prior banking inflation will lead to monetary inflation as government debt is shifted to the Federal Reserve, which again was more or less exactly Willis' concern.

Charlie would ultimately move beyond Willis, as good students always move beyond their teachers, but there can be no question that he started from Willis. To understand Charlie, therefore, we also must start from Willis.

The central event in the life of Henry Parker Willis (1874–1937) was the establishment of the Federal Reserve System in 1913. A student of J. Laurence Laughlin at the University Chicago, Willis was coauthor with Laughlin of the 1898 *Report of the Monetary Commission of the Indianapolis Convention,* which launched the movement for monetary reform, and for the rest of his life his attention never wavered. Not only did he help draft the Federal Reserve Act, working closely with Senator Glass, but also, after the Act was adopted, he served as chairman of the Technical Organization Committee,[11] then Secretary of the Federal Reserve Board (1914–18) and then Director of Research (1918–22). The process

---

[10] His published autobiography claims no recollection of summer 1935. The Interim Biography, however, does treat this episode: pp. 27–28.

[11] Hammes (2001) provides a comprehensive account of the work of this committee.

left him with a firm view of what the Fed was all about, what problems in the past it was meant to solve, and what vision of the future it was meant to bring into reality.

Inspired by the British model of central banking, Willis always considered the central purpose of the Fed to be the creation of a class of notes and deposit accounts backed by self-liquidating commercial loans (so-called "real bills"), which notes and deposits would serve as the solid foundation of the larger monetary and financial system. Says Willis: "The banker is essentially one who concerns himself with facilitating the movement of goods into actual consumption, the basis of his loans being found in the consuming power of the community."[12] In this point of view, loans against goods on their way to sale are naturally self-liquidating, since the eventual sale of the goods provides the funds needed to pay back the loans. A core holding of such loans therefore provides a constant flow of liquid funds to the banker, enabling him readily to meet any deficit at the daily clearing, so allowing his balance sheet to expand and contract elastically according to the needs of business.

Willis knew well that American commercial banks would be making other kinds of business loans as well, financing "production, storage, or speculation" in order to meet the long-term capital investment needs of the dynamic young economy.[13] But he was at pains to point out that such loans involve commitment of funds for a longer term – funds that are therefore not available to meet a deficit at the daily clearing. Some fraction of this kind of business may be appropriate for commercial banks, but definitely not for the new Reserve Banks, whose deposit and note liabilities were supposed to serve as the reserve for commercial banks and others. That is why the Act explicitly limited Reserve Banks to holding real bills; the assets of the Reserve Banks were supposed to be the core holding of self-liquidating bills for the entire banking system.

The Reserve Banks were also explicitly not supposed to constitute a central bank, rather just a cooperative system of private banks, more or less on the model of a mutual clearinghouse: "co-operative

---

[12] Willis and Chapman (1934, 31).
[13] Willis and Chapman (1934, 658).

organization of existing banks for the purpose of providing a jointly guaranteed or secured type of credit representative which could be used as reserve funds."[14] Foreign trade was similarly not supposed to be a matter of settlement between central banks, but rather a natural extension of decentralized reserve banking, and that is why foreign bills that finance the movement of goods into and out of the United States were also made eligible assets for the Reserve Banks. The idea was to bring some of the existing trade finance business home from London, and to do it in dollars rather than sterling. But there was no intention for the Fed to serve, as the Bank of England did, as de facto central bank for the world. Rather, a core holding of self-liquidating bills was supposed to provide a constant flow of funds to the US banking system, allowing it to expand or contract elastically according to the needs of trade, internationally as well as domestically.

All of this was meant to be a revolutionary change from the former National Banking System, under which bank notes had been backed instead by government bond debt and holding foreign trade bills had been illegal. Under that former system, what elasticity there was in domestic trade operated through the international money market in London, an inefficient procedure for the United States and a periodically disruptive influence on the rest of the world. With a more or less fixed domestic money supply and a pronounced seasonal fluctuation in money demand on account of the predominance of agriculture, the United States always had either too much money, in which case the excess supply flowed to New York and the call loan market for stock market speculation, or too little money, in which case the excess demand pulled in supply from London. Pronounced seasonality of short-term interest rates reflected this feast–famine seesaw and also exacerbated political tensions between Main Street and Wall Street since rates were always lowest when Main Street had money to invest and highest when Main Street needed to borrow. The new Fed was supposed to fix all of that by allowing the money supply to fluctuate in tandem with demand.

It didn't work out that way. Almost immediately after adoption of the Act in December 1913, the banking system was called upon to help

---

[14] Willis (1923, 48).

finance the World War, and as a consequence not real bills but rather Treasury bills became the core asset of the Reserve Banks. "Balance sheet inflation," Willis called it. Even as he accepted wartime necessity, Willis regretted keenly the evolution of the banking system toward a more frozen and less liquid portfolio – the exact opposite of the future envisioned by the language of the Federal Reserve Act. In war time, government became the ultimate consumer, buying whatever it needed on credit using the banking system, with the Reserve Banks operating as a backstop by expanding their own balance sheets to provide banks with the funds needed. War allies, especially France and Britain, also served as ultimate consumers, buying essential war material from the United States on credit, to such an extent that the United States became for the first time a net creditor on the world stage. These foreign debts were largely public debts, one Treasury borrowing from another, but the important point is that they were financed ultimately by the US Treasury borrowing from the US banking system.

In theory, all of this short-term bank credit expansion was supposed to be periodically reversed by government bond issues, the proceeds of which would be used to pay off short-term bank credits. In practice, however, banks lent their retail customers much of the funds needed to purchase the government bond issues, and anyway the proceeds of the bond sales were never used to liquidate government bank credits, which just kept growing. Bank liabilities (which is to say the money supply) grew along with bank assets, and so too did the prices of the commodities purchased by all this credit-financed demand. For Willis it was never a matter of money supply growth causing price inflation, as believers in the simplistic quantity theory of money would have it, but rather balance sheet inflation driving both money and prices. In the end the banking system survived, but it was a near-run thing. Says Willis: "Had the war continued much longer ... the country would have plunged definitely into the morass of 'fiat credit' as one economist has termed it."[15]

On the bright side, one of the positive features of the period of war finance was the extraordinarily rapid unification of domestic money markets, and capital markets as well, as funds were drawn from every

---

[15] Willis (1923, 1220).

corner of the United States to support short- and long-term borrowing by the government. The goal of the Federal Reserve Act had been merely to establish nationwide settlement with par clearing, and it had been expected that the different Reserve Banks would set different short-term interest rates according to local conditions. In short order, however, we got more or less uniform discount rates across the entire country, deliberately set by the Fed below the coupon rate on government war bonds in order to create incentive for investors to "borrow and buy." All of this led to nationwide unification of money and capital markets, with much tighter spreads between one region and another than previously. A process that might well have taken more than a decade happened instead in a few short years.

In addition to monetary unification, the experience of war finance also brought centralization, as the system of decentralized reserve banks evolved rapidly to become in effect a central bank with regional branches.[16] The Board of Governors in Washington may have bemoaned the wartime power grab by the Treasury, but the real beneficiary was the New York Fed, which became in effect the Treasury's bank: "Thus by a certain stretching of the terms of existing law the entire body of banks in the United States were to be used as depositary banks, while the reserve banks were to act as local collecting and disbursing agencies, thus for the first time fulfilling their functions as fiscal agents."[17] Again, perhaps this process would have happened without war, but it would have been more than a decade instead of a few short years.

The end of the war did not mean the immediate end of war finance, since government deficit spending continued and one big final bond issue had yet to be floated, and so for a while the Fed continued its wartime policy of supporting "borrow and buy." But the end of the war did mean the end of wartime restrictions on private credit, which immediately took off, making full use of the enormous credit machine that had been built to facilitate public borrowing during the war. Banks that saw

---

[16] Willis (1923, 1211, 1509). The pre-Fed system of clearing using bankers' balances was replaced by clearing using Reserve Bank balances, and then final clearing between the Reserve Banks themselves.

[17] Willis (1923, 1119). Increasingly, the government held its deposits with the few Reserve Banks, not with the many commercial banks.

their public credit holdings paid off from the final bond issue used the proceeds not to shrink their inflated balance sheets, but rather to expand private credit. Balance sheet inflation thus continued, albeit now with frozen private credits rather than frozen public credits.

In an attempt to control this speculative excess, the Fed began to transition away from the wartime discount rate policy, starting November 1919 with a 0.5 percent discount rate advance and ending a year later "on the verge of a Panic" with the rate standing at 7 percent. The Depression of 1920–1 that followed was, for Willis, the inevitable adjustment of a wartime economy to peacetime conditions, a wrenching process but one in which the Fed played an admirably supportive role by discounting freely.[18] Prices that had been inflated by wartime demand pressures dropped precipitously, and credits that had been extended on the basis of wartime prices inevitably defaulted, but the system held. For Willis, this was the Fed's finest hour.

Writing in 1923, in his massive tome *The Federal Reserve System: Legislation, Organization and Operation*, Willis told the story of the founding of the Fed, urging his readers to put wartime experience behind them and to return to the original vision of the Federal Reserve Act. Domestically, "experience has shown the capacity of the note issue to contract as prices fell and demand for circulation was reduced. It is a fact that the theoretical elasticity of the new note currency has been entirely vindicated."[19] Internationally, the high discount rates used to combat postwar speculation had allowed London to regain its dominance of foreign trade financing, but it was not too late to make another effort. "Come on, guys," you can hear him exhorting his New York banker friends, "make an effort!"

Once again, it didn't work out that way. Looking back a decade later, Willis saw only "credit debauch."[20] The beautiful machinery of the Fed, tuned by the experience of war finance, had instead been diverted to speculative finance, not only domestically but also internationally. The resulting mess ultimately collapsed, first internationally, starting with the

---

[18] Willis (1923, 1406).
[19] Willis (1923, 1522).
[20] Willis and Chapman (1934, 106).

stock market collapse of 1929, and then domestically, ending with Roosevelt's national bank holiday in March 1933. At the root of both collapses was the prior expansion of unsound credit, first during the war, when government debt replaced real bills as the core of the system, and then after the war, when banks extended credit on government bond collateral for more or less anything.

This perversion of his creation must have been a terrible thing for Willis to watch. As editor of the *Journal of Commerce*, starting in 1919, he not only had a ringside seat from which to watch the unfolding debacle, but also a megaphone through which to express his dismay. But it was hard to make his voice heard over the Roaring Twenties, and so mainly he just watched, as "slower and less liquid forms of bank holdings invaded the portfolios of the different institutions during the ten years in question ... result[ing] in a reduction of liquidity (or viewed from another angle, in an increase of inflation) by approximately 40 per cent before 1929."[21]

What was worse, Willis' beloved Reserve Banks had not only let it all happen, but also had participated themselves. The orthodox doctrine that had privileged self-liquidating bills had been replaced by a new "shiftability" doctrine that instead privileged assets that were readily saleable.[22] As a consequence, banking came to be based not on the consuming power of the community, but rather on the "ability of the community to purchase, pay for, and hold or absorb issues of bonds, stocks, and other securities," which is to say on the "general conditions in the stock market."[23] In the process, central banking had come to be based not on discounting self-liquidating bills, but rather on outright purchase of long-term assets for the Fed's own portfolio through so-called "open market operations." Even internationally, "foreign funds had been largely engaged in frozen paper ('revolving' bankers' accept-ances and others of the same level), with the guarantee of the Federal Reserve Bank of New York which, of course, meant the guarantee of the

---

[21] Willis and Chapman (1935, 127).
[22] Moulton (1918).
[23] Willis and Chapman (1934, 32).

system."[24] The underlying cause of the credit debauch was, in this sense, the deliberate monetary policy of the Federal Reserve System.

Against this background, we can understand the seminar that Willis offered at Columbia in 1933–4 as a kind of last-ditch effort to get the Fed and the larger banking system back on track. The credit debauch of the Twenties had been about using banking and currency manipulation to avoid confronting hard political realities. Banking collapse could therefore be seen as a good thing, since it finally forced us to face reality and offered the opportunity to rebuild on solid ground rather than shifting sand. Just so, Willis urged his readers to put the period of speculative excess behind them, and to use the Banking Act of 1933, which he had himself played a role in drafting as advisor to Senator Glass, as an opportunity to restart the Fed on sound principles. That Act, known today as Glass-Steagall, called for strict separation of commercial and investment banking, which in context we can understand as an adaptation of the real bills doctrine for American conditions. Willis hoped that Glass-Steagall, though not itself as far-reaching as he would have liked, would in time spark a radical transformation of American banking.

For Willis, collapse had been inevitable because the underlying credit was unsound, but what was not inevitable was mismanagement of the policy response by leaders who should have known better. Hoover was one such leader, using the Reconstruction Finance Corporation to prop up banks that had been made insolvent by the prior policy of stuffing them with illiquid assets. The Fed was another such leader, needlessly abandoning the gold standard in 1933 in the face of a little speculative attack, even while the United States held 40 percent of the world's gold: "Speculators in New York bought sterling, and the British government, in pursuance of its policy of maintaining a relative degree of stability in the pound sterling, bought the dollars offered for the sterling – almost necessarily so – with the result that they earmarked a corresponding amount of metal."[25] Central bank cooperation could have shut down the speculators in short order, but the Fed was unprepared, having "never developed and trained an adequate foreign

[24] Willis and Chapman (1934, 57).
[25] Willis and Chapman (1934, 18).

exchange staff,"[26] and so instead they abandoned the stable anchor of the system just at the very moment it was most needed. Instead of simply borrowing the gold back from the Bank of England, the Fed treated the speculative movement as a genuine loss of reserves, and then on June 5, 1933, Congress enacted a resolution nullifying the right of creditors to demand payment in gold.

Against this background, it is no wonder that Willis took an interest in Charlie. Students like Charlie were exactly what the Fed needed as it sought to build a more adequate foreign exchange staff. For Willis himself, the international dimension of the US banking system was always of secondary concern; he was more about the Fed and domestic money. But at the highest level of abstraction, the fundamental issues at stake in domestic and international payments are much the same. The "international short-term capital movements" that would be the central focus of Charlie's dissertation are the international analogue of the bankers' balances that had served to facilitate domestic settlement in the United States before the establishment of the Fed.

Even more, Willis' life project of knitting together the sprawling US monetary system, with its twelve separate clearing districts, into a single whole can be seen as the inspiration for Charlie's eventual life project of knitting the international monetary system, with its multiple national sovereignties, into a single whole. Looking back on his thesis after fifty years, he made the connection explicit: "The model for the world should be the integrated financial market of a single country, with one money, free movements of capital at long and short term, the quantity theory of money employed on trend, but free discounting in periods of trouble."[27]

For Charlie, 1933 was what 1898 had been for Willis: the beginning of a lifelong engagement with the process of monetary reform, albeit international reform for Charlie rather than domestic reform as it had been for Willis. From Willis, he had learned how it required the financial crisis of 1907 to get the Federal Reserve Act of 1913; and how it had required the exigencies of war finance to bring the Act alive; and how, even so, in 1933 the work of full implementation remained. Analogously, it seems to

---

[26] Willis and Chapman (1934, 14).
[27] Kindleberger (1987a, 62).

have required the international financial crisis of 1929 to put the matter of international monetary reform firmly on the agenda of the London Economic and Financial Conference, scheduled for June 1933, but the result was no international analogue of the Federal Reserve Act. Instead, Roosevelt's preemptive action on gold and his subsequent refusal to consider a proposal for exchange stabilization put forward by his own central bank meant that the Conference ended early without substantive agreement.[28] The time was apparently not ripe. In 1933, everyone was still absorbing the fact that the old system, which had been centered on London and the pound sterling, was well and truly dead, while the eventual new system centered on New York and the dollar was not yet ready to be born.

International economics may have begun for Charlie, as he says, in his shipboard adventures of summer 1929, but his formal education in the subject began in fall 1933 in the classroom with James Angell. It was his worst grade, but a lasting influence in multiple ways. Most fundamentally, Angell's teaching is the likely origin of Charlie's early sense that "international economic theory . . . does not fit the facts." Even more, Charlie's early ambition to deduce "a new – and probably more complicated theory – from la situation actuelle" more or less mirrors Angell's own ambition to offer an alternative. Four years later, Charlie would produce his own treatise: *International Short-Term Capital Movements* (1937). He might have been talking about the relationship of his work to Angell's when he wrote about how the more rigorous textbooks produced by his MIT students had eaten into the market for his own: "that is the way academic life works: one climbs on the shoulders of the older generation and occasionally steps on a face."[29] Like Angell, Charlie would eventually become a Professor of International Economics, and it was Angell's example more than any other that shaped his conception of the job. To understand Charlie, we thus need also to understand Angell as a kind of aspirational role model.

---

[28] Clavin (2013) provides a detailed time line of the relevant events, though always from the somewhat distorting perspective of the League of Nations, which organized the Conference and had its own view on the central importance of free trade, not so much currency stabilization.

[29] Kindleberger (1991a, 135).

Unlike Charlie, James Waterhouse Angell (1898–1986) was an academic born and bred. His father, James Rowland Angell, was a well-known psychologist and President of Yale University (1921–37), and his grandfather, James Burrill Angell, had been president of the University of Vermont and the University of Michigan. At Harvard, young Angell earned his PhD in economics in 1924, working initially mainly with the great international economist Frank Taussig, and then with Allyn Young, whose favorite he became. The support of these men got him the job at Columbia University in 1924, where he remained until his retirement in 1966, living in the idyllic Fieldston historic district of the Bronx and summering on Martha's Vineyard. Unlike Charlie, Angell never strayed from the family business, and also unlike Charlie, that family business was never upended by the Depression.

Like Taussig and Young, Angell was an internationalist, regretting the failure of the United States to join the League of Nations, but nonetheless committed as a private citizen to advancing the internationalist cause wherever possible. The central focus of his thinking in this regard was the very much enlarged role of the United States in the realm of international trade and finance that arose as a direct consequence of World War. During the War, European belligerents had depended heavily on American production, and also on American finance to buy that production. As a consequence, during the war the United States was able to remain on the gold standard even as everyone else abandoned convertibility. Even more, the United States shifted from a net debtor to a net creditor position, becoming in effect investment banker for Europe, as well as substantially replacing Europe as investment banker for the rest of the world.

After the war, like everyone else, Angell expected a return to the status quo ante, which is to say the gold standard and global free trade, all centered in London, albeit with the share of the United States substantially increased. But until that eventual return, the United States would inevitably be called upon to play a major role in the transition from the disordered conditions of war and its aftermath. Dependence on American production and finance thus continued and even widened (notably to include Germany) in the period of reconstruction that followed the War. All of this posed for the United States a new challenge of economic management, and even moreso a new challenge of intellectual development to guide that management. Prewar isolationist habits of thought would have to change if America was to play the role required by new conditions.

As a graduate student, Angell had used his 1924 PhD dissertation, expanded into his first book, *The Theory of International Prices: History, Criticism and Restatement* (1926), to prepare himself to engage the range of new economic problems stemming from this new postwar reality. Substantially a history of economic thought on the topic, the book tells the story of developing English thought and Continental reaction, but the guiding question throughout is how much of classical doctrine can be taken over to the new world, and what needs to be reconsidered. Classical doctrine had developed the theory of international trade more or less separately from the theory of money, whereas it was clear that postwar problems of international trade and finance were completely intertwined and could not be treated separately. Integration of the two bodies of economic doctrine was thus needed, and such integration was bound to require changes in both.

In classical doctrine, the place where trade and finance come into closest contact is the so-called specie-flow mechanism, which is supposed to restore equilibrium in the balance of payments under a gold standard. If a country exports less than it imports, then it must pay for the difference in international money, which means gold. But gold reserves are also the basis of the national money supply, both notes and deposits, so these international gold flows cause contraction of money at home and expansion of money abroad, which tends to lower prices here and raise them abroad. In this way exports are encouraged and imports discouraged, and that is what restores balance, according to the theory.

Nice theory, but the facts turn out to be otherwise. Gold flows are clearly driven by other factors in addition to trade balances, most importantly capital flows, both short- and long-term. Further, the link between gold reserves and the domestic money supply is not so tight as the theory supposes, nor is the link between domestic price levels and the domestic money supply. And anyway, the price of international goods is only a small component of the overall price level. Angell concludes: "The specie flow analysis, at least in any short time sense, is now discredited in the eyes of most writers."[30]

And yet, some mechanism of self-regulation does seem to be operating, since prices do tend to remain more or less in line across country boundaries. Angell proposes that the relevant mechanism is not the flow of gold, but rather the operation of the market for foreign exchange, and in particular the shifting balance of importer and exporter bills, which has an immediate effect on short-term interest rates and also, so he proposes, on the total volume of purchasing power, meaning bank credit. "This explanation rests on the effects which changes in the demand and supply of bills of exchange produce in the volume of bank deposits, and in the levels of general prices."[31]

One virtue of Angell's alternative explanation of international prices is that it applies even when currencies are not convertible, as they were not for some period after the war. Under such circumstances, not only interest rates but also exchange rates shift with movements of the balance of international payments.[32] The classical doctrine for the case of inconvertible currency depended on so-called "purchasing power parity," according to which exchange rates simply reflect relative price levels, so that exchange depreciation simply reflects relative inflation rates, which presumably arise from relative monetary policies. But that is another nice theory at odds with the facts, since exchange rates can and do move independently from price levels in response to speculation, and changing exchange rates can and do affect domestic price levels independently from domestic monetary policy.

After Angell took up his new job at Columbia, Allyn Young encouraged him to develop his theory of foreign exchange into a full-blown treatise, as did Ralph Hawtrey, who reviewed Angell's book for the British *Economic Journal.* But Angell had other ideas. As a student, he had spent the academic year 1922–3 touring Europe to meet all the leading international economists, as background research for his dissertation. Once he was in New York, he lost no time in establishing contact with the

---

[30]   Angell (1926, 393).
[31]   Angell (1926, 474).
[32]   Indeed, it seems that Angell began with the inconvertible case, as in Angell (1922).

Council on Foreign Relations, founded in 1921 as a kind of successor to "The Inquiry," which had organized academic input into the Paris Peace Conference. After Congress rejected official membership in the League of Nations, the Council operated as a kind of informal member of the League. Under its auspices, Angell turned his attention to the pressing policy questions of his time in *The Inter-Ally Debts and the United States* (1925), along with the problem of reparations and *The Recovery of Germany* (1929), the latter volume being the output of a year's travel in Germany sponsored by the Council.

In doing so, Angell was very much following in the footsteps of his mentor Young, who had served as chief economist of The Inquiry and chronicler of the League's first World Economic Conference in Geneva.[33] Indeed, Angell's starting point in thinking about the problem of international debts was Young's 1924 article, "War Debts, External and Internal" (published in the CFR journal *Foreign Affairs*). Like Young, Angell saw intergovernmental debts as the major obstacle unsettling world economic affairs and eventual commercialization of German reparations obligations as the essential step toward resolution. Until that could be worked out, however, the important thing was to keep the credit flowing. Germany needed US loans in order to rebuild its economy to pay reparations, and Europe needed reparations in order to repay war debts to the United States. The Dawes Plan of 1924 and then the Young Plan of 1929 were therefore key to the continued operation of the international monetary system. Writing in 1929, Angell was optimistic that things would work out, but also very much aware that international success depended crucially on the continued ability of German borrowers to issue securities in New York.

Even after the 1929 stock market crash, and the untimely death of Young, who had by then moved to the London School of Economics, Angell remained optimistic. The crash and the devastating economic contraction that followed were definite setbacks for the internationalist program, but all was not lost. The Hoover Moratorium bought time to put things back on a sustainable track. After the Lausanne Agreement resettled the reparations problem, Angell joined a group of economists urging creation of a World

---

[33] Young (1921a, 1921b), and Young and Fay (1927). See also Mehrling (1997, ch. 3).

War Foreign Debt Commission to readjust funding agreements between the allies, and he went on to produce a book-length report on *Financial Foreign Policy of the United States* for the Second International Studies Conference in 1933 (a project of the League of Nations), and to write the introduction to *The Program for the World Economic Conference* (1933) in an attempt to garner support for that conference in the United States.[34]

As he was doing all of this, apparently assuming that a solution would be found to the immediate problem of war debts, Angell focused his own attention on the deeper and longer-term problem that he anticipated would be revealed after settlement. As a net creditor, the United States was for the first time in its history in a structurally surplus position in terms of the international balance of payments, and that meant that the rest of the world would need to find means to make payments to the United States. Given US resistance to buying foreign goods, as expressed in high tariffs, payments would have to be made not by selling goods but instead by selling securities and other property, which is to say by further expanding the US net creditor position. In a prescient speech of November 14, 1930, Angell warned that "when we take our income from abroad in the form of additional foreign securities, we are not solving the foreigners' payment problem at all. We are merely deferring the problem, and in the end making it worse."[35] At some point, he cautioned, further lending would cease, and at that point settlement would become impossible, making foreign sales impossible, and the world system would shatter.

In fact, even as Angell was speaking, that breaking point was already at hand, the collapse having begun with the New York stock market crash in October 1929. But in 1930 Angell thought it was still possible to turn the tide, and he kept that faith until the bitter end. On the very eve of the fateful 1933 World Economic Conference, Angell judged that currency stabilization remained an achievable goal, even if greater international financial cooperation did not. In the event, however, even currency stabilization proved too much since the United States was unwilling to play the necessary leading role, Roosevelt in effect blocking the internationalist program on which Angell and others had pinned their hopes

[34] Angell (1932, 1933a, 1933b).
[35] Angell (1931).

for so long.[36] It must have been a sore disappointment for him. The mission he had accepted from his mentors – to help the United States navigate the tricky transition from war to peace, and from autarky to global free trade – seemed now more or less a complete failure.

Not only an internationalist, Angell was also a liberal, and as such a strong supporter of Roosevelt's interventionist New Deal. For him, economic stabilization at the national level was the prerequisite for any program of stabilization at the international level that went beyond mere currency stabilization and central bank cooperation. Angell's response to the policy failure of 1933 was therefore to shift his attention away from international matters and to focus instead on using monetary control to stabilize the domestic economy. Ultimately, he produced two books on the topic: *The Behavior of Money: Exploratory Studies* (1936) and *Investment and Business Cycles* (1941).

It is this latter work that did not survive, as Charlie pointed out in his autobiography, and the reason was Keynes, whose *General Theory of Employment, Interest and Money* (1936) better caught the spirit of the times. On the matter of effective control of internal economic activity, Charlie, along with everyone else, followed Keynes rather than Angell. Charlie had been introduced to Keynesian thinking as early as 1934 by Henry Villard who had been part of the Keynes seminar at Cambridge but then shifted to the City College of New York, "bringing with him reports of the new book by Keynes which fundamentally altered economic analysis of business fluctuations."[37] They had met and become friends in Charlie's second year at Columbia, and then in the third year they had organized a graduate student seminar which met at the apartment of Professors Arthur R. and Eveline M. Burns, which "proved to be as stimulating as any formal seminar listed in the catalogue."[38]

All of this – the bitter disappointment of the World Economic Conference and the looming figure of Keynes – would have been uppermost in Angell's mind in fall 1933 when Charlie enrolled in his class, and no doubt it colored their initial interaction. Although Charlie was

---

[36] See Clavin (2013), and footnote 28 herein.
[37] Interim Biography, p. 25.
[38] Kindleberger (1991a, 32).

initially a protégé of Willis, the topics of the papers he wrote during his first graduate years show him moving toward the Angell agenda step by step. Already in fall 1933 he was writing a term paper for his course with Beckhart, "Competitive Currency Depreciation between Denmark and New Zealand," concluding that the only winner of competitive depreciation was the British consumer who got cheaper butter.[39] More fundamentally, in his master's thesis "Inflation and Foreign Trade" (1934), he examined exchange depreciation in Great Britain, Japan, and the United States, concluding that it was not a consequence of domestic inflation, as the theory of purchasing power proposed, but rather a cause of subsequent inflation. Compare Angell: "The English data ... show that the order of change which that theory expects was on the whole reversed here, not confirmed. The exchanges moved first, then prices, and last of all the note circulation."[40]

With these finger exercises behind him, Charlie was ready to tackle the Angell agenda head on, producing a sketch of a possible theoretical framework: "Flexibility of Demand in International Trade Theory." Feeling the inadequacy of his mathematical preparation, Charlie proceeded instead "with the (possibly) archaic tool of logical analysis,"[41] but there is no mistaking his ambition. He urges attention to the role of changes in nominal income, not just the international prices emphasized by Angell, as central to the mechanism through which disequilibrium in the balance of payments is adjusted. It was on the basis of this paper that Angell agreed to serve as supervisor of his thesis.

The thesis itself was written largely off-campus in evenings and weekends, initially at a temporary job at the US Treasury in summer 1936, and then during the first year of a permanent job at the Federal Reserve Bank of New York which started in October 1936. Charlie remembers:

> Angell lacked a warm nature, and called me Mr. Kindleberger all through the process of supervision. He did however respond fully to the separate

---

[39] The paper was Charlie's first publication, in *Harvard Business Review* (July 1934), and the only pre-World War II publication that he would include in his retrospective (2000a, ch. 2).

[40] Angell (1926, 430).

[41] Kindleberger (1937a, 353).

chapters of the thesis as I submitted them ... In the end we disagreed on
the main point of the thesis, whether disequilibrium in the balance of
payments should be measured by gold flows alone, as he thought, or gold
flows plus or minus short-term capital movements, as I maintained.[42]

In context, we can understand this disagreement as stemming from
Charlie's Willis-inflected understanding of the international monetary
system as fundamentally a payment system, with short-term capital movements playing the role that bankers' balances play in the domestic system,
shifting funds from short-term surplus agents to short-term deficit agents
in order to facilitate immediate settlement. Thus, although Charlie got
his start in international economics from Angell, he used what he had
learned about banking from Willis to propose his own alternative to the
classical model, which was more far-reaching than Angell's.

The usefulness of this alternative perspective was revealed most immediately in the clarity it gave to the phenomenon of "hot money," which is
to say the speculative short-term capital movements that first got Charlie
interested in understanding the international monetary system. He
writes in his thesis:

> To take a simple case, if a central bank of a country on an exchange
> standard decides to shift its foreign exchange reserves from one country
> to another, the sale of the exchange on the country where the reserves
> were originally held and the purchase of the exchange on the country to
> which they are to be moved may well cause a gold flow from the former to
> the latter. If gold be the evidence of disequilibrium in the balance of
> payments ... then the first country should deflate and the second
> country should expand its means of payment. If short-term capital
> movements be the sole criterion, then the first country having
> experienced a reduction in its net short-term liabilities – an outflow of
> short-term capital – should inflate and the second country, with increased
> net short-term foreign liabilities, should deflate. But if the gold outflow
> and inflow be set off against the short-term capital outflow and inflow,
> respectively, then it is seen that no change in the means of payment should
> be permitted to take place, which requires that the gold movements

---

[42] Kindleberger (1991a, 39).

should be offset in both countries. This is evidently what should take place.[43]

Observe here that "logical analysis" takes the form of thinking like a banker, in balance sheet terms, attending to both assets and liabilities. From this perspective it becomes clear that the central bank in the country losing the gold should at most borrow it back from the central bank in the country gaining the gold, thus reversing the speculative flow, both of gold and of short-term capital.

In the theory of international money, Charlie thus moved beyond Angell, as good students always move beyond their teachers, but the example of Angell had a lasting influence on Charlie's trajectory in other ways, most importantly by introducing him to an alternative career goal: teaching, instead of central banking. The teaching plan did not immediately work out – this was the Depression and there were simply no jobs – but eventually Charlie did manage to shift into teaching, starting at MIT in 1948 as a professor of international economics, more or less exactly the position that Angell still held at Columbia.

Further, Angell's internationalist perspective had lasting influence, while the failure of Angell's internationalist interventions informed Charlie's own rather different interventions when the opportunity presented itself. Significantly, Charlie would have nothing to do with the multilateral Bretton Woods agreement, nor the United Nations which arose as successor to the failed League. His energies were devoted instead to the Marshall Plan, the unilateral move of the de facto world leader. That said, Charlie's economic justification for the Marshall Plan, laid out in *The Dollar Shortage* (1950), very clearly echoes the concerns expressed by Angell as the international monetary system was collapsing in 1930. In 1950 as in 1930, the fundamental problem was that the rest of the world needed to make payments to the United States, now not so much for war debts but rather for the materials needed for reconstruction, so even zero tariffs would not help very much. The Marshall Plan worked because it addressed this most pressing obstacle to recovery, and so bridged the gap from war to peace, from command economy to market economy (Chapter 4).

---

[43] Kindleberger (1937b, 234).

In February 1932, Charlie had graduated early from Penn with the idea of getting a job at the Fed and marrying Caroline Thompson. Three years into his graduate studies, it was time to try again. Eileen O'Daniels was by this time out of the picture. Her parting gift to Charlie was to arrange for him to get professional help for his stuttering problem, and this softened the blow: "Not to stutter in teaching or in a big public lecture before as many, on some occasions, as a thousand people, reminds me of my deliverance."[44] Taking her place was Sarah B. Miles, the sister of Charlie's friend Francis Miles, and the daughter of Wardlaw Miles, the World War I hero who became headmaster of the Gilman School and then Professor of English at Johns Hopkins, and who would become a kind of adoptive father for Charlie as his own family collapsed under the strain of Depression.[45] But Charlie did not feel that he could propose to Sarah until he had a job, and he did not feel that he could marry until he finished the thesis: "A considerable part of the spur to complete the dissertation was the suggestion from my prospective father-in-law that it might be useful to get the thesis out of the way before marrying."[46] Strong incentive.

Job first. As it happened, W. Randolph Burgess, a vice president of the Federal Reserve Bank of New York, attended one meeting of the Villard–Kindleberger Keynes seminar and, when Charlie expressed interest in a job, invited him down: "I met Lewis Galantiere and discussed with him the possibility of a job working partly in his Foreign Information Division and partly for the Foreign Report Section of the Foreign Exchange Department with Emile Despres."[47] But nothing immediately came of it, and so instead Charlie accepted a summer position in the Division of Research and Statistics at the US Treasury, working mainly on calculating purchasing power parities, while writing his thesis in the evenings and visiting Miss Miles in Baltimore on the weekends. Eventually, the Fed job did materialize with a starting date of October 1, 1936, and on the strength of that Charlie got engaged on September 26th and resigned

---

[44] Kindleberger (1991a, 42).
[45] Like Charlie, Miles had managed to avoid his father's profession (medicine) and developed a mastery of the essay form (French 1944, Miles 1930).
[46] Interim Biography, p. 34.
[47] Interim Biography, p. 29.

from the Treasury on the 28th. "Harry White, I recall, asked me to stay on for $2600 [a $200 raise from his summer salary]. I said I would for $3200, but he could not or would not make such an offer."[48] And so Charlie shifted from Washington to New York, now working mainly on calculating international capital flows.

Thesis second. A lot of the preparatory reading and note-taking was already done. A first step had been a review of the recent literature on international capital flows. Three books on the topic were published in 1935, and Charlie got hold of them by promising to review them for the *Political Science Quarterly.* The best of them all was Ragnar Nurkse's *Internationale Kapitalbewegungen,* "a brilliant excursion into a theoretically dimly lighted territory."[49] It is Nurkse's classification of different kinds of capital flows that Charlie would use as the frame for Part I of his thesis.

Part II of the thesis followed Willis, by applying a payments perspective to short-term capital movements. The first of two basic principles that Charlie sought to establish has recognizable origins in Willis: "that short-term capital in the balance of payments and in a national banking system should be regarded as equivalent to gold (from which the corollary follows that when gold flows are due solely to movements of short-term funds their effects on the banking system should be offset)." Part III then followed Angell by tracing the effects of these flows on domestic money and nominal income. The second principle has recognizable origins in Angell: "that equilibrium in the foreign-exchange market and in the balance of payments can be said to obtain when at a given rate of exchange the balance of payments exerts neither an inflationary nor a deflationary force on the national money income."

---

[48] This is the account in the Interim Biography, p. 33. In his autobiography, Charlie says he was willing to stay for $2,600 but White was unwilling to offer the extra $200. I have favored the IB account, as it was written closer to the time of the event, but it should be kept in mind that a central purpose of that account was to establish that Charlie was not so interested in a job at the Treasury, so as to "dispel any possible question in any mind that I was participating in a Treasury plot, if there was one, whether to pastoralize Germany, or for any other purpose." In the IB account, Charlie more or less rejects the Treasury, while in the autobiography account the Treasury more or less rejects Charlie.

[49] Kindleberger (1936).

It is only in the final section – Part IV, "International Monetary Interdependence" – that Charlie looks forward, toward his career as central banker. Here he argues that the task of the central bank is not to choose internal or external stability, but rather to find the best combination of partial stability in both, using the available range of stabilization tools, and he devotes the remaining chapters to an exploration of those tools. In this argument we see him breaking away from his teachers: from Willis, who held that "some form of external stability is all that can be hoped for in the present state of knowledge," and also from Angell, who held that "internal stability is approachable only if external stability be abandoned."[50] Charlie rejects both extremes and adopts instead a position that seems closest to that of John H. Williams, Professor of Economics at Harvard and also Chief Economist at the New York Fed, whose views Charlie distilled from his 1934 paper "The World's Monetary Dilemma – Internal versus External Monetary Stability."[51]

As it happens, Charlie had attended the conference in spring 1934 where Williams presented this paper, but he had not given it any special attention at the time. As he told his diary: "Brown and Hansen made the best talks, Pitt the senator from Nevada on silver and Warren on gold being the most provocative."[52] Likely his renewed attention to Williams came instead from Emile Despres, his Fed colleague who had studied under Williams at Harvard, writing his undergraduate thesis on "Capital Movements and the Mechanism of International Trade Adjustment under Gold" (April 15, 1930).[53] All the while Charlie was writing the thesis on *International Short-Term Capital Movements*, his day job was to work with Emile Despres tracking short-term capital movements in the real world. In the thesis, this influence can be seen in the statistical appendix which outlines the available data, and their deficiencies, as well as the careful treatment of the mechanics of the forward exchange market (Chapter 8). In this regard, it is significant that Charlie thanks Despres equally, along with his formal supervisor Angell, "for the light

---

[50] Kindleberger (1937b, 176–177).
[51] Williams (1934).
[52] KPMD, Box 40, "Personal Diary." The conference was held at Hotel Astor, Mar. 21, 1934.
[53] Truman Library, Despres Papers.

they have given me on the problems covered below and for their patience in reading and suggesting improvements in the manuscript."[54]

Job first, thesis second, and finally marriage. Working fast, Charlie finished the thesis in March 1937, just in time to marry Miss Miles on May 1, 1937. Marriage came with a dowry of $6,000, half of which he used to fund publication of the thesis by Columbia University Press, so it was fitting that the published book was dedicated "To S.M.K." Realizing that the two key dates of his engagement and his marriage coincided with two important events in the world of money – the Tripartite Agreement that stabilized dollar–sterling–franc exchange and the Fed's decision to raise reserve requirements – Charlie included an entry in the book's index for "S. Murgatroyd" that references the two worldly events. He liked to joke that it served as an aide memoire to remind him of the important personal anniversaries. Everywhere else it may have been Depression, but not in Charlie's life. Not for the last time, Charlie's planful resilience had overcome worldly setback.

---

[54] Kindleberger (1937b, viii).

CHAPTER 3

Hot Money

This much is evident: governments propose, markets dispose.[1]

As Charlie started his new job at the New York Fed, the Tripartite Agreement for currency stabilization between the United States, Britain, and France was being implemented. In fact, his new job largely involved providing statistical support for the US role in the new monetary system, working with Emile Despres to tally short-term capital flows and report to the Treasury. A further idea seems to have been to free up Despres to do other things, such as spending the academic year 1937–8 pursuing formal graduate study at Harvard, specifically participating in the famous Hansen–Williams Fiscal Policy Seminar. For Charlie, the important thing was that he was now finally in the game, doing more or less exactly what he had set his mind on doing. Rejected out of hand by the Fed in his first attempt back in 1932, he had regrouped and retrained and was now on his way.

The way the new currency stabilization system worked, every day each country published the price at which it was willing to sell gold to other signatories of the Agreement, and then for the next 24 hours met all requests using the gold reserves in its Exchange Stabilization Fund. Large enough gold outflows could of course exhaust the gold reserves of any one country, but so long as outflows were matched by inflows into one of the other Tripartite currencies, reserves could always be replenished simply by borrowing and lending between the deficit and surplus Funds. As the system came into effect, this replenishment came to operate mainly

[1] Kindleberger (1981a, 69). Possibly Charlie is here echoing a famous line from *The Imitation of Christ*, which he likely encountered in chapel at Kent: "Man proposes, but God disposes."

through the fixed buying and selling price of gold in terms of dollars, $35 an ounce, which operated as an anchor for the system as a whole. The effect was to create a 24-hour fixed exchange rate between the three countries. As an international monetary system, it wasn't much – only three currencies and only 24 hours – but it was a start, and it was soon joined by Belgium, Switzerland, and the Netherlands. It didn't restore the prewar globally integrated trading system, but it did temporarily help to stabilize exchange rates that had been whipsawed by the flow of so-called "hot money" ever since Britain's suspension of gold convertibility in 1931.

The underlying logic of the Tripartite system, it is important to emphasize, was the so-called "key-currency" idea that had first been floated by Harvard Professor John H. Williams back in 1932 in his role as US representative to the Preparatory Commission of Experts, preliminary to the June 1933 World Economic Conference in London.[2] Prior to the Conference, in May 1933, Williams was brought on to the New York Fed staff as an assistant Federal Reserve agent, and then in 1936, prior to the Tripartite Agreement, he was promoted to Vice President. Thus, in effect Williams was chief economist of the New York Fed when Charlie joined, and, although Charlie never reported to him directly, his job required him very much to engage with Williams' thinking.

In his autobiography, Charlie remembers how Williams split his time between Harvard and the Fed:

> He patronized the overnight sleeper, the Owl, to such an extent that some of us thought he had hung pictures in his lower berth ... I saw more of Professor Williams [after the war] when I was at MIT and he at Harvard, and found myself slowly and partly unconsciously more and more impressed with his notion of "key currencies."[3]

---

[2] Following Clarke (1967, 40), Kindleberger (1984a, 336, 430) suggests that the key-currency idea perhaps has its origin even earlier in the thinking of Benjamin Strong, while drawing attention to the account of Williams' "pays-clef" views in *Documents diplomatiques francais, 1932–39*, 1st Series, 1932–1934, Volume 2, para. 180, Geneva to Paris, p. 386. See also Kindleberger (1987b, 122, 140). Clavin (1996, 90, 110, 112) tracks the diplomatic history of stabilization discussions leading up to the World Economic Conference, emphasizing their tripartite nature. The most complete account of Williams' thinking is Asso and Fiorito (2009).

[3] Kindleberger (1991a, 50).

In fact, the record shows that Williams' intellectual influence during Charlie's two-and-a-half year stint at the Fed before the war was already quite substantial. Charlie's postwar monetary writings – *Europe and the Dollar* (1966), *International Money* (1981), and *International Capital Movements* (1987) – all build on that prewar influence, quite as much as they do on the influence of Willis and Angell. And so, finally, to understand Charlie, we must also understand Williams.

Like Angell, John Henry Williams (1887–1980) had been a student of Taussig at Harvard, from whom he absorbed the same lesson that Angell did about the shortcomings of the classical analysis of the gold standard. Williams' 1920 PhD thesis, "Argentine International Trade under Inconvertible Paper Money, 1880–1900," was the first in a remarkable series produced by Taussig students, followed by Viner (1924), Angell (1926), and White (1933).[4] But it was Williams more than any of the others who focused his attention on banking, and it was Williams alone who returned to Harvard, starting in 1925 and rising to full professorship in 1929.

The key-currency idea seems to have arisen to make sense of the experience of international monetary reconstruction in the 1920s. After World War I, everyone had expected restoration of the prewar gold standard system, which was understood almost universally (if not by Taussig and his students) in orthodox specie-flow terms. The gold-exchange standard agreed to at Genoa in 1922, according to which countries were supposed to accept one another's currencies in settlement of international payments and not insist on gold, was understood as only a temporary stopgap on the road toward reconstruction of the prewar system. In 1925 Britain did return to gold convertibility, albeit at the overvalued prewar parity, followed shortly after by France. Gold outflow from Britain began immediately and became a persistent problem, caused in part by undervaluation of the French franc, and also by a sustained shift of French sterling balances in London to dollar balances in New York. Periodically, the Fed tried to help the Bank of England by lowering its own interest rate in order to make the dollar less attractive, but the rising US stock market pulled in foreign capital anyway. And, all

---

[4] Alacevich et al. (2015).

the while, the unresolved problem of Allied war debts and German reparations stood in the way of more extensive central bank cooperation. Williams' breakthrough in thinking about these matters was to recognize that the prewar gold standard had actually been a gold standard only for Britain: "England was on the gold standard and the rest of the world was on the sterling standard," insofar as it was the London sterling bill market that facilitated trade across the globe.[5] Through its empire, Britain had run a trade surplus with the rest of the world, and through its financial center in London it had recycled that surplus into long-term investments across the globe, while the Bank of England managed the daily fluctuations of the international monetary system by raising the bank rate in response to net gold outflows and lowering it in response to net gold inflows.

From a key-currency perspective, the central problem facing the Bank of England after the war was the new position of the United States as net creditor to the rest of the world, which meant that sterling no longer stood alone at the apex of the system. As a consequence, reasoned Williams, stabilization of *both* sterling *and* the dollar, against gold but more importantly against each other, was the key to achieving international monetary stability, the essential first step but also the essential stable core around which others could subsequently orient themselves:

> Fixed exchanges and gold flow would provide a means of imparting to the rest of the world stabilizing influences developed, maintained and controlled through money management in the center countries. Under such conditions, the foreign exchange problem would boil down in the main to the question of the dollar-sterling rate relationship. Some community of action in monetary and in general economic policy as between these two countries would clearly be involved.[6]

---

[5] Williams (1934, 65). Here he is explicitly following the historical account of Smit (1934), which references a longer study he published with the Council on Foreign Relations. In context, we can understand the interventions of Williams and Smit as an attempt to shift the multilateral League-style thinking of the Council in a key-currency direction.

[6] Williams (1934, 66).

The Agenda for the 1933 World Economic Conference very much reflected Williams' conception of the road forward. The very first item on the Agenda was Monetary and Credit Policy: "We feel that, in practice, certain countries are in a key position in that the reestablishment of a free gold standard by them would influence action in a number of other countries." In this regard, "countries with a free gold standard and with abundant monetary reserves" are obliged to take the lead; no specific countries are named, but clearly France and the United States are intended. "Countries which have left the gold standard" are obliged to restrain themselves from seeking individual advantage by depreciating their currencies against the leaders; again, no specific countries are named, but clearly Britain is intended. And "countries which have introduced exchange restrictions" as a means of defending their exchange rates are obliged to allow these rates to find their own levels and to stabilize at those levels; here, the main target is likely Germany. The central banks of all three kinds of countries are obliged to cooperate, initially to facilitate reallocation of world monetary reserves, and after that on an ongoing basis concerning credit policy. "The Bank for International Settlements represents a new agency for central banks and should be able to play an increasingly important part, not only by improving contact, but also as an instrument of common action."[7]

This published Agenda is likely more or less what Williams urged privately to his fellow experts in 1932, and it is also likely more or less what the American representatives to the World Economic Conference, O. M. W. Sprague from Harvard (representing the Treasury) and George Harrison from the Federal Reserve, pushed during the first weeks of that Conference. For a brief moment, it even seemed possible that the Agenda might become reality as central bankers, meeting separately from the main conference, made rapid progress nailing down the details of specific exchange rate pegs. But in the end, the new US President Roosevelt refused to go along, perhaps having in mind the British experience of the 1920s when domestic prosperity was sacrificed to a quixotic attempt to restore the prewar gold standard. Instead, Roosevelt moved in exactly the opposite direction by suspending US gold payments in

---

[7] Angell (1933b, 31–39).

April 1933 and then raising the price of gold in an attempt to raise domestic prices, causing gold to flood into the United States. His "bombshell" telegram more or less tanked the Conference, with the result that instead of international monetary stabilization we got the era of hot money.[8]

Notwithstanding the failure of 1933, it is important to appreciate that the Agenda of the World Economic Conference was subsequently kept alive as a minority view inside the New York Fed by Williams and also by Allan Sproul, Charlie's ultimate boss, who would succeed Harrison as President of the Bank. Finally in 1936, when recovery in the United States seemed to be under way, there was space to press the Agenda forward again. The result was the Tripartite Agreement.

Whether or not Charlie knew about the larger Williams agenda in advance of taking the Fed job, he certainly found out in a hurry once on site. For the first six months, his focus understandably was on finishing his thesis, but all the while he was coming up to speed. Already in an internal Fed manuscript dated January 12, 1937, and titled "International Monetary Organization and Policy," which opens with an essay by John H. Williams of the same title,[9] Charlie contributed a coauthored chapter 6, "Trade Areas," and a single-authored chapter 7, "Some General Implications of Recent Currency Developments." Charlie might have been channeling Williams when he writes: "The devaluation of the franc and the other gold bloc currencies, long expected and postponed, clears the way for possible advances in the development of international monetary organization."[10]

What possible advances? One possibility, which Charlie subsequently urged in a variety of internal Fed memos, was the demonetization of gold: "A Program for Gold" (June 18, 1937), and "The Gold Problem" (March 24, 1938, with Emilio G. Collado). He argued that the continued availability of gold as a monetary asset was a destabilizing feature of the system, since it enabled runs on national currencies, that is, the hot

---

[8] Clavin (2013, 120–121).

[9] Under a different title, this chapter was published as Williams (1937).

[10] "International Monetary Organization and Policy," p. 144. KPMD, Box 4, Folder "Federal Reserve Bank of New York, 1936."

money problem. His solution: "set up a system of foreign exchange based upon less expensive counters than gold by exchanging cash assets with foreign countries, closing all central banks to gold, and going on a world foreign exchange (largely dollar and sterling) standard."[11]

Short of that ideal, the important thing was to prevent short-term capital flows from destabilizing exchange. Toward that end, in an internal memo titled "Hot Money" (April 18, 1938, with Collado), Charlie urged a two-tier exchange system: the official dollar to be kept stable by official gold flows, and the private dollar to be allowed to fluctuate.[12] The idea was to channel short-term capital flows into the private market, in effect absorbing the pressure of speculative inflows and outflows in the fluctuating price of the private dollar, while maintaining stable official rates for foreign trade purposes. "In effect this proposal would provide a system of foreign exchange control, sorting out the commercial from the hot money transactions with none of the usual administrative details and difficulties incident to most foreign exchange control systems."[13]

It is important to appreciate that both of these ideas about possible future developments are fully consistent with the key-currency approach. True, Williams always framed his proposal as a return to the gold standard, but gold convertibility of the key currencies was never the main thing; rather, it was stable exchange rates between them so as to serve as an anchor and reserve for the larger international monetary system. Demonetization of gold internationally was just a next logical step after demonetization of gold nationally, which essentially all countries had achieved by then. Similarly, Williams was always centrally concerned about the destabilizing effect of short-term capital flows, and concerned particularly that they might overwhelm the capacity of central banks to

---

[11] "The Gold Problem," p. 4. KPMD, Box 4, Folder "FRBNY, 1938–1939."

[12] The origin of the idea (probably Collado's contribution) was apparently ATT's practice of limiting foreign ownership of its stock and letting the price of the foreign quota fluctuate relative to the price of the domestically held stock.

[13] "Hot Money," p. 12. KPMD, Box 4, Folder "FRBNY, 1938–1939." Despres (1973, ch. 14) would revive both of these proposals in the 1960s, prior to the imposition of a two-tier gold market in March 1968, and the suspension of convertibility on August 15, 1971.

absorb them. The so-called "golden avalanche" that followed Roosevelt's increase of the dollar price of gold was just such an overwhelming flow. If only there were a way to absorb some of the flow in price, it would be easier to absorb the rest in central bank credit. Charlie's two-tier exchange market proposal was designed to do exactly that.

In the end, the Tripartite Agreement didn't really deliver, in part because of the reversal of the US recovery in 1937, but more fundamentally because of European preparations for war. Meanwhile, however, daily engagement with the nitty-gritty of foreign exchange markets left Charlie with a base of institutional knowledge on which he would build for the rest of his life. The most significant indicator of this is his paper "Speculation and Forward Exchange," written in 1938, tracking the effects of speculative capital flows and official interventions over the period 1935–7, a period spanning the implementation of the Tripartite Agreement. His most significant empirical finding is the very different operation of sterling as opposed to the franc and the guilder; the sterling forward premium against the dollar is clearly driven by active interest rate arbitrage, whereas the same arbitrage is restricted or impossible in the case of the franc and the guilder. Though he does not say so explicitly, in effect Charlie is documenting the emergence of a dollar–sterling key-currency system, with the two currencies held together by covered interest parity arbitrage so that differences in domestic interest rates are reflected in the difference between spot and forward exchange rates.[14]

As the prospect of European War loomed, Charlie reframed his views on gold demonetization and hot money as ruminations about "American Gold Policy in the Event of European War" (August 19, 1938) and "The Dollar in the Event of European War" (April 13, 1939). But once Despres returned from his year at Harvard, realizing that his prospects for promotion within the Fed were distinctly limited, Charlie began looking for a change. When he learned of an opening at the Bank for International Settlements, he asked Sproul to nominate him and, after an interview with New York banker Leon Fraser, former President of the Bank, he got the job, which entailed

---

[14] Charlie's explicit target is the erroneous argument of Paul Einzig (1937) to the effect that intervention in the forward market offers a nearly costless way of stabilizing exchange, since it does not require use of scarce gold reserves.

a three-year commitment in Basel, Switzerland.[15] A particular attraction was the regular meeting of central bankers at the Bank, in effect the very locus of international monetary cooperation. A further attraction was a return to the land of his ancestors, whose origins he traced back to Berne by way of the German Palatinate.[16]

Established in 1930 as part of the Young Plan to commercialize the German reparations debt – a project almost immediately rendered moot by cancellation of that debt – the Bank for International Settlements remained important as the Trustee for the privately funded Young Loan and as a meeting place for member central banks. Because of the reparations connection, the United States had refused to join the Bank; so, private New York banks took up the allotted shares instead. Thus, although de facto Charlie was sent as a representative of the Fed, as indicated by his month of orientation meetings at the Board before setting sail, de jure he was required to resign from the Fed in order to take up the new position. The incoming president of the Bank, Thomas H. McKittrick, was an American but an outsider to New York banking circles. Charlie, however, was by now an insider to those circles, and so presumably a reliable conduit of information from his listening post in Basel.

For Charlie, international economics had begun in 1929 with his summer adventures on commercial freighters traveling to foreign shores. Imagine his delight, therefore, to find himself only ten years later traveling on the SS *America* to a new job at the central bankers' bank as a first-class passenger, upgraded by the line to show appreciation for the Fed's gold shipment business. His life was quite definitely coming together, and not only his professional life, for he was traveling with his new wife and her dog Mr. Whimperton. Had he remained in Switzerland for the planned three years, both of his sons would have been born there, and international economics might well have extended beyond the agreed three years. In the event, however, the outbreak of war would limit his time in Basel to a single year, as we shall see.

---

[15] Interim Biography, p. 38. The autobiography says that Sproul approached him about the opportunity; Kindleberger (1991a, 50).

[16] Kindleberger (1991a, 5).

It is perhaps significant that, well after the war, while on sabbatical in Geneva, Charlie took the opportunity to challenge himself and his eldest son with the famous Haute Route, a strenuous hike through the Alps, "he at fourteen just old enough ... I at forty-four hoping to be just young enough." And then later, to mark his seventieth birthday, he organized another less strenuous hike from the Saint Bernard Pass down to Champery with his two sons, "this time they taking care of me, rather than as in 1953–4, my looking out for them."[17] Baptismal hikes thus took the place of actual baptisms, significant for their suggestion of a life that might have been, a life that in summer 1939 Charlie was intent on building.

By the time Charlie and Sarah left the United States on July 3, 1939, Germany had already invaded Czechoslovakia and wider war seemed a distinct possibility. But the United States was determined to remain neutral, as was Switzerland and especially the BIS, the latter in reaction to its earlier decision to accede to an obviously coerced Czech request to transfer its gold reserves – held physically at the Bank of England but booked at the BIS – to the Reichsbank. At any rate, in summer 1939, the prospect of wider war seemed sufficiently distant that Charlie and Sarah invited her parents to join them in Switzerland for a touring holiday in the last weeks of August. When Germany invaded Poland, triggering England and France to declare war on September 3, the in-laws cut their holiday short and scrambled home, but Charlie and Sarah stayed, moving into a rented apartment at 14 Casinostrasse, across from a park and easy walking distance to the Bank.

Unfortunately for Charlie, war meant suspension of the regular meetings of central bankers, which was a big disappointment, but maybe only temporary. Meanwhile, citizens of the belligerent countries who were returning home were eager to sell their furniture, and the Kindlebergers were eager to buy. These items, shipped back to the States a year later courtesy of the Fed, would remain in the family as mementos of a life plan cut short.

After September 3, Basel was transformed by a general mobilization, on account of its strategic location on the border of both France and

---

[17] Kindleberger (1991a, 146).

Germany: "soldiers everywhere, the huge tank barricades in the streets near the station and bridges. Our park now is spotted with machine gun nests and barbed wire."[18] But life went on. New refugee arrivals replaced belligerent departures, and the Kindlebergers built an extensive social life with interesting new friends, enjoying elaborate restaurant meals hosted by the Bank, and even indulging in a February ski vacation in Davos. Meanwhile, the Bank offered a platform from which to observe and analyze the workings of the European war economies, so different from the peace economy of the United States. By March, Sarah was officially pregnant, expecting in August. The Kindlebergers were staying.

After the German invasion of the lowlands in May, however, the Bank moved up into the mountains to Chateau d'Oex, in effect a retreat to the famous National Redoubt, and Charlie began to think about leaving. Through his Fed friends he managed to get a concrete job offer from the Board of Governors of the Federal Reserve in Washington, DC. But the BIS would not release him. As late as June 13 (which is to say after Dunkirk), Charlie wrote to his father-in-law:

> If the war were to end before the end of June with a German victory and an armistice, I should resign I think from the bank, and we should head right for Baltimore. If the Germans should win later, I am afraid it would be more feasible to stay here until after Cookie [the baby] arrived and got into travelling condition. But most of all for general reasons, let us hope the Allies hang on until the Germans collapse from exhaustion, in which event I have to stay until June 1942.[19]

The fall of Paris on June 17 changed everything. The real possibility of German victory and armistice brought the prospect of a very different Europe – a Europe organized around the Reichsmark, as envisioned in the famous Funk Plan that would be released in July.[20] It would be a Europe that engaged with the rest of the world on a cash (which is to say gold) basis, starting with the looted gold reserves of the Banks of France and Belgium. The BIS thus seemed in danger of becoming at best

---

[18] KPTL, Box 11, "Dr. and Mrs. Wardlaw Miles."
[19] KPTL, Box 11, "Dr. and Mrs. Wardlaw Miles."
[20] Gross (2017).

irrelevant and at worst an agent of the Reichsbank. For Charlie, the idyll was definitely over. After some renewed pressure from the Fed (organized by Despres), on June 29 he was finally able to get a release from his BIS contract. On July 3, the Kindlebergers left Geneva by bus, arriving eventually in Lisbon where they caught the SS *Manhattan* for New York, and then on to Baltimore where Charles Poor Kindleberger III was born nine days later (July 27).

Back in the States, and back also at the Fed, now the Board in DC rather than the Fed in New York, Charlie commuted for a while from Baltimore before moving with the family in October to a rented house on Seminary Hill in rural Alexandria, Virginia. There the Kindlebergers would remain until 1948, even as war service and then State Department posting took Charlie abroad for extended periods. The friendships forged with the New Dealers who made Seminary Hill their home during those first years of family life continued on for the rest of their lives; three of these friends served as godparents for the children born on Seminary Hill.[21] After the move to MIT in 1948, Charlie's continuing appetite for international economics would take the family abroad repeatedly for sabbatical trips, but Sarah's responsibility for domestic economics would keep the family firmly rooted on domestic soil.

Meanwhile, life went on at the BIS without Charlie. In October 1940, the Bank moved back to Basel and Charlie's boss, Per Jacobsson, Economic Advisor of the BIS, stayed on through the war, as did the American President McKittrick.[22] Uncomfortably, the majority of Bank assets were loans to Germany (against the long-term deposits of the founding members of the BIS), which Germany continued to service throughout the war. Accepting gold in payment of interest due was arguably less shameful than laundering German gold for war material imports (as the Swiss banks did), especially since those interest payments were the main source of BIS income during those years; the Bank would have had to shut down without them. But it cannot have come as any surprise that, in the 1944 Bretton Woods Conference that laid the

---

[21] Chandler Morse for Sally, Clifford Durr and Mary Walton Livingston for Randall.
[22] Auboin (1955), Jacobsson (1979), Toniolo (2005).

groundwork for postwar monetary arrangements, the BIS was slated for closure, and only managed to survive thanks to the staunch support of its central bank founders. In the years that followed, the diminished BIS would redeem itself by managing the monetary stress of postwar reconstruction in Europe, specifically by running the European Payments Union that served as the seed of the subsequent Monetary Union. But that is getting ahead of the story. The important thing for now is that Charlie's dream of a life in international central banking was over.

In his autobiography, Charlie passes quickly over his year at the BIS, and also his two subsequent years at the Board before he joined the War. Understandably, his war experience starting August 1942 stands out much more sharply in his memory. But an outsider can see what he does not: a period of some three fallow years when Charlie, previously narrowly focused on monetary matters and heading for a career as a central banker, laid the foundations for the wide-ranging mature economist that he would become. For the first (and last) time in his life he had more time than he needed – time to draft and revise. By temperament, he was not happy with so much time on his hands, and he found the solution by jumping into the war as soon as he could. But until that moment he continued his education, and it all began in Basel, with his work with Jacobsson on the Bank's *Tenth Annual Report* (May 1940).

In typical understatement, Charlie suggests that the report was "modestly better than those it followed."[23] In fact his hand is very visible throughout, perhaps most obviously in a short digression on the theory of "shiftability," but more generally in the attention given to short-term capital flows as disruptive shocks to the system, and the way that markets and central bankers were responding to them. We can, I think, read this report as the missing empirical chapter of Charlie's dissertation, but also more importantly as a foreshadowing of his mature *The World in Depression* (1973), and the opening statement of his lifelong debate with monetarism, as in *Keynesianism vs. Monetarism* (1985).

The report opens by reminding the reader of the tremendous advance in human flourishing that had been achieved in the period leading up to World War I: "This improvement was built on the basis of the

---

[23] Kindleberger (1991a, 55).

international gold standard, the relative freedom of trade, and the intensification of international lending both at short and at long term." After the war, it seemed for a while that this prewar trajectory could be regained, but the Depression of 1929–33 halted forward momentum, a disruption greater even than World War had been. "It is to be hoped that further attempts will be made to analyse the causes of the great depression of 1930–33," Charlie writes in a memo-to-self he would check off more than thirty years later (Chapter 8).

"As a result the international credit system was largely put out of action – there has been an almost complete cessation of long-term foreign investment and a gradual liquidation of a great mass of short-term credits often at a considerable loss." However, "by the end of 1936, after the devaluation of the gold bloc and the simultaneous conclusion of the Tripartite Agreement, a new equilibrium in the world's monetary conditions seemed within reach and a rapid improvement in trade set in over a wide area." Writing before the Blitzkrieg, Charlie's emphasis was on how the preparation for war had prevented an improvement in economic conditions from showing up in the general standard of living, which he hoped might yet prove only temporary.[24]

On the eve of World War II, in effect the world economy had been split in half, with one half operating under new wartime rules and the other half still operating under old peacetime rules – a division also between state control and the free market. The war economies of Britain and Germany had both mobilized their respective captive trade areas to support wide-ranging programs of rearmament and restocking, and inevitably the pressure spilled over into the peace economies. What was most remarkable was how well the world economy was holding up under this new demand pressure, so much better in 1939 than it had in 1914, with no speculative bubble in commodity prices and no spiking of interest rates. War rumblings brought repatriation of capital to France and flight capital to the United States, both of which put tremendous pressure on the British pound, but the Tripartite machinery more or less held up under the strain, at least until late August 1939.

[24] BIS, *Tenth Annual Report*, pp. 6–8.

Only then was Britain finally forced to abandon its defense of the pound, to allow devaluation, and to implement far-reaching currency controls. Other countries responded along a spectrum, some (such as France) following the pound, others switching to peg against the dollar instead, and still others splitting the difference. In effect, under pressure from war, the global shift from a sterling standard to a dollar standard was moving forward faster than it would have in peace time. In September 1939, the United States issued a statement reaffirming the Tripartite Agreement, but in effect it was already over. Foreign trade between the war economies and the peace economies shifted quickly to a cash basis, as commercial traders were unwilling to offer credit terms, and states were yet unprepared to offer political terms. Central banks everywhere supported the flight to safety in their individual countries by expanding their note issue against purchases of long-term government debt, much of it new debt issued to support rearmament expenditure beyond tax revenue. In effect, central banks, "the indispensable adjunct" of government, were shifting from bankers' banks to government banks, even in peace economies.

Just so, in the United States, Depression deficits had already transformed the central bank balance sheet and central bank policy as well, showing the way forward for others; "In fact, the bond market has to an increasing extent been utilized by the banks not only for investment but as a means of adjusting their cash position, thus usurping the functions of the money market." "[T]he old conception of liquidity has changed . . . In the United States, the theory of 'shiftability' was developed – any assets for which there was a high degree of marketability were considered liquid." As adjuncts of government, central banks take on the task of maintaining orderly bond markets but, "anxious not to become 'shifter of last resort'," insist on substantial price concession before absorbing excess bond selling pressure.[25]

Charlie's embrace of shiftability shows how far he had traveled from his teacher Willis, but not so far as monetarism, not by a long shot. Working on the *Report* meant tangling with Per Jacobsson, head of the Monetary and Economic Department and a committed monetarist with special interest in the Report's chapter on "Production and Movements

---

[25] BIS, *Tenth Annual Report*, pp. 102, 134, 135.

of Gold." But even in this chapter, Charlie's hand is visible: "Gold in itself has no mystical influence on prices; it is only when the supply brings about an increase in active purchasing power than an effect on the price level can be expected." From Angell, Charlie had absorbed the idea that money influences income as well as prices, and from Keynes the idea that it is not so much money as spending that drives income, specifically investment spending:

> Experience has proved that monetary measures such as the depreciation of the dollar, cheap money and deficit spending have not been sufficient by themselves to achieve or even to support effectively a sustained recovery. Such measures can be of lasting effect only in so far as they influence the continuing flow of private funds into durable producers' goods and into housing.[26]

The mention of housing as a potential driver of recovery is significant. In his presidential address to the American Economic Association (AEA) the previous year, Harvard Professor Alvin Hansen had put forward what came to be known as the secular stagnation hypothesis: the idea that the maturation of the US economy, including the closing of the frontier, had permanently weakened investment spending as the engine of economic growth.[27] Without explicitly referencing Hansen, the *Report* is at pains to suggest that increased spending on housing can substitute for decreased spending on producers' goods – indeed, that the effectiveness of such a policy had been demonstrated in the European context, specifically the UK, Sweden, and Switzerland.[28]

Subsequently, Charlie's shift to the Board of Governors would bring a shift from this relatively complacent view to a recognition that restoring economic growth was a problem at the level of the entire world, not each nation separately, and that it would require deliberate steps to promote investment spending in the underdeveloped parts of the world. The key influence driving that shift in his thinking was none other than Hansen

---

[26] BIS, *Tenth Annual Report*, pp. 80, 14.
[27] Hansen (1939).
[28] BIS, *Tenth Annual Report*, p. 15.

himself, chair of the Joint Economic Committee of Canada and the United States, for which enterprise Charlie would serve as Secretary. Back home, Charlie built on the work he had done at the BIS:

> The work which the Board was so anxious to have me undertake was to contemplate the nature of United States foreign trade in a world where Germany had conquered Britain. It is hard to recall the deep pessimism of those months of June, after Dunkirk, and July, August and September, until it appeared that possibly the British would be able to resist defeat ... I wrote a long memorandum on the "Future of World Trade."[29]

The concern was with American loss not only of export markets, but also of raw material supply channels, in a world divided between a German "New Order of Europe" and a Japanese "Co-Prosperity Sphere" – two essentially imperial projects with their own dedicated, more or less enslaved peripheries serving the imperial core. Supposing that happened, America would survive, but its existing industrial structure would have to be significantly changed, and trading patterns would have to be shifted strongly toward Canada and Latin America. Definitely not a bright prospect, and fortunately one that did not actually have to be faced as, after the bombing of Pearl Harbor on December 7, 1941, the United States officially abandoned neutrality and declared war, thus decisively shifting the likely outcome.

But even supposing that Britain somehow managed to resist defeat, all would not be well. Providing statistical support to the negotiations of the Lend-Lease Act in March 1941, Charlie had reason to appreciate not only the desperate position of wartime Britain, but also how much that untenable situation would persist even after eventual peace.[30] In a seminal essay "Britain's Trade in the Postwar World," published anonymously with Hansen's encouragement by the National Planning Association in December 1941, Charlie set out the problem and his proposed solution.[31]

---

[29] Interim Biography, pp. 41, 46. KPMD, Box 21.
[30] Charlie's interest in British matters dates from New York Fed days: "Tentative Outline of a Memorandum for Mr. Williams on British Economic Future" (Apr. 24, 1937) and "The British Economy, 1925–1937" (July 20, 1937), both listed in Interim Biography, p. 37.
[31] Whitham (2016) provides useful historical context about the efforts of the National Planning Association.

The whole reason for Lend-Lease was that Britain had by then largely liquidated her portfolio of foreign investments, and so had nothing with which to pay for essential war imports.[32] One consequence of that liquidation was that, after the war, there would be no investment earnings to support essential imports. Even more, the anticipated postwar shift to a dollar standard seemed likely to involve shift also of the trade financing business from London to New York – another crucial source of earnings lost. And even though Lend-Lease meant that there would be no postwar indebtedness to the United States, Britain was in effect borrowing heavily from her former colonies by paying them for war material with sterling balances, which they would want to spend on imports from the United States after the war: "How Britain can improve her balance of payments is one of the crucial postwar problems ... Narrowly construed, the problem of Britain and the entire sterling area will be: 'What will we use for dollars?'"[33]

Lend-Lease for Britain during wartime, and perhaps also during reconstruction, solved this problem for a while, but obviously it could not be expected to continue after the war. The danger (and the obvious default scenario) was that Britain would resort to bilateralism and exchange control, as it had after it went off gold in 1931, so likely coming into conflict with the United States over trade preferences with former colonies. Meanwhile, the clear interest of the United States was in a larger global settlement: "International economic collaboration for production and trade on a new and higher level," to be achieved by a two-pronged program of "simultaneous internal measures to achieve world prosperity, and the development of economically backward countries under international sponsorship and with international capital."[34]

Just as British prosperity in the nineteenth century had depended on development of the New World, so too more general prosperity after World War II would depend on development of the rest of the world: "Indian, Chinese, and African peoples must be helped to develop their

---

[32] Some of this liquidation was more or less forced on Britain. "White was determined to make the British turn their pockets inside out, and this led to their being compelled to sell a prize investment in the United States, the American Viscose Company, owned by Courtaulds" (Kindleberger (1991a, 66).
[33] Kindleberger (1941, 15, 16).
[34] Kindleberger (1941, 20, 34).

own countries ... Capital and technical assistance from more developed nations could be made available under adequate international safeguards." International loans would be key, but "subject to local laws governing hours of work, wages, working conditions, health, sanitation, housing and other social standards," perhaps under the guidance of the International Labor Organization. The goal, in effect, was to get the economic boost of imperialism, but without the political and social downside of actual imperialism – in effect an international version of Roosevelt's New Deal measures that had created the conditions for restoration of domestic prosperity in the United States. In a prosperous world economy, Britain could prosper as well, and meanwhile Lend-Lease could provide the leverage for the United States to encourage (not to say force) Britain to choose postwar collaboration rather than isolationism.[35]

US isolationism was another potential problem. Charlie writes: "The United States is learning for the second time in a single generation that she is unable to escape from the impact of world forces. She is therefore compelled to assume world responsibilities, and to concern herself with policies designed to promote world security and world prosperity."[36] It is perhaps these words that caught the eye of Hansen, who proposed to Charlie that they coauthor for *Foreign Affairs* an article on "The Economic Tasks of the Postwar World." The resulting article advocates the same two-pronged policy approach – full employment domestically plus economic development internationally – but now with a focus on US security rather than the British balance of payments. The whole problem with the settlement after World War I was that it had focused too narrowly on political stability and monetary stability, leaving economic stability to take care of itself. Stalin's example of forced economic development, undertaken despite more or less complete lack of foreign loans, stands as a possible choice for other countries after the war. US security interest would be better served by promoting instead a kind of "International R. F. C." on the model of Hoover's Reconstruction Finance Corporation.[37]

---

[35] Kindleberger (1941, 33–34).
[36] Kindleberger (1941, 29).
[37] Hansen and Kindleberger (1942a, 473). See Mehrling (1997, 117–123) for the larger context in Hansen's own work.

In subsequent work, Charlie would sketch in further detail how such an International Development Authority, as he came to call it, might work: "The Bases of an International Program for National Development after the War" (June 24, 1942); "Problems of World Economic Development" (July 27, 1942); and "The Organization of An International Development Authority" (August 5, 1942). A central idea running throughout these essays is the prevalence of fundamental disequilibrium. The price system could not be expected to work very well under such conditions; hence the necessity for a program of public loans, but also the necessity to limit those loans to productive purposes in order that their repayment not be excessively burdensome, productive not only in terms of domestic income but also in terms of foreign exchange earning.

A revised version of the first memo would eventually be published as "International Monetary Stabilization."[38] More immediately important, the second memo apparently caught the eye of Hansen, leading to another coauthored article, "International Development Loans."[39] Having warned against the dangers of isolationism in their previous piece, their target now was the opposite danger of economic imperialism: "Economic sovereignty can rest fundamentally in nations which adjust economic differences internally by virtue of their sovereign power, and internationally as equals among United Nations ... International assistance should be free from the implications of imperialism – military or financial."[40]

This vision of a possible postwar world never left Charlie, but for the moment there was a war on and he was anxious to play a more active role in it. The birth of his second son, Richard, on June 17, 1942, meant that military draft would not reach him for another year, but he was anxious to get started anyway. After an abortive attempt to join the Navy, in line with family tradition, he took the opportunity instead, following Emile Despres and Chandler Morse, to join the Office of Strategic Services in

---

[38] Kindleberger (1943b).
[39] "Together we wrote a pamphlet for the National Planning Association on *International Development Loans.*" Interim Biography, p. 49.
[40] Hansen and Kindleberger (1942b, 5, 34).

the Research and Analysis Branch, starting in August 1942 as chief of the Military Supplies section in the Economics Division.

"The task of the Military Supplies section, as outlined to me by Morse, was to estimate German economic capabilities in the fields of military hardware ... but we very shortly started to move into target selection." While Morse traveled to London to set up what came to be called the Enemy Objectives Unit, Charlie stayed in DC to draft "the first beginnings of a theory of bombardment known to me, in which the recuperative powers of an industry, the depth of its output behind the fighting front, and the need for a fighting front as an anvil to the air force hammer were related to each other."[41] With this sketch in hand, Charlie then traveled to London to relieve Morse, taking up residence at 50 Great Cumberland Place and working at the US Embassy at 40 Berkeley Square. There was a war on, and now he was in it.

One last thing before he left: Charlie took part in a panel on "The Future of International Investment" held on January 6, 1943 in Washington, DC, as part of the annual meeting of the American Economic Association. His contribution, "Planning for Foreign Investment," is notable for its unusual forthrightness:

> The world "chronic shortage of dollars" of which so much has been heard abroad, is basically ascribable to the United States' failure to lend abroad more abundantly, or rather more continuously ... The private investor is not in a position to undertake the provision of large blocks of capital for major development undertakings ... The government is appropriately the borrower for such large-scale projects, as government is appropriately the lender.[42]

Let economists quibble about fine points of price theory; Charlie was embarked on a much grander venture. There was a war to be won, and after that a world to be reconstructed. For the next five years, both tasks would occupy him completely.

[41] Interim Biography, pp. 52–53, 55.
[42] Kindleberger (1943a, 350–353).

CHAPTER 4

A Good War

If one processes enough hay, one can find a few needles.[1]

There can be no question that for Charlie, like so many of his generation, war service was the peak experience of his life, a fact that he signals by dedicating his 1991 autobiography to "the comrades-at-arms of EOU," meaning the Enemy Objectives Unit of which he became chief starting February 28, 1943. He was relieving Chandler Morse, and the plan was for Emile Despres to relieve him in turn; so, it was just a temporary assignment, but it was his first significant managerial position and he was determined to rise to the occasion. In the event, Despres never did relieve him, and Charlie remained in London as chief until D-Day, after which he shifted to the ground war in France. His colleague Walt Rostow remembers: "His rule in exercising authority was 'tough upwards, soft downwards'," and he set an example with his own "fierce integrity" and unrelenting work ethic.[2] Many of the friendships he formed in the foxhole at 40 Berkeley Square would continue on into postwar government work and remain lifelong.

The job itself was Research and Analysis: desk work behind the lines and behind the scenes, not Secret Intelligence "spy stuff" or Secret Operations "sabotage" (the other OSS units), but nonetheless clearly an essential contribution to the war effort. Charlie loved it. Even with two babies at home, there is no sense at all that he ever questioned where his duty lay, not until the war was well and truly won. Indeed, he was plenty irritated by the fact that in September 1943, when the official draft

---

[1] Kindleberger (1991a, 80).
[2] Rostow (1992). See also Winks (1987), Katz (1989, Ch. 4), and Milne (2008, 31–34).

finally got around to him, he was required to leave his vital war work behind and return to the States for six weeks in order to receive his official commission (as Captain).[3]

The central task of the EOU was to provide analytical support for the strategic bombing effort, in effect advising how best to disrupt the German war machine. Put another way, the question was how best to make practical use of the 50,000 airplanes that Roosevelt had committed to supply. The British favored shock and awe, for psychological effect, but as an economist Charlie thought about the problem differently. The economics of war, Charlie would reflect, are essentially simple: "win the war without unduly deranging the domestic economy . . . Our task in OSS was to try to decide how best the enemy economy could be taken apart . . . In the end, we recommended ball-bearings and aircraft."[4]

The remaining problem was to find out where exactly the Germans were producing ball-bearings and aircraft, and that's where the hay-processing came in: "every possible source of information, including mountains of Photostats produced by Polish intelligence, aerial photography, prisoner-of-war interrogation, etc . . . Instead of passively examining the flow that came across our desks, we pushed . . . The task kept us going nights and weekends."[5] In his autobiography, Charlie lovingly relates various needles found by processing this hay, but these war stories need not detain us. The important thing for our account is the demonstrable success of EOU's methods of research and analysis, a success that would inform Charlie's later academic style of research and analysis. He was never much one for digging in the archives, but he was definitely prepared to read everything written on a subject and then to spin the bits and pieces into a plausible narrative. As an academic, he would remain in effect an intelligence analyst.

As D-Day approached, the attention of the EOU shifted from strategic to tactical bombing in support of the invasion, which required an

---

[3] Interim Biography, p. 58. The autobiography spins this moment more positively, referencing instead a "week of blessed leave" (1991a, 80).

[4] Kindleberger (1991a, 71, 76). Tooze (2007) tells the story of a German war economy already stretched near to breaking point, and significantly disrupted by Allied bombing.

[5] Kindleberger (1991a, 77, 79). See also Babington-Smith (1987).

upgrade in Charlie's security clearance from Top Secret to BIGOT since he obviously needed to know the location of the eventual landing. Strategically, the EOU recommended a shift to bombing fuel depots, while tactically they recommended bombing railway bridges as a way of interfering with German resupply. Their British counterparts argued instead for bombing railway centers (marshalling yards), and for a while the British view prevailed; pilots were even forbidden to bomb bridges.[6] In the end, the EOU position won out, thanks to the political stratagem of temporarily breaking up the group and spreading key personnel throughout the Allied War effort, so-called "Operation Octopus." Charlie himself was temporarily appointed to Allied Tactical Air Command of the Twenty-First Army Group, based outside of London in Uxbridge, Middlesex. "It was striking how the various headquarters after a time were sounding the same notes."[7]

In the last days before D-Day, all bridges crossing the Seine from Paris to the sea were destroyed, and after D-Day the bridges crossing the Loire were attacked as well. It was not the comprehensive plan that EOU had recommended, but it proved to be enough, as Charlie would argue convincingly in a contemporary assessment of the first ten days of the invasion.[8] Here again, war stories are not the important thing, but rather the demonstrable success of EOU's methods of persuasion, which would inform Charlie's later academic efforts. Even if one is defeated by a more powerful opponent in a public "trial by combat," one can nevertheless hope ultimately to prevail by means of quieter and more decentralized

---

[6] The key proponent of the British view was Lord Zuckerman. Rostow (1981b) tells the story of Eisenhower's fateful decision of March 25, 1944, in favor of Zuckerman, and of the eventually successful EOU effort to reverse that decision. Rostow's decision to publish seems to have been provoked by Zuckerman's (1978) self-serving memoir, and Kindleberger's (1978d) review of that memoir.

[7] KPTL, Box 3, "War Diary, R&A Branch, OSS London, Vol. 5. Economic Outpost with Economic Warfare Division." Kindleberger (1991a, 88).

[8] "German Rail Movement in France in the First Ten Days after D-Day: an Interim Report by Charles P. Kindleberger, June 16–19, 1944," published as Appendix F in Rostow (1981b). A less hasty and more comprehensive post-mortem can be found in Kindleberger's letter to Major Derek J. Ezra, Apr. 13, 1945, which treats also the political battle over targeting that continued from D-Day all the way to the end of the war, KPTL Box 1.

methods, operating through one's students and the readers of one's books.

On the eve of the invasion of France, Charlie wrote to his son Richard, then just two weeks shy of his second birthday, about what his father had learned (so far) from his war experience:

> It is not a pleasant thought: and it is a very obvious one, which we all take for granted without translating it into its many practical applications. It is that beauty, and logic, and symmetry and truth have to fight to win against power. The rise of Hitler and the enormous effort and loss of life which it is going to cost to defeat him are the obvious manifestation of this. But I, in my very small way, have been conducting a fight in planning for some four months now, a fight against power, held by a few men, with a very bad plan, with a good plan which has truth on its side.
>
> It is sometimes thought, and frequently stated, that the right will prevail … What I have finally gotten a sense of is power, naked and unashamed, which can laugh at logic, reason and truth. Goebbels and Hitler do so. But so can all power.[9]

Once the invading Allied force was well and truly established, Charlie shifted to the G-2 (Intelligence) section of the Twelfth Army Group, and from London to the Continent, in effect an attempt to keep "Operation Octopus" going even as the ground war progressed. This move required a further upgrade in his clearance all the way to Ultra, which gave him access to the code-breaking operation that had been reading German communications. In his new position, he worked out of the forward tactical headquarters, so-called "Eagle Tac," traveling with General Omar Bradley, working in a mobile trailer and sleeping in a tent with two others: "My charge was intelligence on enemy supply and transport, and specifically to make recommendations as to how air force could assist the ground troops."[10] The frustrating political battle over bomb targeting continued, but for Charlie the long hours at EOU learning the intelligence business had paid off. For the first time he had full access to all intelligence, and also a direct line to a key decision maker whenever he

---

[9] KPTL, Box 10. CPK to Richard, June 4, 1944.
[10] Kindleberger (1991a, 83, 91).

had advice to offer. It's what he liked best – being a useful member of a highly qualified and motivated team, working toward a common objective.

Eventual Allied victory was never seriously in doubt, and Charlie found time to enjoy his access to French food and drink, as well as the occasional jaunt through the French countryside, but as the end approached he found himself increasingly eager to get home. Initially he thought it would be over by October, then Christmas 1944 at the latest. The last-ditch German offensive at Ardennes on December 16th came as a complete surprise, notwithstanding access to Ultra intelligence. After the first weeks of battle, Charlie judged that German fuel supplies were nearly exhausted and urged a final big Allied push. Instead, the decision was made to continue grinding and even to launch the horrific firebombing of Dresden and other German population centers in February.

As the war finally wound down, Charlie took the opportunity to visit some of the sites he had most been looking to destroy, most importantly the very impressive underground factory near Nordhausen (soon to be within the Soviet zone of occupation) that had been producing buzz bombs, jet engines, and V-2 rockets. "Fantastic" as a piece of German engineering – "the eighth wonder of the world," as he wrote to his wife – it was at the same time a horrific death camp, where prisoners were literally worked to death: "A strong man could last six months. A thin or weak one usually folded after three."[11] It was obvious that the Germans who worked at the factory knew about the death camp, but somehow they had managed not to confront its horror until the war was lost. Having lost the war, Germans were forced to confront the fact that they had lost their honor as well; suicide of responsible leaders seemed to Charlie an honorable acknowledgment of complicity in such war crimes.

Charlie would end the war with the rank of Major and be awarded a Bronze Star by General Bradley himself, but by then his thoughts were very much on other things, specifically postwar employment. The easiest thing would have been to stay in Europe, specifically Germany, as part of the postwar Army occupation. But that Charlie most definitely did not want to do, and not only because he wanted to get home. Wartime

---

[11] April 19, 1945. Letter reproduced in Kindleberger (1989b, 203).

animus toward the German army was clearly spilling over into peacetime animus toward the German people, and Charlie wanted no part of it. The Morgenthau Plan to pastoralize Germany, made public after the September 1944 Quebec Conference, was the guiding document on the ground even if not official policy. Writing to Despres in October, Charlie is clear:

> The important point of a postwar program for Germany is not military or economic controls from without, but firm support for the right people within, and a reeducation program, run by Germans, which can point to a cooperative world outside so long as the right Germans are in control. We can ruin our friends pretty easily by insisting they keep power and then accusing the German nation as a whole of being evil.[12]

Ideally, Charlie wanted some kind of Research and Analysis position back in DC, and he wrote to Despres about that as well. But Despres was intent on getting out of the intelligence business altogether, and in the end what he had to offer Charlie was a job providing analytical support for postwar settlement discussions. Charlie took it. It got him out of Germany, and it got him home, albeit at the cost of giving up three months accumulated leave since work had to start right away. He arrived home June 12, 1945. His third child, Sarah, was born nine months later, on February 28, 1946.

Years later, in response to a request from General Bradley for his recollections of the last months of war, Charlie prefaced his remarks with the following reflection:

> [W]hile no man is a hero to his valet in the usual aphorism, I have often stated that I have four heros in the Pantheon of men I have worked for – well down the line to be sure, in my youth. They consist in (in alphabetical order), Omar Bradley, William Clayton, George Marshall and Allan Sproul. There is universal agreement that I have been blessed beyond the deserts of any man to have had an opportunity to work with these great men.[13]

---

[12] KPTL, Box 1. CPK to Chan and Emile, Oct. 27, 1944.

[13] KPTL, Box 9, CPK to Bradley, Dec. 18, 1978. He would offer the same list in a letter to Alfred Malabre of the *Wall Street Journal* (Oct. 7, 1988), in his autobiography

Sproul, of course, had been Charlie's superior at the New York Fed during the years of the Tripartite Agreement, and Clayton and Marshall would be his superiors during his immediate postwar service at the State Department. But in my judgment it was the experience with Bradley, more than anything else, that made Charlie realize the deep satisfaction that could come from service to one of the greats, and it was that experience, moreover, that impelled him to seek out similar opportunities in postwar service. In this interpretation, it was the opportunity to work under Clayton that persuaded Charlie to put aside his own feelings and to accept the position of Chief of German and Austrian Affairs in November 1945, in effect confronting the power of the Morgenthau boys who had a very bad plan for Germany. And it was the opportunity to work under Marshall that caused Charlie to accept the position of director of the committee that put together the Marshall Plan and ushered it successfully through Congress, in effect confronting the power of American isolationists who had a very bad plan for Europe. In both jobs, he would be joined by former EOU comrades-in-arms and would pursue the well-honed EOU strategy of using a small, dedicated team to shift a large and determined consensus.

It is notable that Charlie's Pantheon were all men of the world, men of broad vision and decisive action, albeit in different spheres: (in temporal order) the banker Sproul, the soldier Bradley, the merchant-statesman Clayton, and the soldier-statesman Marshall. Charlie would dedicate his 1996 *World Economic Primacy* to the memory of these four. In addition, and closer to Charlie's own merely human condition, the demigods in his private religion were advisors and implementers, all of them economists: Emile Despres and Alvin H. Hansen, about whom we have heard already, and Edward S. Mason and Willard L. Thorp, his immediate superiors at the State Department, working under Undersecretary for Economic Affairs Clayton, and eventually Secretary of State Marshall. Charlie would dedicate his 1999 *Essays in History* to the memory of these four. It seems clear that the experience of working for his Pantheon, and alongside these economists, made Charlie into the economist he was, well

(Kindleberger 1991a, 48), and in a letter to Clarice Thorp (May 11, 1992). KPMD, Box 12.

before he shifted to MIT in Fall 1948. An admitted lifelong overachiever, Charlie never felt that he could aspire to be one of the greats, but he could and did aspire to be a useful economist.

Back in Washington at the State Department, Charlie began his post-war work as the DC backstop to the reparations discussions taking place at the Potsdam conference in August, and then moved on to support of negotiations for the Anglo-American loan. But these assignments were both essentially marking time until his appointment in November as Chief of the Division of German and Austrian Economic Affairs (GA). There his charge was to provide guidance to the Office of Military Government, US (OMGUS), which had been running Germany since the end of the war under the command of General Lucius Clay. As Charlie put it, "From 1942 to 1945 I was engaged in helping to take the German economy apart; from 1945 to 1947 I was busy helping put it back together again."[14] His staff consisted largely of familiar faces from EOU days, recruited for the purpose – John deWilde, Harold Barnett, William Salant, and, most importantly, Walt Rostow – a group that came to be known as "Clayton's economists."[15]

An immediate problem they confronted was JCS 1067, a directive of the Joint Chiefs of Staff issued in April 1945, which contained strong language that appeared to stand in the way of the reconstruction of Germany:

> You will take no steps (a) looking toward the economic rehabilitation of Germany, or (b) designed to maintain or strengthen the German economy ... [C]onsumption held to the minimum in order that imports may be strictly limited and that surpluses may be made available for the occupying forces and displaced persons and United Nations prisoners of war, and for reparation.[16]

It was this kind of language that had emboldened the so-called "Morgenthau boys" working under Bernard Bernstein in the Finance Division of OMGUS.

---

[14] Kindleberger (1987b, 162).
[15] Rostow (1981a, 52).
[16] Reprinted as Appendix C in Department of State (1946, 63–64).

Notwithstanding the emotional appeal of such a position, the economic logic was questionable, as even a noneconomist like General Clay could see. Even supposing a maximal shift toward agricultural output (as urged by JCS 1067 in obvious echo of the Morgenthau Plan), there was essentially no prospect that Germany could ever be self-sufficient in food. So unless the Allies were prepared indefinitely to subsidize German food imports, economic recovery and reconstruction were essential in order for Germany to be able to produce sufficient exports to cover its necessary food imports. That logic was already leading Clay to cozy up to conservative industrial interests in the American zone, in an attempt to get the German economy off the American dole. By October 1945 Clay had managed to outmaneuver Bernstein and his men, and to install instead his friend Joseph Dodge as his chief financial advisor. In time, Dodge would coauthor the famous Colm–Dodge–Goldsmith report "A Plan for the Liquidation of War Finance and the Financial Rehabilitation of Germany," issued May 20, 1946, which would became the template for the eventual Monetary Reform promulgated June 20, 1948. But on myriad other matters there was a vacuum, and the job of Clayton's economists, as they saw it, was to fill that vacuum.[17]

The first item of business was to interpret the August Potsdam Agreement, which superseded JCS 1067, in such a way as to mute the force of the most problematic passages of the latter. The way forward was found in the specific Potsdam language: "It is the intention of the Allies that the German people be given the opportunity for the eventual reconstruction of their life on a democratic and peaceful basis."[18] Clayton's economists argued that this passage implicitly involved a commitment to specifically economic reconstruction: "It is recognized that democratic and peaceful institutions will have little chance of developing unless the economic foundations are properly laid."[19] Interpreted thus, the "level of industry" agreement at Potsdam became not a ceiling

---

[17] The report was eventually published as Colm, Dodge, and Goldsmith (1955). See also Gottlieb (1956/1957, 404), Kindleberger and Ostrander (2003). It should be noted that Gottlieb worked under Dodge, while Ostrander ran Price Control. It was Ostrander who recommended Colm and Goldsmith to Clay.

[18] Department of State (1946, 78).

[19] Department of State (1946, 27).

that prevented economic reconstruction beyond a bare minimum, but rather a floor on which economic reconstruction could be built. The key document marking that policy shift was "The Reparation Settlement and the Peacetime Economy of Germany," released by the Department of State on December 12, 1945, approximately a month after Charlie took over as chief of the German and Austrian division:

> [T]he United States intends, ultimately, in cooperation with its Allies, to permit the German people under a peaceful democratic government of their own choice to develop their own resources and to work toward a higher standard of living subject only to such restriction designed to prevent production of armaments as may be laid down in the peace settlement ... It is our desire to see Germany's economy geared to a world system and not an autarchical system."[20]

So far as Charlie was concerned, this was the policy of the State Department going forward, and his job was to lay the groundwork for implementing it.

The December report envisaged a three-stage approach. In the first stage, which was to last until Spring 1946, the focus would be on recovery of the rest of Europe, even at the immediate expense of Germany in terms of coal and food allocation. It would be a cold and hungry winter for the Germans while the Allies worked out a detailed level of industry plan for the eventual peacetime German economy. But then, in the second stage, allowed peacetime industries would reopen while excess or disallowed wartime industries would be available for reparations. And upon completion of that second stage – say, by February 1948 – control would be shifted to the Germans themselves, for further economic development of the peacetime economy as they saw fit.

From the start, the goal was eventual freedom of the German people to chart their own course, not only economically but also politically. Clay's closeness to business interests and the conservative CDU was therefore highly inappropriate. After all, the British Labour government was nominally socialist and they were running the British zone, so there was no reason for the United States to resist something similar for the

---

[20]   Department of State (1946, pp. 94, 97).

American zone if that was what the Germans themselves wanted. The problem was not just Clay. The entire War Department, headed by Stimson and his deputy McCloy, was intent on preventing Communist political parties operating as agents of the Soviet Union from taking advantage of disordered postwar conditions to gain a foothold in Western Europe, and they viewed socialist parties as a dangerous entry point for such. This political calculation would in the end lead to the division of Germany, and of Europe also, between the two superpowers, but in 1945 alternative futures still seemed possible and Clayton's economists were working toward their own favored outcome.[21]

From an economic point of view, the central challenge to be confronted in the level of industry plan was that prewar Germany had depended on exports from heavy industry to pay for necessary imports, and that was going to be impossible for postwar Germany. Under Hitler, heavy industry had been easily repurposed for war production, and that made it the immediate target of postwar plans for "industrial disarmament" and also of demands for reparations.[22] In broad terms, the main idea was to dismantle as much of German heavy industry as possible and ship it to the USSR. That left light industry as the potential source of postwar export earnings; so, that's where Clayton's economists focused their attention, urging not only retention of existing capacity, but also a wholesale retraining of the labor force to work in that capacity, using multiple shifts in order to make maximal use of existing capacity until it could be increased. The plan was fleshed out and then adopted by the Allied Control Council in a comprehensive document, "Plan for Reparations and Level of post-war German economy," issued March 28, 1946, with lists of Prohibited, Restricted, and Unrestricted sectors for industrial reconstruction and development. Stage One thus complete, attention turned to Stage Two, and that's where the trouble began.

Key to the plan was the "single economic unit" principle established in the Potsdam Agreement, according to which the four zones of occupation were to be treated as a single unit for economic purposes. That meant pooling scarce export proceeds from all four zones and using

---

[21] Leffler (1996). On the War Department and McCloy, see Bird (1992).
[22] On the complex politics of reparations, see Cairncross (1986).

them to meet the most pressing import needs in all four zones. And it also meant taking maximal advantage of interzonal trade within Germany: "The United States zone lacks coal. The French and British zones have coal but lack food. The Soviet zone has food and brown coal, lacks iron and steel."[23] Thus, from the beginning, the plan was concerned not just with the American zone, but also with Germany as a whole, and in particular with restoring economic relations between the four zones of occupation. The trouble on this front came from France and Russia, both of which resisted the single economic unit principle and in practice treated their own zones as a resource to be exploited for their own domestic purposes.

Even more, and also from the beginning, the plan was also concerned with restoring economic relations between Germany and Europe. It seemed clear to Clayton's economists that reconstruction of Germany was a key element of the larger project of reconstruction of Europe, and by Europe they meant all of Europe, both East and West. Walt Rostow, in particular, made this wider European dimension of the plan his own personal mission, sketching the outline of such a plan as early as February 1946, which in later draft would become known as the Acheson–Clayton plan, forwarded by Charlie to Secretary Byrnes in April. But Byrnes did nothing with it, neither forwarding it to the attention of President Truman nor introducing it at the April Council of Foreign Ministers meeting in Paris. In retrospect, Rostow would come to view Byrnes' pocket veto as a crucial missed opportunity to avoid the drift toward division of Europe. In the event, instead of the economists, it was the foreign service side of the State Department that had Byrnes' ear, starting with Kennan's famous "Long Telegram" in February. As Rostow remembers, "The task of the West was to contain the outward thrust of Communist power rather than seek a grand settlement embracing all of Europe."[24]

But Rostow was not one to accept defeat so easily. In true "Operation Octopus" fashion, he simply shifted his attention from the State Department to the United Nations, where he urged the creation of an

---

[23] Department of State (1946, 32).
[24] Rostow (1981a, 42).

Economic Commission of Europe (ECE), and there he met with more success. His idea was to build on three existing instruments of Europe-wide cooperation: the European Coal Organization, the European Central Inland Transport Organization, and the Emergency Economic Committee for Europe. ECE was formally created March 1947, and in May held its first meeting in Geneva. By then a similar initiative was emerging inside the State Department, which would come to be known as the Marshall Plan after a public announcement at Harvard Commencement on June 5, 1947. Significantly, the initial idea was to run the Marshall Plan out of the ECE. But that is getting ahead of the story.

Back in 1946, Charlie's own response to Byrnes' pocket veto was to travel in August to Berlin, Vienna, Frankfurt, and Brussels in an attempt to canvass potential support for the GA plan from the forces on the ground, most importantly from General Lucius Clay. Clay had visited Washington in the early days of GA and had come away unimpressed by the "little people" he had met there, including Charlie himself, and thenceforth had proceeded to run Germany more or less on his own.[25] Specifically, confronted with a fractious Allied Control Council and facing the prospect that the American zone might have to go it alone, Clay had taken the decision in May to halt reparations deliveries to the USSR, while, in July, Byrnes had floated the idea of possible joint management of just the British and American zones. Division of Germany was thus already under way when Charlie arrived in Berlin on August 3, and he seems to have been determined to do what he could to stem the tide.

The GA plan, to recall, was for a unified Germany in a unified Europe. General Clay's interest, by contrast, turned out to be more narrowly in a united Allied Control Council, and, if that proved impossible, then even more narrowly in an economically self-sufficient American sector no longer a burden to the American taxpayer. Indeed, in an effort to keep the Council together, Clay early on had proposed acceding to Russia's demand for reparations out of current production (as opposed to capital equipment), which ran in direct opposition to explicit State Department policy: "The United States in particular has no desire to repeat, in

---

[25] Clay (1950).

different form, the experience undergone after World War 1, when Germany paid reparation out of the proceeds of American loans and investments, then defaulted on the latter."[26] But so long as the United States was shipping its own current production to the Western zones to keep the Germans alive, Russian demands for reparations from current production more or less amounted to exactly that repeat.

Clay's focus on keeping the Council together had the further effect of blinding him to any larger agenda of a united Europe. "Localitis," Charlie would call it, attributing the phrase to General Marshall.[27] The best that Charlie was able to achieve with Clay was a united front against "carpet-bagging": the attempt by American and other business interests to buy up German property on the cheap. But even there, Clay tolerated smaller-scale carpet-bagging by the occupying troops, and even facilitated their activity by his policy of freely converting occupying Reichsmarks into dollars.[28] Charlie's mission to Europe was thus largely a failure, judged against the objective of a unified Germany in a unified Europe.

Back home, however, his reports did have some apparent success in stimulating Secretary Byrnes to make a public statement of policy, specifically in the famous Stuttgart speech of September 6th, which he framed as a restatement of the principles agreed at Potsdam. Central themes of Byrnes' speech included the GA interpretation of Potsdam as a floor not a ceiling, and the central importance of the "one economic unit" principle and of interzonal trade, along with implicit endorsement of the Colm–Dodge–Goldsmith plan for monetary reform. Announcing the formation of common administrative apparatus for the British and American zones, Byrnes called for the French and Russian zones to join in due time, with the aim of turning over responsibility to the Germans themselves as soon as possible – in effect, Stage 3 of the original GA plan. "We do not want Germany to become the satellite of any power or powers or to live under a dictatorship, foreign or domestic," which is to say neither Russian dictatorship nor a reconstituted Nazi dictatorship.[29]

---

[26] Department of State (1946, 23).
[27] Kindleberger (1987b, 186).
[28] Kindleberger (1987b, 177).
[29] Stuttgart speech, available at ghdi.ghi-dc.org/pdf/eng/Allied%20Policies%209%20 ENG1.pdf.

Unified Germany was thus reaffirmed as official American policy, even if not unified Europe. Byrnes was now on record resisting the drift toward division, presenting the Bizone as the core of an eventual unified Germany rather than as de facto acceptance of inevitable division. That's where matters stood going into the brutal winter of 1946–7, which necessitated much larger American support than had been antici- pated, including even transatlantic shipments of coal. One consequence was to convince skeptics that a larger-scale program of relief was needed. At the same time, change of leadership at the State Department, as President Truman prevailed upon General Marshall to return to govern- ment service as Secretary of State in January 1947, provided new oppor- tunity to push the economists' agenda, first at the Moscow Council of Foreign Ministers in March, and then in the Marshall Plan announced in June.

In Charlie's telling, both were attempts by Marshall to find some possible accommodation with Russia, and so to avoid both division of Germany and division of Europe. Crucially, Marshall Plan aid was offered to Eastern as well as Western Europe, but was rejected by Russia and, then, under pressure from Russia, rejected also by Poland and Czechoslovakia.[30] After that, division of Germany and division of Europe both became fait accompli for forty years, ending only with the fall of the Berlin Wall on November 9, 1989, which is to say two years after publication of Charlie's *Marshall Plan Days* (1987) in commemoration of the fortieth anniversary of the Marshall Plan, and shortly after publica- tion of Charlie's *Letters from the Field* (1989), his letters from Berlin in August 1946 and from Moscow in March 1947.

With the fall of the Wall, it could perhaps be said that the logic of the GA plan for a unified Germany in a unified Europe ultimately prevailed, but in 1947 it had most definitely failed. The Marshall Plan was second best, especially after Eastern Europe pulled out, though even then Charlie held out hope that trade relations between West and East could eventually be restored, a hope that proved illusory once the Korean War broke out. In the event, notwithstanding its origins as a pro-European measure, the Marshall Plan got implemented as an anti-Soviet measure.

---

[30] Kindleberger (1987b, 100).

Indeed, Charlie points to the Soviet overthrow of the Czech government and the death of Jan Masaryk in March 1948 as key to achieving the votes needed in Congress to approve the Marshall Plan in April.[31] Even as second best, the Marshall Plan proved to be an enormous success, and Charlie always counted his own contribution to that success as one of his proudest achievements. His first contribution was the role of GA in inserting the idea into policy discussion in the first place.

> My conclusions on the origins of the Marshall Plan are that it emerged largely from the economic side of the Department, with causa remota being the German and Austrian economic division, an intermediate cause (my Latin fails me) being the economists in the trade and commodities divisions, and the causa proxima being the Undersecretary, Mr. Clayton, and George Kennan, the chief of the Policy Planning Staff, virtually the only political officer to take a leading role.[32]

But his even bigger contribution came after. On June 25, just weeks after Marshall's speech, Charlie shifted from GA to a new position as executive secretary of the State Department's working committee on the Marshall Plan. Relieved finally to be off the endlessly frustrating German beat, and to be working instead toward a clear and important goal, Charlie threw himself into the task of producing a detailed plan that could be presented to Congress for approval.[33] It was a monumental task, involving coordination with the Committee of European Economic Cooperation (CEEC) to knit together a unified plan from sixteen different country proposals for American contributions of twenty-six different commodities. Initially the CEEC asked for $30 billion; ultimately Congress gave $17 billion, spread out from April 1948 to June 1952.

After Congressional passage, the German monetary reform was finally implemented on June 20th, which triggered the Berlin blockade on June 24th, which in turn triggered the Berlin airlift operation mounted with great distinction by General Clay. Notwithstanding these consequences, for many years afterward Charlie imagined that the German

---

[31] Kindleberger (1987b, 101). See also Jones (1955).
[32] Kindleberger (1987b, 157). See also Jones (1955, 243).
[33] Kindleberger (1997, 185).

monetary reform had proceeded more or less along the lines of the original Colm–Dodge–Goldsmith plan, of which he had heartily approved. In fact, however, only part of the plan had been implemented: the part that converted all money and debts from Reichsmarks to Deutschemarks, at a 10:1 ratio. The proposed capital levy, which had been intended to effect an internal German redistribution between those who profited from the war and those who suffered from it, never got done. (It was that part of the plan that the War Department had choked on when the plan first came out.) Imagining that the capital levy had gone through as planned, Charlie would write in 1984: "I regard the German monetary reform of 1948 as one of the great feats of social engineering of all time."[34] Informed otherwise by his old friend Tyler Ostrander, he would walk back the hyperbole in a paper that would see publication only posthumously, expressing instead "regret that burden sharing did not go further in rooting democracy more firmly."[35]

Meanwhile, the apparent success of the German monetary reform, which almost immediately brought goods out of hiding and into the shop windows, stimulated Charlie to reconsider the reasons for the failure of the Anglo-American loan way back in 1945. The whole idea of the loan had stemmed from Williams' key-currency approach, which suggested the importance of stabilizing sterling against the dollar by facilitating exchange of the sterling overhang. In retrospect, the mistake had been to try to stabilize currencies in an environment where markets were basically not working. The right approach was to address that more fundamental problem first, which the Marshall Plan did, and only then to address the monetary problem, precisely as had been done in Germany. Indeed, in retrospect Charlie would understand the Marshall Plan itself as an extension of the key-currency idea, focusing on getting a key *area* – in this case, Western Europe – on its feet first and then extending the effort to other areas later. In this regard, Stalin had perhaps done the West a favor by refusing Marshall Plan aid for Eastern Europe, which might well have proven to be more than could be tackled at one time.

---

[34] Kindleberger (1984a, 418).
[35] Kindleberger and Ostrander (2003, 191).

Likely the reason Charlie did not contemporaneously notice how the German monetary reform had been watered down was that he was glad to be rid of responsibility for Germany and hence was no longer paying close attention. In fact, by the time the reform was implemented he was out of the State Department completely and starting a new life as a professor at the Massachusetts Institute of Technology. Exhausted by his work on the Marshall Plan, and anticipating Truman's defeat in the 1948 election, he had been contemplating such a move for a while, giving seminars at Princeton and Yale, but with no luck.

The result was different at MIT primarily because of the intervention of Richard Bissell, himself a 1939 Yale Economics PhD perennially on leave from his MIT appointment during the war, who had asked MIT for even more leave in order to serve as deputy to Paul Hoffman, the first administrator of the Marshall Plan in Europe. Bissell had come to know Charlie through the Marshall Plan work, Bissell serving as Executive Secretary of the Harriman Committee which lobbied for the Plan, and he recommended Charlie to MIT.[36] Charlie visited Cambridge, this time no formal seminar just office visits, most importantly with W. Rupert Maclaurin, and he was offered the job: "associate professor with a promise of full professor in three years."[37] He took it and bought a house at 37 Bedford Road in nearby Lincoln, and that was his life for the next forty-one years. "Bissell got me this job, and I've never regretted it."[38]

The resistance of Princeton and Yale, however, is something that needs to be understood – indeed, is something that Charlie himself worked hard to understand and to counter, determined as he was to make good in his new academic career. Charlie's seminars at Princeton and Yale had mounted an economic defense of the Marshall Plan, a defense he would later expand into the book that got him tenure, *The Dollar Shortage* (1950). The fundamental objection of people like Frank Graham and Jacob Viner, the professors who tanked his academic

---

[36] Bissell would ultimately resign his position in 1952 when he shifted from the Economic Cooperation Administration to the CIA. See Bissell (1996).
[37] Kindleberger (1991a, 129).
[38] Kindleberger (1987b, 119).

seminars, came from their stolid belief that "any structural disequilib-rium could be cured by leaving it to the market." It was a belief that Charlie had met before in the work he did as a government economist, but one so obviously out of touch with conditions on the ground that it had not been hard to overcome. As chief of GA, Charlie's mantra had become "If markets don't work, don't use markets." In academia, as he was learning, theoretical priors were much harder to shift. He put it down to what he would call the "fallacy of misplaced concreteness"; for lack of concrete information about actual conditions on the ground, economists fell back on the concreteness of their merely theoretical ideas about how the world works.

To be sure, Charlie always had in the back of his mind the ideal system of multilateral trade, the theoretical ideal that is the trained economist's instinctive reference point, and an ideal that had in fact been approxi-mated by the multilateral system of the nineteenth century. However, his point always was that construction of such a multilateral system had involved a lot more than just leaving things to the market. Indeed, "the multilateral system of the nineteenth century was an accident, built of British economic hegemony, the London capital market where dis-tressed debtors could raise funds, and the British commodity markets where distressed goods could be sold."[39] In the immediate postwar period, none of these conditions pertained.

Rather, under actual postwar conditions, the fundamental problem was structural disequilibrium. "The ultimate restoration of convertibility and multilateralism presupposes that the resources within the countries in the system will already be located in those occupations at which they can earn the highest return,"[40] which presupposition was clearly counterfactual for Europe. The necessary reallocation of productive resources would take time, and meanwhile opening up markets prematurely could easily disrupt the necessary adjustment, for example by destroying what already exists, leaving nothing behind with which to build toward the future. Specifically,

---

[39] Kindleberger (1987b, 58). Compare Kindleberger (1973, 292), which emphasizes the central role of the United States in the postwar multilateral system, without, however, ever using the word "hegemony."
[40] Kindleberger (1987b, 51).

in a world in which every country except the United States faced a structural deficit on the balance of payments, each country on its own would most likely address its deficit by cutting imports, and the result would be a general breakdown into autarky, exactly the opposite of what was needed. From this point of view, the Marshall Plan worked precisely because it covered the structural deficits of Europe for four years, thus buying time for recovery and structural adjustment. Put another way, by covering the deficits, the Marshall Plan allowed the deficits to appear, thereby creating the conditions for a possible system of multilateral trade to emerge.

Of course, the Marshall Plan only covered the deficits for four years – hardly long enough to address fundamental disequilibrium. That's why Charlie was no fan of the European Payments Union, established in 1950. In his mind, the key problem was not economic integration inside Europe, but rather integration of Europe into the larger world economy. Once the United States no longer covered the structural deficit of Europe as a whole, the danger was that Europe would instead solve its problem by cutting imports from the rest of the world, retreating into a regional autarky. The success of the Marshall Plan had merely been to provide for restocking the inventories of the existing European system of production and exchange; by 1952 the European economy was back on its feet, but the problem of structural disequilibrium remained.[41] By then, however, an alternative source of dollars had begun to emerge in military expenditures for the North Atlantic Treaty Organization, established April 1949, in effect extending US balance of payments support even after the end of the Marshall Plan, helping to avoid retreat into regional autarky.

To repeat, it was the concept of persistent structural disequilibrium that orthodox economists found so hard to accept, and that blighted Charlie's prospects at Yale and Princeton, but that was not the full extent of the intellectual challenge that Charlie faced as he entered academia. Charlie's experience in the State Department had led him to expand his conception of equilibrium and disequilibrium to incorporate political as well as economic dimensions. The economist's mantra to simply "cut inflation and devalue" wouldn't work, not only for balance of payments

---

[41] Kindleberger (1987b, 193–196).

reasons, but also because such a policy hits different social groups differently, and those most affected may well respond in ways that destabilize
the political equilibrium which is presupposed as a condition for implementing the policy. Simply put, a reasonable degree of economic equal-
ity may well be a prerequisite for economic equilibrium: "Political
stability in Europe requires not only an increase in the standard of living
of the peasant and laborer in Italy and Greece, but also a reduction in the
conspicuous consumption of the Italian landowner and the Greek shipping magnate."[42]

That's why Charlie had objected to General Clay's cozy relationship
with the German industrialists, and that's why he had seen the capital levy
as a crucial element of the German monetary reform. Indeed, Charlie
always saw political cooperation, not economic cooperation, as the essential element of the Marshall Plan. Crucially, no country would get anything
from the Plan unless they all came to an agreement on who would get what,
and that forced construction of a new kind of political equilibrium across
Europe. "The division of aid without objective economic or political
criteria was a creative cooperative act, forced on Europe by the United
States, no doubt, but nonetheless cooperative. The type of sharing implied
in this act is the basis of forging many into one sovereignty."[43] "In the
Marshall Plan, the economics profession got an opportunity to spend
$17 billion to test a theory about the relationship between economic
dislocation and political behavior. The experiment was a success."[44]

At MIT, Charlie would develop this idea of political equilibrium into
a little paper, "The Distribution of Income, Political Equilibrium, and
Equilibrium in the Balance of Payments." Rejected by Harvard's *Quarterly
Journal of Economics*, Charlie published it anyway as an appendix to
The Dollar Shortage.[45] For him the problem of structural disequilibrium
was fundamentally both political and economic and could only be
addressed effectively by engaging both dimensions at the same time.
Economists did not apparently agree but, fortunately for Charlie, MIT

---

[42] Kindleberger (1950, 259).
[43] Kindleberger (1987b, 88).
[44] Kindleberger (1987b, 103).
[45] KPMD, Box 1, Edward Chamberlin to CPK, Dec. 9, 1949.

was willing to buck economic orthodoxy by promoting him to tenure anyway. Charlie never forgot it. By nature he was always a team player, and now MIT was his team. Significantly, one of his first acts after joining MIT was to recruit Walt Rostow to join the team with an appointment in History. Clayton's economists were shifting to MIT.

For the first part of his career, Charlie's path had very much paralleled that of Emile Despres, starting at the New York Fed and then, after a year on his own at the BIS, continuing at the Board of Governors, the OSS during the war, and the Department of State after the war. It is important, therefore, to appreciate that although he could have followed Despres into academia at Williams College, he actively chose not to. (Both Emile Despres and Chandler Morse had shifted to academia earlier, even as Charlie stayed behind to help with the Marshall Plan.) He told Despres it was for family reasons, due to the physical isolation of the College way out in western Massachusetts, but Charlie had his own reasons, as he would later reflect: "It was intellectually debilitating to be too long a colleague of Despres, as it was often easier to ask him his solution to a problem than to work it out for oneself."[46]

In context, the choice of MIT can thus be understood as a kind of declaration of intellectual independence. After coauthoring a short paper with Despres in 1951, "The Mechanism for Adjustment in International Payments – The Lessons of Postwar Experience," Charlie did not collaborate with him again until 1966, in their famous "The Dollar and World Liquidity: A Minority View" (with Walter S. Salant) for *The Economist.* They did remain friends, however, and kept in touch, visiting regularly and then, after 1961, when Despres moved on from Williams to Stanford, maintaining a regular correspondence.[47] But each pursued his own local professional agenda.

---

[46] Kindleberger (1991a, 49).

[47] Recommendation letters from Charlie and also Paul Samuelson were instrumental in effecting Despres' move to Stanford. KPMD, Box 3. CPK to Lorie Tarshis, Mar. 4, 1960.

II

INTERNATIONAL ECONOMIST, 1948–1976

CHAPTER 5

Tech

A friend of mine was fond of enunciating, "What doesn't kill, strengthens." But that is not true either. Something that might not kill you might nevertheless leave you crippled.[1]

In 1948, MIT was not the economics powerhouse it would later become. For one thing, back then the economists mingled with other social scientists in one single department, which existed mainly to service students majoring in engineering of one kind or another. Paul Samuelson had been charged with producing an introductory textbook suitable for that student body, the first edition published in 1948; but conservative alumni objected to the Keynesian thrust of the book, and the administration had to get involved.[2] In a communication to the alums, department chair Ralph E. Freeman assured that "the group we now have includes no freaks or extremists . . . all of the members of the Department share a desire to preserve and improve the free institutions of America."[3] He might have been talking about Charlie who, with his twelve years of government service, carried more weight with business practitioners than academics like Samuelson ever could.

In addition to service teaching, the department had begun offering a bachelor's degree in Economics and Engineering, which yet attracted very few students; it also supported professional courses in Business and Engineering Administration, but particular attention of the faculty focused on the fledgling graduate division. Lawrence Klein had been

---

[1] Kindleberger (1991a, 131). See also Kindleberger (1964, 327 n. 3).
[2] Giraud (2014, 139–143).
[3] MIT Archives. Office of the President, 1930–1959. Box 93 "R.E. Freeman, 1945–1954."

the department's first PhD, graduating in 1944, supervised by Samuelson. In the next decades, Charlie along with Robert Solow, hired in 1949, were the two most popular choices for thesis supervision.[4] In sum, when Charlie joined the MIT department, it was essentially a startup, a work in progress, and Charlie was hired to help with the heavy lifting involved in getting the project off the ground.

Officially, his job was to teach International Economics and to provide graduate advising, while sustaining at the same time a credible personal research trajectory: "At MIT teaching was a valued activity but research was vital. People worked their heads off, some like Paul Samuelson with the most relaxed air in the world, others practically running from place to place."[5] It rubbed off on Charlie. After years of running around at the State Department, he embraced the virtue of *Sitzfleisch*, putting in long hours at the desk, in the office four days a week in order to be available to students and then at home in his study on Fridays and weekends.

Long after retiring from MIT, Charlie published what he called "my working rules," the very first one stating: "be available to students. That is what you are paid for."[6] That's why he maintained four days a week in the office, where he kept his office door open and prided himself on his class preparation. He had been hired to teach International Economics, and we know what he taught because economic necessity forced him to turn his lecture notes into a textbook. Working rule #3, "do not be a perfectionist," allowed far too many errors in the first edition (1953), errors that were fixed by student assistants in the second (1958). In the classroom, that's how he taught also, using his lectures mainly to inspire students, and relying on the students themselves to fill in the details after lecture.

He took his teaching responsibility seriously, ensuring student mastery of the standard corpus, but there was always a larger agenda as well. Speaking to the economics profession as president of the American Economic Association, he recalled: "I have from time to time suggested that host countries resist the intrusion of strangers . . . usually adding that it is the task of international economics to extirpate these primitive

---

[4] Cherrier (2014, 25).
[5] Kindleberger (1991a, 133).
[6] Kindleberger (1986b, 13).

instincts and to teach cosmopolitanism."[7] Not only did Charlie teach cosmopolitanism, he personified it, offering a model that students were invited to emulate and make their own.

Foreign students particularly noticed and appreciated this. Here is Ryutaro Komiya, a student visiting from Japan whom Charlie had met and befriended in 1955, reminiscing at a dinner to celebrate Charlie's eightieth birthday:

> You are always fair, internationally minded, and quite free from insular, nationalistic, and racial prejudices. You look at both sides of the matter when the interest of different groups are in conflict. To be unprejudiced and internationally minded is an advantage for an economist, especially for those specialized in international economics, but I found, both with regard to myself and others, that it is not easy to be free from a nationalistic bias.[8]

Not easy, indeed. Elsewhere in the MIT economics department, the predominant spirit of "policy relevance with rigor" tended to emphasize measures for improvement of *national* economies, which is to say Keynesian fiscal and monetary policy for full employment in the short run and microeconomic measures to promote long-run economic growth. In this context, it was especially the task of the international economist to teach cosmopolitanism, simply because no one else was.

We postpone to later chapters a deeper dive into Charlie's distinctive approach to international economics in order to place it properly in the context of concurrent policy debates in the outside world and concurrent theoretical debates within academia (Chapters 6 and 7). The present chapter proceeds instead to provide the scaffolding for that more detailed treatment, as well as for the chapters that treat Charlie's post-MIT career as an economic historian (Chapters 8 and 9).

Charlie's job was in Cambridge, but his home was in Lincoln, a leafy suburb to the northwest. The choice to live there was a conscious attempt to replicate the country life the Kindlebergers had so enjoyed on

---

[7] Kindleberger (2000a, 446).

[8] KPMD, Box 24, "Reminiscences of Charles P. Kindleberger on his Eightieth Birthday, October 12, 1990."

Seminary Hill, driving in to work, sometimes carpooling or taking the train. The house was an old Victorian (circa 1840) on an undersized lot, drafty and with a creaky heating system, but Charlie loved it. He loved chopping wood, cutting the grass with a push mower, tending his garden, and he even tried his hand at beekeeping. In summers, when his mother-in-law visited and took over his study, he moved into the old chicken coop in the back yard. The picture on the back cover of his autobiography shows him standing in the doorway of that outbuilding, and you can just make out the stacked beehives in the background. There he worked, banging away at his manual typewriter, taking typewritten notes on whatever he was reading and arranging them in an expanding set of loose-leaf binders: "Napoleon's armies marched on their stomachs. I do research in economic history with a three-hole punch."[9]

He took pride as well in participating in town affairs, founding the Rural Land Foundation to buy up land for conservation, and building lifelong friendships with his noneconomist neighbors. His best friend was Charles Jenney, a Latin teacher at The Belmont Hill School, and other close friends included the Episcopal minister Rollin J. Fairbanks and his wife Phyllis (to whom Charlie dedicated one of his books), and Groton School teacher Fitzhugh Hardcastle and his wife Edith. Money was always tight – extra money went into the children's education before anything else – and Charlie's biggest regret was that he never felt able to buy a sailboat of his own. But he did rent boats from time to time, and it was his noneconomist neighbors as well as family in-laws Aunt Jen (Sarah's sister) and Uncle Will Walker who most often would accompany him. Typically, these excursions took place off the coast of Maine, but once in summer 1961 off the coast of Sweden for two weeks with the Hardcastles. Echoes here of privileged childhood summers in Jamestown.

The Swedish sailing trip was a break during Charlie's second sabbatical year (1960–1), which he spent mostly at Oxford and Paris. He had spent the first sabbatical (1953–4) in Geneva, "under practically ideal conditions . . . As guests of the Economic Commission for Europe of the United Nations, at the invitation of its executive director Gunnar

---

[9] Kindleberger (1986b, 16).

Myrdal."[10] And he would spend the third sabbatical (1970–1) in Kiel and Rome. Each of these sabbaticals produced a book, but the locations were always chosen as places that Charlie especially wanted to visit. Echoes here of the foreshortened BIS adventure.

Children came along on all these adventures, but child rearing, both at home and abroad, was almost entirely the domain of Charlie's wife, Sarah, as was perhaps typical in those prefeminist days. Charlie's books thus came at the expense of some neglect of his children, and perhaps also some neglect of his wife, who found outlet for her own energies in social work, volunteering at the library, and civil rights activism. After the last child was safely off to college, it was Sarah's idea to spend a year at one or more of the historically black colleges, which took her and Charlie to Atlanta for 1967–8, and led to Charlie's ongoing engagement as a trustee of Clark College. The assassination of Martin Luther King in April 1968 was, Charlie recalls, "the towering event of the year," especially so because King had been a graduate of local Morehouse College where he was teaching a class.[11]

Life at 37 Bedford Road had its definite routine, but birthdays and anniversaries were always special opportunities for fun. At Charlie's sixtieth, a favorite nephew penned a limerick that Charlie saved:[12]

> There was an old geezer from Lincoln
> Who said "Birthdays set me to thincoln
> Bout the meaning of life
> And the love of a wife
> But the best part of them is the drincoln."

[10] Charlie would have occasion to return the favor in his memorial tribute to Myrdal: "I first met Gunnar and Alva Myrdal at a party in New York given by a *Fortune* editor and his wife, Jack Jessup and Eunice Clark, to celebrate the release of John Strachey from Ellis Island, where he had been detained as a Communist sympathizer because of the tone of his book, *The Coming Struggle for Power*" (Kindleberger 1987c). Strachey's account of his experience "A Reporter Confined" was published in *The New Yorker* (Nov. 12, 1938).

[11] Kindleberger (1991a, 186). Charlie's report on that year "Teaching Economics at Atlanta University Center, 1967–68" may be found at KPTL, Box 8.

[12] KPMD, Box 1. The limerick is dated 1970, and the menu 1965.

A menu saved from another special occasion adds detail about food choices:

The Diningroom of the Kindleberger Maison
Cocktail a la Kindleberger
Scotch Eggs, Frikadeller [Danish meatballs], Brasede
    Kartofler [German Potatoes], Haricots verts
Trifle Surprice
Kaffe Coffee Cafe

The choice to live in Lincoln created physical separation from MIT colleagues, but social life nevertheless definitely included them. Charlie would invite his economist colleagues out for cocktail parties on occasion, and in summer he would have the graduate students out for a picnic. Work life and home life were thus for him an integrated package, a rich life even if without much money. Most importantly, it was a life that enabled him to write his books – twenty-five of them as of 1991, when he wrote his autobiography, and six more after.[13] He self-diagnosed "an acute case of hypergraphia," but also "occupational therapy" and "keeping alive by keeping busy," and he was quick to specify that, of all his books, only about ten (!) constitute "real books," the rest being mostly collections of papers or lectures and textbooks. "I would emphasize in concluding that an economist's life is a good one. Unlike a dean or a college president, one can measure output in printed words."[14]

Returning to academia in 1948 after twelve years away, and now able to choose his own intellectual direction, Charlie seems to have picked up where he had left off before the war when he was working with Hansen (see Chapter 3). His June 1942 memo had identified a series of "disequilibria for which remedies must be found within the continuing post-war trade system":

Among these are the chronic world shortage of dollars; the continuous balance of payments deficit of the British Isles and a few other countries of

---

[13] KPMD contains outlines for three more collections that never found publishers: *The Economic Review as a Literary Art Form*, edited by Stephen Magee (Box 8); *The Finance and Economy of France* (Box 25); and *The Economist and the Academy* (Box 19).
[14] Kindleberger (1991a, 209).

Western Europe; the problem of "hot money" which may be still further aggravated after the war by the increased proportion which liquid claims bear to national wealth in all countries; and the world trend of the terms of trade against agriculture in favor of manufacturing.[15]

The first of these would be the topic of *The Dollar Shortage* (1950). The third was not yet a problem given the capital controls established at Bretton Woods (but see Chapter 6). The second and fourth Charlie would initially pursue by accepting "moonlighting" teaching assignments outside MIT, respectively a year-long course on "The Economy of Europe" at Columbia University and courses on development economics at the nearby Fletcher School of Law and Diplomacy.[16] The purpose of taking on all this extra teaching was not only intellectual broadening, but also helping with family finances since Charlie had taken a substantial cut in pay when he shifted from government to university work, even as the Kindlebergers welcomed their fourth child, Elizabeth Randall, born August 1949.

In his preface to *The Dollar Shortage*, Charlie frames the book explicitly as an attempt to "bridge part of the gap between government and university economists, widened by the irritation of the former with the latter for their lack of responsibility and the occasional patronage of the latter for the former as students who failed of academic distinction."[17] It is easy to see that it is Charlie himself who has felt irritated and patronized, not least in those failed job talks at Princeton and Yale, and to see also that he is determined in his new job to keep one foot deliberately in each world. Indeed, Charlie probably imagined that his future academic work would be supported by government contracts of one kind or other, just as *The Dollar Shortage* had been supported by his ongoing consulting work for the Economic Cooperation Administration (the Marshall Plan). That seems to have been the plan.

Even more, his 1951 paper "Group Behavior and International Trade" points to the likely intended direction of his immediate posttenure

---

[15] KPMD, Box 5, folder "Post World War II Planning." "The Bases of an International Program for National Development after the War" (June 24, 1942), p. 5. The published version (Kindleberger 1943b) leads with more or less the same list, though with dollar shortage listed fourth rather than first.

[16] Kindleberger (1991a, 137–139).

[17] Kindleberger (1950, v).

research. Inspired by reading Polanyi's *Great Transformation*, Charlie was interested in developing a "theory of group behavior at the national level ... in particular, a theory that systematically makes allowances for variation in the relation of subgroups that make up the larger entity ... as an adequate adjunct to the analytical tools of the market."[18] Basically a work of comparative political economy, the paper takes an inductive approach, comparing the response of different European countries to the dramatic fall in the price of wheat that resulted from the entry of American supply in the nineteenth century. Finding himself in an interdisciplinary department, Charlie was embracing a broadening of the decision horizon of economics. This also seems to have been the plan.

But it was not to be, most immediately because in April 1951 Charlie lost his security clearance and was unable to be hired for government work in any capacity. Why so? Eventually he would find out, as we shall see, but in 1951 he could only guess. The precipitating event was his application the previous August for so-called Q (top secret) clearance through the Atomic Energy Commission "in response to a request of Dr. H. P. Robertson of the Weapons Systems Evaluation group to make myself available for work with his office on a consultant basis."[19] In his autobiography, Charlie says "I disliked intensely being refused clearance," but that is just a WASP's way of saying that he was mad as hell.[20] At the very least, the refusal threatened his livelihood, but it was about more than money.

One gauge of his true feeling is his outrage on behalf of General Marshall: "A recent revisionist book on postwar economic recovery took potshots at many of the characters involved and said of Marshall that he had 'as yet an unsullied character.' I find the 'as yet' obscene."[21] Given Charlie's own war service, which had involved top secret clearance, and which had been recognized with a Bronze Star, the potshots taken at him by anonymous denouncers might themselves be considered

[18] Kindleberger (1951b, 30, 56). On Polanyi specifically, see Kindleberger (1974a).
[19] Interim Biography, p. 93.
[20] Kindleberger (1991a, 126).
[21] KPMD, Box 3, "Correspondence 1973–89," CPK to Alfred Malabre (Oct. 7, 1988). The offending passage can be found at p. 56n in Alan S. Milward, *The Reconstruction of Western Europe*, London: Methuen, as cited in Kindleberger (1987b, 263).

obscene. Remembering his postwar work on the Marshall Plan, Charlie allows himself an emotional outburst: "Every night a brief case went home. Many nights I stayed late. Work proceeded every Saturday and most Sundays. One gets annoyed that derogatory information is produced only from 9–5, with lots of time off for coffee, and clearance takes many months, when many of the people cleared or not cleared used to work their tails off."[22]

To make up for the lost income, Charlie turned to textbook writing, starting with *International Economics* (1953), but the more serious loss was intellectual. It was now going to be impossible to build a career bridging the worlds of government and academic economics, as he had planned. Charlie's subsequent reflections on the multiplicity of new postwar international organizations – the IMF, World Bank, but also OEEC and ECE, United Nations and ECOSOC – have the flavor of ruminations on an alternative life not lived.[23] In effect, the loss of his clearance meant nothing less than loss of the hay supply he had been depending on to fuel his research. Of necessity, both of his feet were now in academia, and he was forced to find a different source of hay. We see him doing that in his next book, the heavily empirical *Terms of Trade, A European Case Study* (1956), written with the support of the Merrill Foundation, and after that in the heavily historical *Economic Growth in France and Britain, 1851–1950* (1964), written with the support of the Ford Foundation. It was not the life that he had planned, but it is recognizably an adaptation of that plan to changed circumstances.

It could have been worse. MIT could have taken the clearance issue as a reason to refuse promotion, as happened to MIT's first PhD, Lawrence Klein, at the University of Michigan. In his memoirs, MIT President Killian includes a chapter entitled "Communist Charges and McCarthy Harassment," which reports that in April 1949, six days after his inauguration, an FBI informant accused mathematics professor Dirk Struik of teaching "red revolution." One of Killian's very first official tasks as president thus involved scrambling to develop an institutional response.

---

[22] Interim Biography, p. 83.
[23] Kindleberger (1951a; 1955a).

MIT suspended Struik, with salary, for five years, until finally the case was dropped for lack of evidence.[24]

In this regard, it is important to note that Charlie's own promotion was happening at the exact moment that MIT was setting up the Center for International Studies, secretly accepting CIA money that Harvard had turned down because of the CIA's security restrictions.[25] Cold War competition with the Soviet Union was on, and MIT was proud to be of service, just as it had been during World War II when it had developed vital radar systems at the famous Radiation Lab. Had Charlie not lost his security clearance, one can imagine that he might have put himself forward as a candidate for directorship of the new Center, perhaps partnering with his wartime buddy Walt Rostow, who produced the first two studies for the Center under classified CIA contract: one on the Soviet Union and one on Communist China.[26] Indeed, possibly it was the prospect of involvement with the new Center that triggered the fateful 1951 security investigation in the first place, which then had the effect instead of blocking that involvement.

In the event, instead of Charlie it was Max Milliken, a former student of Bissell brought back from the CIA, who got the director job and held the post until his premature death in 1969. Under Milliken's administration, the CIS became the intellectual center for social sciences at MIT, attracting large grants from the Ford Foundation (where Bissell had moved after the Marshall Plan), which built up first the economics department and then the political science department. But without security clearance, Charlie's involvement in all of this was inevitably limited.

For a brief period in 1956, Charlie thought he saw a way to clear his name. Following the advice of lawyer friends Walter Surrey and Monroe Karasik, he produced "An Interim Biography": 100 typewritten pages plus multiple appendices.[27] The idea was to get hired at the Council of Economic Advisors and then try to arrange for a hearing if he could not

[24] Killian (1985, 150–157).
[25] Blackmer (2002).
[26] Rostow (1952, 1954).
[27] KPTL, Box 9. CPK to Monroe Karasik, June 25, 1956.

get cleared; the biography was for the anticipated hearing. But nothing came of it because Arthur F. Burns, chairman of the Council, thought "it meant too much trouble."[28] While Charlie was waiting, however, and apparently hoping for the best, he took on an assignment for the Center, producing in short order a report, "The Objectives of United States Economic Assistance Programs," under contract for a Senate hearing January 1957.[29] The CIS was already on record advocating increased aid for economic development up to the so-called "absorption limit" in any given country, in a book by Milliken and Rostow, *A Proposal: Key to an Effective Foreign Policy* (1957). In his report, Charlie offers his own spin.

Ever since the outbreak of the Korean War in 1950, US aid had been focusing mainly on military support to counter the Communist military threat, but the end of that conflict brought opportunity to shift instead toward economic development proper. Just as the Marshall Plan had successfully assisted longer-term reconstruction in Europe (1948–52), so too a program that channeled capital funds to the underdeveloped world could assist in their transition to self-sustaining growth. In the Marshall Plan, the initial idea had been to use the Economic Commission for Europe as the coordinating body. In his report, Charlie analogously proposed creation of an International Development Advisory Council to oversee distribution of largely US funds. Echoes here of his prewar work with Hansen on a possible International Development Authority.

In context, we can thus understand the 1957 report not merely as an attempt by the CIS to shift US policy, but more locally as an attempt by Charlie to shift CIS policy away from Cold War competition with the Soviet Union and toward the more globalist Hansenian vision that he preferred. In the event, neither attempt was successful, and Charlie's security clearance plan also failed because of Burns' timidity. Once again, Charlie compensated by turning to textbook writing, now *Economic*

---

[28] Kindleberger (1991a, 127).

[29] Kindleberger (1957a). The report lists Charlie as one of many CIS researchers involved in its production, but Charlie lists the report on his CV without mentioning any coauthors. According to Blackmer (2002, 102), it was this report that prompted William F. Buckley, Jr. publically to reveal the previously secret CIA funding of the CIS.

Development (1958), which makes extensive use of facts and figures gathered by CIS researchers but within an entirely different analytical frame. For Charlie, economic development was always a business thing, not a Cold War thing. It was about the developing countries catching up with the developed world, not about US competition with the Soviet Union for influence over them. Further, for Charlie, the critical ingredient in the growth process was not so much capital formation as what he called "the social capacity of labor for economic development." The key thing is to change people, and that suggests focus on "two major growing points ... transport (and communication) and education."[30]

Charlie's 1957 report for the CIS focused on using public funds from the global North to create public goods in the Global South in order to prepare the ground for later private investment, both domestic and foreign, and self-sustaining growth. The economics of that subsequent private foreign direct investment, however, remained largely unexamined until Charlie, in collaboration with Stephen Hymer, his thesis student from 1958 to 1960, turned his attention to the problem. Hymer's thesis, "The International Operations of National Firms: A Study of Direct Foreign Investment," though rejected in 1960 for publication in the MIT economics department series on the grounds that "the argument was too simple and straightforward," laid the foundation for more or less all of Charlie's subsequent thinking on the topic.[31]

The central idea was that direct foreign investment was primarily driven by the attempt of essentially national firms to more efficiently organize their international operations by bringing them under centralized control. Just so, typically American firms make equity investments in foreign firms, which they then integrate with their own domestic operations, even as they use the foreign platform to raise creditor capital in the foreign country. It follows that foreign direct investment is not so much a part of the theory of international capital movements, but rather part of the theory of the firm. For Charlie, the most compelling thing about these international operations was the prospect that they would eventually lead national firms to become essentially international actors,

---

[30] Kindleberger (1958b, 56, 161).
[31] Hymer (1976, xiii).

hence potentially a powerful force pushing toward the creation of an integrated world economy.[32] The "Global Reach" of American corporations that leftists would deplore was thus something that Charlie as an internationalist was always more inclined to embrace.[33]

Charlie would go on to incorporate the Hymer analysis as chapter 21 in the third edition of *International Economics* (1963) and to pursue an active sideline on the topic, starting with *American Business Abroad* (1969) and continuing with assorted shorter pieces collected in *Multinational Excursions* (1984). He also edited multiple volumes, the output of conferences that broadened the community that built on Hymer's work, most importantly *The International Corporation* (1970), but also *Multinationals from Small Countries* (1977), and *The Multinational Corporation in the 1980s* (1983). That's a lot of books, but it was really always only a sideline for Charlie, pursued in part because of a sense of personal responsibility for a favorite student, particularly after Hymer's untimely death in 1976. Significantly, in Charlie's final collection of his own favorite papers, he includes nothing from this sideline, "a subject in which I have lost research interest."[34]

Blocked as Charlie was from the intellectual center for social sciences at MIT, he instead sought and found community down the road at Harvard, joining the interdisciplinary seminar on France at the Center for International Affairs (CFIA). It was this stimulating group of political scientists, sociologists, and lawyers that supported Charlie's first real work of economic history, "The Postwar Resurgence of the French economy."[35] Sabbatical in 1960–1 gave him time to develop the argument further into a book-length manuscript, *Economic Growth in France and Britain, 1851–1950* (1964). And European travel in summer 1964, financed by the CFIA, gave him the chance to bring the project to conclusion in *Europe's Postwar Growth: The Role of Labor Supply* (1967). Here he proposes the Lewis model – "the model of growth that Marx identified and regarded as highly exploitive of labor" – as a unifying framework for understanding the variety of European experience, both

[32] Kindleberger (1967a).
[33] Kindleberger (1984b, 171–176).
[34] Kindleberger (2000a, 2).
[35] Kindleberger (1963a).

over time and across countries.[36] It was surplus labor supply that had produced the super-growth of the immediate postwar period, and it was the drying-up of that supply that was bringing that super-growth period to an end.

It was thus Harvard not MIT, and the CFIA not the CIS, that kept Charlie going during his years in the wilderness. In context, we can understand his championing of the Lewis model as an attempt to pose an alternative to both Rostow's *Stages of the Economic Growth* (1960), which was the favored frame at CIS, and also to Solow's (1957) neoclassical growth model, which was the favored frame in the MIT economics department. In the event, it was the Solow model, applied to Europe in the statistical growth accounting exercise of Denison (1967), that would carry the day. Increasingly, Charlie would find his audience not only outside MIT but also outside economics.[37]

Eventually Charlie did get his clearance back, in September 1962, after the Kennedy administration hired him through the office of the Undersecretary of State, but by then he was no longer the same person he had been ten years before.[38] He did take advantage of the clearance to dabble a bit in government consulting around international monetary reform, starting with a memo for his old EOU buddy Robert Roosa, "Suggested Lines of Evolution for the International Monetary System" (January 7, 1963), which he developed further in a memo for the Treasury, "Summary of Views on US Balance of Payments Position and Policy" (April 2, 1963).[39] And two years later he was appointed to President Johnson's Advisory Committee on International Monetary Arrangements.[40] But it was really too late for him to build

---

[36] Kindleberger (1967b, 8), Lewis (1954).

[37] One exception, his student Peter Temin (2002) would subsequently build on Charlie's preferred analytical structure.

[38] His application is dated December 5, 1961. The ultimate resolution is stated in a letter from the US Civil Service Commission, Bureau of Personnel Investigation, dated Sept. 26, 1962. KPTL, Box 8.

[39] The Roosa memo may be found in KPMD, Box 21. The Treasury memo was published as ch. 6 in Kindleberger (1966).

[40] In his autobiography, Charlie refers to this committee as the LBJ Presidential Committee on International Monetary Policy, but historians call it the Dillon Committee, after Douglas Dillon its Chair. Apparently its first meeting was July 16,

the kind of government–university bridge he had originally planned. Not only was Charlie different, but so was the government and so was the university.

In government, the big difference was political leadership: "In 1962, President Kennedy said that the two most important problems in the world were the nuclear bomb and the balance of payments of the United States. When I first heard this, I thought it was funny. Now I think it tragic."[41] As we shall see (Chapter 6), in Charlie's view the United States was not running a balance of payments deficit, rather merely supplying the world's demand for dollars as a liquid reserve. When President Johnson proved no better on this point than his predecessor, Charlie took the earliest opportunity to resign from the Advisory Committee and to pursue instead a public campaign on the pages of *The Economist* with his friends Emile Despres and Walter Salant. Their article, "The Dollar and World Liquidity: A Minority View," raised a ruckus, but did essentially nothing to stem the tide.

In economics, the big difference was methodological. When Charlie first joined MIT, the kind of economics that he did – so-called literary economics, as opposed to modelling, whether mathematical or statistical – was already old-fashioned, but fourteen years later it was barely even recognizable as economics by a new generation reared on the latest technique. And, of course, by then MIT, under Paul Samuelson's intellectual leadership, was positioning itself as to go-to place for young scholars seeking professional training in this changed conception of economics. The older generation at MIT never lost their respect for Charlie, a respect based on his wide knowledge about the world and intuition about current economic problems, but increasingly he was a fish out of water, "MIT not being the sort of place that attracts students of economic history."[42]

As at the Kent School, Charlie found other ways to help the team, ultimately trying his hand at academic administration as chairman of the

---

1965, memorialized by a press conference and statement by President Johnson, so it was a relatively brief sojourn for Charlie.

[41] Kindleberger (1970b, 7).

[42] Kindleberger (1991a, 193).

faculty (1965–7) with a view toward possible deanship or college presidency. In the end, however, he decided instead to rededicate himself to scholarship, though it took several tries before he found his footing. During his year away in Atlanta, he dusted off some lectures he had earlier produced on the multinational corporation and published them as *American Business Abroad* (1969). And then, back at MIT, he tried writing a third textbook, now exploring the boundary between international economics and international politics. Published as *Power and Money* (1970), the book found not much market in either discipline, though it would later be rediscovered and hailed as a founding text of the new subdiscipline of International Political Economy.[43] Next, in his third sabbatical (1970–1), he returned to the comparative political economy project he had floated twenty years earlier, adding more case studies and eventually publishing the result as *Economic Response* (1978). Upon his return from sabbatical, a group of his former students presented him with a festschrift: *Trade, Balance of Payments, and Growth.*[44] It was an "affectionate tribute" but also a not-so-subtle hint that his time had passed.

In the event, it was the fortuitous invitation to write what became *The World in Depression, 1929–1939* (1973) that finally showed the road forward, that is, financial history. To make room for this new life venture, Charlie would recruit coauthors for his two successful textbooks and thereafter leave periodic revisions entirely up to them. The decks thus cleared, after retiring from MIT in 1976, Charlie followed up the *Depression* book with his best-selling *Manias, Panics, and Crashes, A History of Financial Crises* (1978), dedicated to "the MIT Old Guard of the 1940s." And he would follow that up with what he would call his "chef d'oeuvre,"[45] *A Financial History of Western Europe* (1984), dedicating it to his wife, just as he had his very first book. Having been a civil servant for twelve years, and then an economics teacher for twenty-eight, he used retirement to reinvent himself as an economic historian.

---

[43] Kirschner et al. (1997), Cohen (2008, ch. 3).
[44] Bhagwati et al. (1971).
[45] Kindleberger (1991a, 204).

Going his own way at last, unburdened by academic responsibilities and no longer held back by loyalty to the department he had done so much to build, he reaped an unexpected reward in the form of election as President of the American Economic Association. The students who had learned from his textbooks, especially *International Economics*, had become professional economists and voted him in. His presidential address in December 1985, "International Public Goods without International Government," urged a renewed two-way conversation between economics and political science, as opposed to the one-way form of economic imperialism urged by Chicago economists Stigler and Becker.

Summing up his life, in the self-deprecating way of the WASP, Charlie suggests: "I should perhaps be ashamed of a life of intellectual hit-and-run, of taking up a topic – foreign exchange, international trade, capital flows, economic development, the multinational corporation, political economy, economic history, financial crises, financial history – skimming the cream and moving on." "I sometime accuse myself of having a grasshopper mind, as I and my sisters know our mother had."[46] Perhaps that is how it felt to him. An outsider, however, surveying the corpus as a whole and appreciating the formative influence of his most important teachers, sees more coherence and unity.

Most obviously, economic history was for Charlie a *method* of inquiry more than it was a *subject* of inquiry; that's where he ultimately found a rich supply of hay ready for processing.[47] True economic historians focus their efforts on digging up new facts from the archives. By contrast, Charlie, a self-identified "historical economist," focused instead on telling his readers what the facts meant. He remained, as I have said, fundamentally an intelligence analyst, adding value by sifting through raw intelligence that had been gathered by others.

Even more, it is no accident that over the years he narrowed his historical inquiry to focus specifically on financial history. Indeed, the bright thread running through all of his "real" books, and providing the analytical frame that he used to detect needles and separate them from

---

[46] Kindleberger (1991a, 209–210; 1999, 1).
[47] Kirshner et al. (1997).

the hay, was an often implicit theory of international money. He never produced a proper theoretical treatise, no "real" book on the subject, though his 1937 thesis comes close. Instead, there were essays and lectures, mostly informal things, most comprehensively collected in *International Money: A Collection of Essays* (1981), but preceded by the essays collected in *Europe and the Dollar* (1966), and succeeded by *International Capital Movements* (1987). Instead of focusing his efforts on mathematical or statistical refinement of this underlying analytical frame, which is the kind of thing that wins Nobels, Charlie chose to use it as an entry point for investigating the problems that interested him, most centrally problems of comparative political economy as revealed in the financial historical record.

In this regard, it is significant that Charlie's last published book of collected essays, titled *Comparative Political Economy: A Retrospective* (2000), includes as chapter 4 the 1951 paper "Group Behavior" with which he had launched his MIT career. Indeed, an overarching theme that runs through all of the chosen essays is the dialectic of economics and politics. Whereas the economic logic of the payment system pushes toward hierarchy and centralization, the political logic of subglobal and subnational groupings pushes toward autarky and pluralism.[48] Economic history, and especially financial history, records the never-ceasing and always interesting seesaw between these two opposing logics.

In the end, and notwithstanding multiple obstacles along the way, Charlie managed to do more or less what he had set out to do half a century earlier. For fifty years, an unusual degree of psychological resilience combined with focused and deliberate adjustment to shocks of multiple kinds had enabled him to continue producing intellectual supply even in the face of shifting intellectual demand. Writing in 1987, in an unpublished paper on Henry George's "Protection or Free Trade," Charlie endorsed wholeheartedly what he takes to be the central message of George's book: "Don't dig in; keep adjusting." It's a good motto for countries seeking economic development, and also for individuals seeking intellectual development.[49]

---

[48] See also Kindleberger (1996b).
[49] Kindleberger (1987d). See also Kindleberger (2000a, 171).

Barred from government work in 1951 by security clearance problems, Charlie had to find another way, and so he did. In retrospect, maybe we could even say that losing his security clearance was a kind of gift to Charlie, shielding him from the distractions of the policy world and forcing him instead to become a world-class economic historian. Rejection and failure, he would always say, force innovation, while success tends to breed stagnation. "I suspect that defeat is a solvent that melts old ideas and old resistances, whereas victory strengthens the pressure groups and vested interests that make adaptation difficult."[50] Nevertheless, the importance of that rejection for his intellectual trajectory poses the question: Why exactly did he lose his security clearance?

For a long time, Charlie wondered about that himself. Initially, he tried to make light of it, coining a witticism: "Derogatory information is just like gonorrhea. It's no worse than a bad cold, and you are not a man until you have had it."[51] But after living with the situation for some years, and watching as other friends and colleagues got caught up in the witch hunt, Charlie decided to do something about it. Writing in summer 1956 for the anticipated hearing, Charlie already had reason to know what some of the derogatory material must be.

Back when he was still at the State Department, as Chief of the Division of German and Austrian Affairs, he had discovered that the FBI was monitoring his phone calls and using what they heard "to peddle gossip from those calls to its sycophantic columnists such as George Sokolsky."[52] The suggestion was that Charlie was working inside the State Department in support of the Morgenthau Plan for pastoralization of Germany, presumably as an agent of the Soviet Union, which sought removal of Germany's capital equipment for its own use, and against President Truman's stated policy. Nothing could be further from the truth, of course, since Charlie had quite explicitly and strenuously avoided taking up the position as GA Chief until after US policy had shifted to rebuilding Germany instead (see Chapter 4). Charlie hired a lawyer and extracted

---

[50] Kindleberger (2000a, 183).

[51] KPMD, Box 1, CPK to Cliff Durr, Dec. 13, 1951. See also Kindleberger (1991a, 155).

[52] Kindleberger (1991a, 45, 117). Sokolsky's articles were published in the *New York Herald Tribune,* June 5 and July 23, 1947. See Kindleberger (1987b, pp. 196–197, n. 3) for excerpts.

a grudging apology, but the incident made him aware that somehow he had attracted the attention of the FBI.

Subsequent events had shed more light on the underlying reasons for the FBI's interest in him. Shortly after joining MIT, Charlie had been investigated and cleared for work as an outside consultant for the European Recovery Program of the Economic Cooperation Administration (ECA). In the course of that investigation, J. Walter Yeagley, Director of the Security and Investigation Division for the ECA, sent Charlie a formal request for further information on his contacts with Frank Coe, Harry D. White, David Wahl, and Mr. and Mrs. Robert T. Miller. That must have been a worrisome letter to receive in February 1949, right on the heels of the highly visible August 1948 hearings of the House Un-American Activities Committee, which had interviewed Robert T. Miller on August 10th and Harry White and Frank Coe on August 13th. But Charlie responded to Yeagley with a letter detailing the nature and extent of his association with each man and that seemed to be the end of the matter. He was cleared.[53]

Having dealt – as he thought, successfully – with the problem of White, Coe, and Miller back in 1949, Charlie no doubt anticipated a similar result when he applied for security clearance two years later. But it didn't work out that way. Thinking back on it in 1956, he concluded that there must be something else: maybe something added after his 1949 clearance? A particular worry was his friendship with Clifford Durr, much closer in fact than that with Miller: "We asked Clifford Durr to be godfather of our daughter Randall, born after we left Virginia, as a sign of our love for him."[54] Durr had been tangling with the House Un-American Activities Committee as early as 1942, and for him Truman's loyalty program, established March 22, 1947, by Executive Order 9835, was the last straw, leading to his resignation on principle in April 1948. Like Charlie, Durr imagined that he would find more suitable employment in academia, but unlike Charlie he found all doors closed to him, and so instead embarked on a career of private civil rights law practice, starting with defense of people unjustly fired on spurious loyalty charges.[55]

---

[53] Interim Biography, p. 86, 92.
[54] Interim Biography, p. 43a.
[55] Salmond (1990).

Durr's principled example may well have been in Charlie's mind when, nine months after his own clearance had been refused, he contributed $10 to the legal defense of Dirk Struik, the MIT professor of mathematics who had been indicted by a Middlesex Grand Jury on charges of advocating the overthrow of the US and Massachusetts governments. In his letter to the Struik Defense Committee, Charlie explicitly dissociated himself from Struik's political views, but went on to explain that "I am nonetheless concerned that the constitutionality of the act under which he has been indicted be tested."[56] It was an act of principle that nevertheless brought him to the further attention of the FBI, as he subsequently learned from friends who were questioned about it. Worrisome.[57]

In addition to his connection with Durr, in his "Interim Biography" Charlie also admitted to connections over the years with "Paul Baran, Andrew Biemiller, Michael Blankford, Lauchlin Currie, Arthur Fletcher, Harold Glasser, Vladimir Kazekevitch, Owen Lattimore, Mrs. Ivy Litvinov, Carl Marzani, Bernard Nortman, William Remington, Rowena Rommel, Paul Sweezy, Donald Wheeler, Nathaniel Weyl, a disparate group of avowed one-time or current Socialists, Marxists and Communists, and of persons who have been publicly attacked on security grounds."[58] He admitted to all of them without apology, and explained each one, as he had earlier explained his connections with White, Coe, and Miller.

But he appreciated that likely the biggest problem was his close circle of professional colleagues, most of whom had wound up with security troubles of their own, in particular Chandler Morse, Emile Despres, and George Eddy:

> It is my understanding that Morse has been refused clearance for Federal employment of some kind, that Despres has had clearance difficulties though he has been cleared and that Eddy has been cleared by a Loyalty Board of charges brought against him in the Treasury in 1954. I assert that

---

[56] KPTL, Box 9. CPK to Struik Defense Fund, Jan. 21, 1952.
[57] KPTL, Box 8. In the event, the Boston Division recommended against any formal interview on the grounds that it "could prove embarrassing to the Bureau" since there was very little evidence. Report of the Boston Division, Oct. 4, 1954.
[58] Interim Biography, p. 98.

I know them well and that I know them to be loyal Americans who have worked hard and faithfully in their country's interest.[59]

In closing, Charlie summarized:

I have indicated in detail the nature of the relations between me and a group of people who are known to me to have "security trouble" at one time or another. This group includes most of my friends and associates in government.

Since I am acquainted or friendly with so many people who have been subject to derogatory information, the impression may be created that I am part of a vast conspiracy. It should be pointed out, however, that if one man in an office is publicly attacked, derogatory information would be developed in the files of say 30 people associated with him in professional work, and the fact that these 30 people know each other adds nothing to the sum total derogation.[60]

Here Charlie is speaking as a professional economist about the statistical value of data as evidence and trying to teach his imagined inquisitors a thing or two. In context, this can be read as a dig specifically directed at the Jenner Committee's infamous hearings on "Interlocking Subversion in Government Departments."[61] In the event, however, the anticipated confrontation with his inquisitors never happened, and Charlie's defense simply moldered in the file drawer.

It is one thing to imagine what might be the reason for your clearance problem, as Charlie was doing in 1956, but another actually to find out. Eventually, after passage of the 1966 Freedom of Information Act, Charlie's curiosity got the better of him and he filed the necessary paperwork to obtain his FBI file. When the redacted photocopies finally came and he worked his way through them, he would have discovered that in fact all three of the counts against him in 1951 were already on record from the earlier investigation when he had been hired to work on the European Recovery Program. Further, all three originated from the

---

[59] Interim Biography, p. 35.
[60] Interim Biography, p. 98.
[61] Published July 30, 1953, Report of the Subcommittee to Investigate the Administration of the Internal Security Act and other Internal Security Laws.

FBI's original file on him, opened in October 1946, as part of its investigation into "Underground Soviet Espionage Organization (NKVD) in the Agencies of the United States Government." Once he had his FBI file, Charlie would have been able to reconstruct what happened, but in his 1991 autobiography he only hints at the full story. Probably it is a case of WASP reticence: "Never complain; never explain"; though he did take care to preserve the relevant documents from which it is possible to fill in the gaps in his own account. Herewith the full story revealed by those documents.

Charlie left the Department of State effective July 31, 1948, to start his new academic life at MIT, and he signed on with the ERP effective November 4, 1948, which triggered a security investigation. In his letter of November 24, 1948, formally launching the investigation, J. Edgar Hoover more or less instructed the field offices where the dirt was to be found in reports that already existed. The resulting report of December 30, 1948, then dutifully compiled it all, along with fresh investigative reports from field offices in New York, New Haven, Philadelphia, Washington, DC, Boston, and Baltimore, none of which turned up any additional derogatory information. The following sentences from the cover-page synopsis of the December 1948 FBI investigation were the fatal ones:

> While employed at Treasury Department, applicant worked with FRANK COE, and under HARRY D. WHITE. Informants report both were involved in a Soviet espionage conspiracy. Informants report applicant member of Chapter #1 of American Veterans Committee. Further report that the applicant's name included in a "roster of helpful persons" maintained by DAVID WAHL, who was reported to be a member of the Communist Party underground movement and a close associate of known Communists. Informants further report applicant and his wife were associates with the ROBERT T. MILLERS. MILLER reported to have been involved in a Soviet espionage conspiracy in Washington.[62]

These were the sentences that must have prompted Yeagley's querying letter of February 1949, which Charlie thought he had adequately cleared up in his response.

---

[62] KPTL, Box 8.

In fact, however, as the FBI file further makes clear, Charlie's response was used in the 1951 investigation as *confirmation* of the suspect associations. The fundamental reason he lost his clearance was thus not any new evidence at all, but rather the fact that, while Yeagley had been willing to override the FBI in 1948, his counterpart at the Atomic Energy Commission in 1951 was not. As a consequence, as we have seen, not only was Charlie unable to be hired for government work in any capacity, but he was also unable to participate fully in the Center for International Studies that would be the intellectual center for social science at MIT.

In his autobiography, Charlie chooses not to tell this story, concerning himself instead with establishing the facts of the matter about White, Coe, and Miller, the men whose purported involvement in a Soviet espionage conspiracy had resulted in his own security troubles. Were they in fact Soviet spies?[63]

White:

> He may or may not have been a Marxist – nothing I have ever witnessed directly would point in that direction – but he was a conspirator. He wanted to run the world ... Although it has been denied in the biography by his brother, I suspect he committed suicide after returning to New Hampshire from having testified in Congress and fighting off accusations. That would fit his conspiratorial character.

Coe:

> Coe may well have been a Marxist ... [While living] in the coal-fields of Kentucky, [he] became radicalized in observing the conditions of the miners. I liked Coe, and kept in touch with him for a while, sending him a copy of my thesis in 1937 ... Poor Coe: when the McCarthy heat was on there was so much he could not explain that he left, first for Mexico and then for Communist China. When Galbraith saw him in China on a trip for the American Economic Association, Coe expressed an interest in seeing more current books, and I sent him some.

---

[63] There is an enormous volume of writing on this topic, reviewed and evaluated persuasively, in my view, in Boughton and Sandilands (2003). My concern here, however, is not so much with the fact of the matter, but rather with Kindleberger's own personal assessment of the cases.

Miller:

Miller had made some money in the stock market in 1933, and went to Russia to see what it was about. There he wrote for a newspaper as a stringer, and married an American woman who may have been interested in Marxism. His conservative Baltimore family was not pleased by all this, and he waited in Europe until his twins were born, meanwhile working in Paris for the Spanish loyalists.[64]

In all three cases, it is notable that for Charlie it all comes down to a matter of character. To evaluate someone's actions you need to know what is behind them. Some of that is about personality, some about past formative experience, and some about the frame they use to understand the world. It is further notable that in all three cases Charlie says nothing about whether they were Communists, much less whether they associated with known Communists. He is interested instead in whether they were Marxists. In effect, he clears all three men of the charge of espionage, but convicts each one of a different variety of human frailty that opened them up to the charge. It is the variety of human frailty that interests him.

Charlie was a New Deal liberal, of the globalist rather than nationalist variety, and a William Clayton free trader rather than a George Kennan Cold Warrior. All three of these positions were controversial, but none of them was the reason for his clearance trouble. He got into trouble instead for his wide interest in humanity, expressed by his continuing friendship and contact with people who interested him, even if he disagreed with them on political grounds. In his autobiography, he concludes that his problems arose because "some of my friends were less than circumspect in the way they responded to the witch hunt," and so they were, Coe and Miller (White was never a friend) and all the others as well.[65] But it is also true that Charlie continued these friendships even in the face of the witch hunt. His friends' lack of circumspection was one of the reasons he liked them, even when he regretted the trouble it made for them and for him. That's who he was, even more than he was a New Dealer.

---

[64] Kindleberger (1991a, 44, 45, 10).
[65] Kindleberger (1991a, 127).

CHAPTER 6

The Dollar System

The economically efficient system of a dollar standard may serve the cosmopolitan interest in a national frame. Its demands on world sophistication are excessive.[1]

As an internationalist, Charlie was instinctively a free trader, imagining a world of fine-grained specialization and increasing returns to scale, in which everyone and every nation trades their own production for the wide range of goods produced by others, to mutual economic benefit. Ideally, not only goods but also capital should flow freely across borders: long-term capital for long-term economic development and also short-term capital as a buffer for temporary deficits in the balance of payments. Writing in 1987, Charlie explicitly embraces this lifelong ideal:

> The model for the world should be the integrated financial market of a single country, with one money, free movements of capital at long and short term, the quantity theory of money employed on trend but free discounting in periods of trouble. Such a world will be full of ambiguity, paradox, uncertainty and problems. Such it seems to me is the human condition.[2]

The reality of the immediate postwar period was of course very far from this ideal, and Charlie was quick to admit that for present purposes his internationalist instinct was little more than a "prejudice" at considerable distance from the facts on the ground. Indeed, it seemed to him clear enough that the world was mired in a state of "pervasive and unyielding" structural disequilibrium, so much so that the normal

---

[1] Kindleberger (1970a, 227).
[2] Kindleberger (1987a, 62).

operations of the market, which in the past had worked well enough in response to small shocks, were simply overwhelmed.[3] Adjustment required instead the active intervention of government to correct structural disequilibrium, working toward restoration of the conditions under which the market system might one day be able to work again. Just so, the immediate postwar structural disequilibrium, which had dollar shortage as its most dramatic symptom, had been overcome by an equally dramatic government-led effort, not just the Marshall Plan, but also a whole panoply of intergovernmental economic assistance. At the heart of the problem, as Charlie saw it, factor prices were out of line with factor endowments, while the price adjustment called for by standard economic theory was incompatible with political stability. The answer was found instead by adjusting endowments to prices by means of a massive program of capital investment.

By this means, the immediate postwar structural disequilibrium seemed well on its way to resolution by the time Charlie was putting together the first edition of his textbook. But a new form of structural disequilibrium was already emerging in the developing world and proving equally resistant to a market solution. Put simply, the "social capacity for development" in the developing countries was running substantially ahead of their own capital resources even while, as a lasting consequence of depression and world war, the international market for long-term capital remained essentially shut down. Governments were stepping in to fill the gap, but still demand was running substantially ahead of supply. "The remedy lies in creating the climate of opinion in which private capital movements can be resumed or in devising the international institutions capable of handling capital movements in the amounts needed, or a little of both."[4]

In Charlie's view, "the young debtor should borrow, the mature debtor should repay, the young creditor should lend."[5] Specifically, capital should flow from the low-interest-rate developed world to the high-interest-rate developing world, as it had before World War I through the mechanism of empire. The problem was that no substitute for empire, whether markets

---

[3] Kindleberger (1958a, 553, 557).
[4] Kindleberger (1958a, 561).
[5] Kindleberger (1958a, 522).

or institutions, had yet been adequately established. Official flows through the World Bank and bilateral aid of various kinds were useful, but were inevitably much too small and also distorted by political objectives. The consequence was persistent structural disequilibrium, which showed up as a tendency toward stagnation in the developed world for lack of demand and a tendency toward inflation in the developing world for lack of supply.

Free trade in goods was part of the answer, specifically lowering tariff barriers in the developed world in order to allow the developing world to raise needed funds by selling their own present production. But the world also needed free trade in long-term capital, in order to enable the developing world to run a persistent current-account deficit: "No fundamental attack on the reserve problem for short-term disequilibria can be made until secular disequilibrium is under control. From the intensity of the interest in growth in underdeveloped countries and the relatively meager flow of long-term capital, this will not be soon."[6]

If capital can't flow to where the labor is, another logical possibility would be for labor to flow to where the capital is, from low-wage countries to high-wage countries. Specifically, "migration should take place until the marginal value product of labor is the same in all parts of the world." That's what a truly "cosmopolitan migration policy" would look like. But free flow of labor was even less likely than free flow of capital: "In domestic trade, the principle of efficiency is highly diluted by equity. In international trade, efficiency has stood by itself, and there has been no room for considerations of equity"; "Goods move more freely than capital, and capital more freely than labor. None moves sufficiently to bring about factor price equalization."[7]

Thus, in the immediate postwar period, cosmopolitanism seemed to Charlie most immediately achievable quite narrowly in the world of goods, mainly by recognizing that most of the barriers to free trade in the developed world arise from attempts by narrow interests to receive special treatment, most importantly attempts by imperfectly competitive domestic producers to avoid foreign competition.[8] For Charlie, "the only

---

[6] Kindleberger (1958a, 584, 563).
[7] Kindleberger (1958a, 547, 439, 582, 571, 432).
[8] Kindleberger (1958a, chs. 12–15).

valid argument for a tariff from a world point of view is the infant-industry argument," and that argument is more salient for the developing than the already developed. In a world of specialization and increasing returns, initial protection may be required in order to build capacity in a new line of activity. Most importantly, tariffs on manufactured imports may be appropriate for developing countries which confront the challenge of shifting labor from a low-wage traditional agricultural sector to a high-wage modern manufacturing sector – so-called "dual economies."[9]

To repeat, it seemed clear to Charlie that tariffs in the developed world should be lowered. The problem was that persistent balance of payments disequilibrium made that goal difficult to accomplish. Faced with a payments deficit, tariffs can seem like a logical policy response even if "anything that the tariffs can do, something else can do better."[10] That's why Charlie so forcefully insisted that "the establishment and maintenance of balance-of-payments equilibrium ... is the central problem in international economics today."[11] Balance of payments disequilibrium was the central problem because it was the biggest threat to free trade. And the main underlying cause of balance of payments disequilibrium was the problem of restoring long-term capital flows from the North to the South.

That's why, notwithstanding the political challenge, Charlie always emphasized restoration of long-term capital flows as job one, more important even than restoration of short-term capital flows. Indeed, he warned that premature restoration of short-term capital flows would likely just fill the long-term capital flow vacuum, and that was asking for trouble since there was no short-term prospect of reversing the flow in order to repay. It is only when the young debtor becomes a mature debtor that repayment can be expected. Reliance on short-term capital flows for long-term capital needs therefore inevitably results in even worse balance of payment problems when the short-term borrowing comes due.

In Charlie's view, the stakes could not have been higher. He remembered well how the structural disequilibrium of the 1930s had brought to

---

[9] Kindleberger (1958a, 234, 216, 550).
[10] Kindleberger (1958a, 233).
[11] Kindleberger (1958a, 469).

a halt both long-term and short-term capital flows and so destroyed the international monetary system, ushering in world depression and eventually renewed World War. Each country, facing its own individual balance of payments constraint, had sought direct control over its interface with the rest of the world, and the result was collapse of the elastic international credit flows required for continued operation of the world trading system: "Parallel with the growth of quantitative restrictions on imports ... has been the development of foreign exchange control. This depression product was born largely of necessity."[12] It is this history that informs the urgency of Charlie's message in the immediate postwar period. Sine qua non for post–World War II reconstruction of the global trading system was long-term capital flows from the developed world to the developing world.

Teaching cosmopolitanism meant not only presenting a realistic account of how the world actually works, that is, structural disequilibrium, but also painting a picture of how the world might one day be able to work, supposing that the long-term capital-flow problem could be solved and short-term capital flow resumed. Toward this end, the central pedagogical challenge that Charlie faced was that the traditional analytical structure of international economics had very little connection to present reality: "There can be little doubt in most minds that the real world resembles less the classical assumptions than their obverse." Three assumptions in particular seemed to him clearly false: full employment, elastic demand, and elastic supply. Supposing these assumptions held, the price mechanism might well be adequate for directing the international adjustment process, and in this case the classical theory would present a powerful argument for free trade: "This approach is pedagogically instructive, but it runs the danger of misleading the student who mistakes the analysis for a description of reality."[13] The pedagogical challenge was to find an alternative line of analysis, more tightly connected to observed reality, without abandoning the cosmopolitan vision of free trade.

Toward that end, Charlie's first step was the Keynesian one, relaxing the assumption of full employment, and drawing attention to the role of income changes in the adjustment process. (This would come to be

[12] Kindleberger (1958a, 281).
[13] Kindleberger (1958a, 557, 148, 554, 148)

called the absorption approach, an early version of which Charlie had grappled with in his thesis, under the influence of Angell; see Chapter 2.) But the Keynesian extreme of treating prices as fixed goes too far, and when we consider a world in which both price and income can change it becomes difficult to achieve any definite analytical result: "The answer is . . . that it depends on the circumstances."[14] That's why his textbook is so full of facts about actual circumstances, not so much as illustrations of a theory deduced from first principles, but rather as examples from which general lessons might possibly be drawn inductively.

It is of course impossible to make sense of facts without some prior underlying analytical structure, and that seems to be the point of the two chapters at the beginning of the textbook: "The Balance of Payments" (ch. 2) and "The Foreign-Exchange Market" (ch. 3). Here we find an analytical image of international relations sufficiently general to be consistent with both classical and Keynesian theoretical frameworks, but also one sufficiently connected to reality to serve as the framework for investigating any particular episode or circumstance. In these initial framing chapters, Charlie emphasizes how the foreign exchange market operates essentially as a system for clearing international payments:

> The primary function of the foreign-exchange market is to transfer purchasing power and clear transactions in opposite directions in essentially the same sort of way as do the Federal Reserve System, the separate Federal Reserve bank, local clearinghouses, or even the informal clearing which takes the form of swapping of checks between the clerks of banks in the same small town.[15]

From this perspective, the balance of payments for a country appears as nothing more than a clearing balance between the domestic banking system and the rest of the world. Balance of payments equilibrium thus requires simply that clearing balances are settled in some acceptable international means of payment – ultimately gold, but more generally short-term capital flows. The key mechanism involves net surplus countries lending temporarily to net deficit countries, typically through the intermediation of some

---

[14] Kindleberger (1958a, 206). See also Kindleberger (1957b).
[15] Kindleberger (1958a, 44).

world financial center or other, formerly London but prospectively New York.

"Temporarily" is key: "Short-term capital movements are like inventory fluctuations in national income . . . [They] should net to zero over a long period, except for growth or decline in working balances." Further, it is the expansion and contraction of the balance sheet of the world banking center, standing in between deficit and surplus countries, that serves as the mechanism for settling international payments by everyone else: "A world banking center must learn to offset the meaningless changes in reserves arising from international transactions in the same way as it responds to seasonal and similar changes in the note circulation [domestically]"; "Short term capital assets can substitute for gold in the money supply of some countries without the necessity for subtracting an equal amount in the other countries which record the liabilities."[16]

The important point to appreciate here is that Charlie always viewed the official balance of payments accounts not through the lens of the new national income concept, as was becoming commonplace among his Keynesian colleagues, but rather through the older lens of the "foreign exchange budget" concept. From this payments perspective, what he ideally would have liked to see in a proper set of international accounts was a full accounting of all payments, both for goods (current account) and for securities (capital account). Instead, throughout history official accounts have mostly focused on the movement of goods. That is one reason that economists had come to focus so much attention on the current account, and to emphasize a conception of static equilibrium in which exports equal imports with no net flows of gold, much less short- or long-term capital flows. By contrast, and notwithstanding data limitations, Charlie always emphasized the importance of long-term capital flows, inherently cyclical and so inherently requiring a short-term capital-flow buffer, hence requiring also a more dynamic equilibrium concept. He summarizes his position thus:

These short-term capital movements have a balance-wheel role to play –
daily, seasonally, and (of great importance) cyclically. If this role can be

---

[16] Kindleberger (1958a, 343, 330, 328).

played by the money market, in a period of stabilizing speculation, well and good. If speculation is destabilizing, it may be possible to offset it and provide the necessary balance by movement of official funds. If official funds are insufficient to cope with the problem, it may be necessary to impose exchange control on movements of hot money and then use official funds to balance – or some other device, such as import restrictions.[17]

This sequence of adjustment mechanisms, from private money markets to official (central bank) funds to direct exchange controls, was the historical sequence through which the mechanism of international payment clearing had broken down in the 1930s. The historical task of the immediate postwar period, as Charlie saw it, was to find a way to run that sequence in reverse, with the objective of eventually returning to a world of stabilizing short-term capital movements, the normal infrastructure of international trade. Such a task would inevitably be slow work, moving forward by fits and starts, but postwar developments did seem to him to be proceeding in that general direction, and anyway Charlie was by nature an optimist. In the short term, structural disequilibrium, formerly in Europe and now in the developing world, required active government intervention. But the long-term goal was always the free trade ideal: free trade in goods but also in capital, both long-term and short-term.

Centrally important for achieving this long-term goal, the United States had a special role to play, with the dollar replacing sterling as the currency of international commerce and New York replacing London as the world financial center. Looking back, Charlie identified the first steps toward a world dollar system already in the interwar years: "The rationalization of the gold standard and the gold-exchange standard was needed to make the transition from the sterling to the dollar standard." By the late 1930s, "if the gold price of the dollar changed, it was the value of gold which was altered, not the value of the dollar."[18] However, World War II and then postwar structural disequilibrium had halted this evolutionary progress, requiring government rather than markets to take the lead for a while, most prominently in the 1946 Anglo-American loan and the 1948

[17] Kindleberger (1958a, 344).
[18] Kindleberger (1966, 207).

Marshall Plan, and continuing in multiple less visible interventions throughout the succeeding decade. The market's time would surely come, but in the 1950s Charlie judged that time was not yet: "Monetary matters continue to hold a fascination of the intricate and complex mechanism. In the postwar period, the most glittering of these toys with which Americans and Europeans joined in playing was the European Payments Union. But the central issues lay elsewhere."[19]

Meanwhile, Charlie's textbook was a market success. One reason was its resolutely middle-of-the-road position between the classical orthodoxy of Charlie's old nemeses, Viner and Graham, and the Keynesian orthodoxy of Charlie's new MIT colleagues, Samuelson and Solow. On policy, the text similarly carved a middle way between the "liberals" and the "planners," appreciating both the strengths and weaknesses of the market mechanism, and both the weaknesses and strengths of state intervention. Even methodologically, the text charted a middle road between the old institutionalist texts loaded down with detailed description of specific instruments and institutions and the new, more analytical texts which sought an abstract and deductive account of theory.

One possible obstacle to adoption of the textbook might have been Charlie's distinctive (and idiosyncratic) payments approach to the subject, as emphasized earlier. But the fact that international short-term capital markets were still more or less shut down, coupled with Charlie's conviction that it would be a mistake to reopen them until there were more satisfactory mechanisms for long-term capital flow, allowed him to place the central emphasis elsewhere. As a result, teachers were not excessively bothered by an unfamiliar viewpoint, while the more careful students were intrigued by Charlie's third way, neither classical nor Keynesian.

Most important for our story, the textbook was an intellectual success for Charlie himself. The effort involved in writing it forced him to get up to speed on developments in international economics, and to stake out his own positions in the field – positions which would become the agenda for his subsequent work. As one example, his focus on long-term capital flows led him to be an early and persistent critic of attempts to solve world liquidity problems by creating new forms of international liquidity, such

---

[19] Kindleberger (1966, 208).

as Triffin's SDR proposal for the IMF; for Charlie, central bank swap arrangements were preferable, and were in fact working fine. As a second example, notwithstanding the political obstacles to restoring an international regime of free trade, Charlie warned against the danger of resorting to a merely regional approach, such as the European Payments Union, another enthusiasm of Triffin. For Charlie, the important thing was not so much economic integration *within* Europe, but rather integration of each European economy into the larger world system. And, a third example, Charlie's conception of the balance of payments as a matter of settling clearing balances led him to be an early and persistent critic of enthusiasts for "freely fluctuating exchange rates" such as Milton Friedman (1953). For Charlie, internationally as much as nationally, trade works better with a single currency, and on these grounds fixed exchange was preferable.[20] As we will see, these three policy debates would absorb much of his energy in the decade of the 1960s.

The return of European currencies to convertibility in 1958 marked the end of one era and the beginning of another. Charlie's preferred key-currency approach would have suggested a more gradual evolution, first stabilizing sterling against the dollar and then adding other currencies one by one. The operation of the European Payments Union, however, had effectively ruled that out, requiring the stronger currencies to wait for the weaker currencies so that all could join at once. From this point of view, it was not so surprising to him that the return to convertibility was accompanied by considerable volatility, as each currency found its own market level relative to everyone else. For Charlie, that was just the growing pains of the emerging new system, nothing really to worry about. The memoir of Charles Coombs, Vice President of the New York Fed in charge of the Bank's Foreign department, tells the tale of central bank cooperation during those volatile years, working gradually to reform the Bretton Woods system by substituting "mutual credit facilities for international gold settlements."[21] Other voices, however, were not so sanguine, none more important than the voice of Robert Triffin, and

---

[20] Kindleberger (1958a, 562, 569, 567).
[21] Coombs (1976, 188).

unfortunately the anxiety of policy makers in the face of volatility meant that Triffin's voice attracted an avid hearing.

Born 1911 (in Belgium) and earning his PhD in Economics at Harvard University in 1938, Triffin was more or less Charlie's exact contemporary. Unlike Charlie, however, Triffin had spent the War years in Washington, DC, at the Board of Governors of the Federal Reserve System, becoming a US citizen in the process. In that capacity, he had attended the inaugural meeting of the IMF and World Bank in Savannah in March 1946, and then joined the Fund as head of the Exchange Control Division, before shifting to Paris in 1948 to advise the Economic Cooperation Administration on establishing the European Payments Union.[22] That mission accomplished in 1950, in 1951 Triffin proved acceptable to the Yale economics department (as Charlie had not), and in 1957 he published *Europe and the Money Muddle*, which contrasted sharply with Charlie's earlier *Dollar Shortage*. Says Triffin: "The factual evidence … accords fully with classical economic theory, and does not lay sufficient ground for generalizing past experience into a new theory of a chronic, structural dollar shortage."[23]

Provocatively, Triffin dedicated the 1957 book to "John H. Williams and Alvin H. Hansen, who tried to teach him money and banking," in effect claiming Charlie's own mentors for himself. But Triffin's framing of the monetary problem was more or less the opposite of those teachers, inspired more by the agreement at Bretton Woods and his experience at the IMF. What Harold James (2012) has called the myth of Bretton Woods as "an act of enlightened creative internationalism," Triffin had swallowed whole and had made into a kind of personal evangelical project. In Triffin's mind, the IMF had been supposed to be a world central bank, and when it turned out instead to be a kind of sideshow, he turned his attention instead to Europe and the EPU, which he imagined as a kind of regional version of the International Clearing Union that had been proposed by Keynes at Bretton Woods.

As opposed to Triffin, Williams and Hansen both always had their doubts about the IMF and always viewed the World Bank as the more important institution because of its potential role in channeling long-term

---

[22] Maes (2013), Maes and Pasotti (2016, 5; 2021,61).
[23] Triffin (1957, 29).

capital flows. Even more, Williams had gone so far as to actively oppose the IMF, in both writing and Congressional testimony, as a distraction from the more relevant project of building the nascent international dollar system. In retrospect, Williams' testimony, in his own admission a "minority view," serves as a prescient guide to the true evolutionary dynamic operating behind the scenes, both in the immediate postwar period and subsequently, that is, the emergence of the global dollar system.[24] As Harold James reminds us: "Bretton Woods was the intellectual sugar, covering and masking the bitter taste of the pill of *Realpolitik* dollar hegemony."[25]

The bulk of Triffin's 1957 book was not directly concerned with these matters, but rather was focused more narrowly on the European Payments Union, which Triffin credits with overcoming bilateralism within Europe, expansion of intra-European trade, and laying the groundwork for eventual convertibility. According to Triffin, the EPU had succeeded in achieving at the regional level what the IMF had not yet been able to achieve at the international level, due to the greater political obstacles to collective negotiation, which is to say US resistance to full implementation of Bretton Woods. I have already noted how Triffin's celebration of the EPU had attracted Charlie's critical attention, on the grounds that promotion of intraregional trade and economic integration came at the expense of the larger objective of international trade and integration, and indeed involved discrimination against non-EPU members, specifically the United States. But it was a few pages at the end of Triffin's book, added almost as an afterthought, that would draw Charlie into a more sustained engagement.

It is here, already in 1957, that Triffin first floated the idea that came to be known as the "Triffin Dilemma": the idea that national currencies such as the pound and the dollar are inherently unable to serve as adequate international reserve currencies, and so should be replaced as soon as possible by a genuinely international reserve currency. Here is the key passage:

> [As early as 1955], it was becoming apparent that further increases on the scale necessary to ward off monetary pressures toward deflation and trade restrictions would be found, sooner or later, to overtax the strength not

---

[24] Williams (1947, ch. 4, appendix 3).
[25] James (2012, 438).

only of the United Kingdom but even of the United States, and to endanger the acceptability of the dollar itself as a safe reserve medium for other countries. The solution of this dilemma should lead us to explore more fully than has been done up to now the possibility of broadening the basis of the gold exchange standard ... by requiring all countries ... to maintain an appropriate proportion of their international reserves in the form of a deposit account with the International Monetary Fund.[26]

The gauntlet was thus thrown. We can read Charlie's subsequent 1966 collection of essays *Europe and the Dollar* as the record of his response to this challenge. The title of the book certainly echoes Triffin's, and the dedication to Emile Despres – "economist's economist, teachers' teacher, and friends' friend" – identifies Charlie's own position with that of a favorite student of Williams and Hansen, in effect claiming himself by proxy as the more legitimate heir of that intellectual legacy, as indeed he was. The essays in the book are arranged in reverse chronological order, from 1965's "Balance-of-Payments Deficits and the International Market for Liquidity" all the way back to 1939's "Speculation and Forward Exchange," showing how far Charlie had come from his New York Fed days. But more or less all of the post-1957 essays are directed toward countering Triffin's interpretation of international monetary events and also his proposal for international monetary reform.

Triffin's argument was attractively simple. Gold production was not keeping up with the growth of world trade, and that posed a potentially deflationary headwind for global expansion. Temporarily filling the gap, and so warding off deflation, was the expansion of national credit money, mainly dollars but also sterling. This mechanism, however, contained the seeds of its own destruction since new national credit money only became available for use as international credit money through the mechanism of a balance-of-payments deficit, the issuing nation paying for purchases of goods or securities with short-term borrowing rather than with its own goods or securities. In the longer run, the buildup of these short-term balances would, Triffin argued, inevitably prove unsustainable, prompting a run on the national currency as holders sought to convert their balances into gold.

---

[26] Triffin (1957, 299).

For Triffin, the collapse of sterling in 1931 foreshadowed the problem that was now confronting the dollar. In his interpretation, 1931 had demonstrated the inherent instability of a gold-exchange standard and much the same collapse could be expected of the dollar sooner or later – maybe even sooner as US gold reserves were already falling dangerously below its burgeoning short-term international liabilities. The solution, so Triffin urged, involved creation of a new, explicitly international credit money, issued perhaps as a liability of the IMF. In this way, the pooled credit of all participating nations, not any individual nation, would be the basis of a reformed international monetary system. Maintaining the growth of that international currency at 3–5 percent annually would keep money growth in line with the growth of world trade, subject neither to the vagaries of gold mining nor to the economic fortune (or monetary policy) of any individual state. In effect, Triffin's proposal sought to shape reality to fit the myth of Bretton Woods.

It's easy to see why this argument appealed to European holders of dollar balances. Deficit countries (such as France) resented the fact that the United States apparently avoided the balance of payments discipline that so constrained their own activity: so-called "exorbitant privilege." And surplus countries (such as Germany) worried about the safety of their dollar accumulations in the event of a devaluation. Developing countries also rallied to Triffin's proposed solution as a potential source of much-needed development finance, naturally welcoming any proposal that promised to monetize their own credit. There were thus multiple reasons why Triffin's analysis and proposal grabbed the headlines.

It is less easy to see the appeal to Americans, except perhaps for the perennial anxiety about living beyond one's means, losing competitiveness in trade, and spending excessively to help non-Americans in Europe (NATO) and the developing world (foreign aid). It was to these anxieties, therefore, that Charlie initially addressed himself, in his June 1959 testimony to Congress, with the more or less explicit objective of assuaging them and directing attention instead to more pressing matters. In Charlie's view, developments since his 1950 *Dollar Shortage* had in fact been "highly satisfactory."[27] The fact that the United States no longer had

---

[27] Kindleberger (1966, 163).

a structural current account surplus was not a problem, but rather the solution of a former problem, bespeaking the increasingly cosmopolitan view of American firms and consumers, and also a welcome technological catchup by Europe.

Contra Triffin, the accumulation of short-term dollar balances by foreigners was also no problem: "There is very little danger from a withdrawal of foreign funds in the United States. It makes no sense to net the $16 billion of foreign funds in this country against the $20 billion gold stock. No other country calculates its reserves net of liabilities, rather than gross, *nor does any bank.*"[28] Central banks already cooperate effectively to stem short-run currency crises. For the longer run, what was really needed was a shift on the margin to sharing the "burden of leadership," specifically some help with US military expenditure and foreign aid.

Although Charlie's testimony made no explicit mention of them, Triffin's two articles of March and June 1959 in the Banca Nazionale del Lavoro *Quarterly Review* were the clear subtext. Probably Charlie thought (hoped) that his testimony would be enough to set the policy conversation on the right track. Instead, Triffin came back in October with his own Congressional testimony and then packaged that testimony with the earlier articles and published the lot as a best-selling book, *Gold and the Dollar Crisis, The Future of Convertibility* (1960), which fatefully struck a chord with incoming President Kennedy. And so, Charlie was obliged to spend precious sabbatical time putting together a major statement, "The Prospects for International Liquidity and the Future Evolution of the International Payments System," now for the first time engaging Triffin explicitly.[29]

For Charlie, the trouble with the gold-exchange standard was not at all the inherent unsuitability of a national currency to serve international

---

[28] Kindleberger (1966, 165), my emphasis. This somewhat offhand comment seems to be the earliest explicit mention of Charlie's conceptualization of the United States as bank of the world. It is, however, clearly the product of a prepared mind, and in retrospect is implicit in Charlie's work as early as 1939. In later work, he often mentions Hal Lary, *Problems of the United States as World Trader and Banker* (1963) as an inspiration. No doubt Lary's strong title did provide welcome encouragement for developing the germ of an idea into a full-blown analysis, but the germ was already there.

[29] Kindleberger (1966, ch. 7).

ends, as Triffin urged, but rather the emergence of *multiple* purportedly key currencies in the period immediately after the return to convertibility in 1958. In this initial stage speculators, anticipating changes in currency parities, shifted from one currency to another: "Hot money, which raged from 1925 to 1939 but subsided after World War II, has taken a new lease of life."[30] In later work, Charlie would reference Gresham's Law on the inherent instability of a system with multiple currencies as a venerable analytic foundation for this point of view. All Triffin had really done was to reinvent that wheel.[31]

Adding to the problem, as early as 1953 Charlie had noted "the 'rediscovery of money' within national economies after 1950 and the increased importance given to the rate of interest, discount policy and the quantity of money in preventing inflation internally."[32] Now, in 1961, he drew attention to the significant international consequence: "renewed responsiveness of international short-term capital movements to interest rate differentials [which] open up a conflict between internal [domestic] and foreign monetary policy."[33] The real trouble with the gold-exchange standard was thus not *national* money, but rather *hot* money, and modern troubles with hot money were driven largely by national differences in monetary policy.

Charlie summarizes:

> There is a respectable view [i.e. Charlie's own view] that with all major currencies more or less in line under the fixed exchange standard, and holders of liquid assets relatively indifferent as to which currency they hold, and therefore ready to speculate by taking open positions, the major money markets have become one market, and small differences in interest rates, such as one or another country may wish to support by reason of domestic monetary policy, will lead to large-scale outflows and inflows of liquid funds.[34]

Charlie of course remembered well how the hot-money problem of the 1930s had given rise to the 1936 Tripartite Agreement, which

---

[30] Kindleberger (1966, 91).
[31] See "Gresham's Law" in Kindleberger (1989a, Third Lecture).
[32] Kindleberger (1966, 209).
[33] Kindleberger (1966, 92).
[34] Kindleberger (1966, 101).

involved key-currency central banks buying the currency that speculators were selling and selling the currency that speculators were buying, in order to stabilize exchange rates for twenty-four hours at a time (Chapter 3). It was therefore natural for him to propose an analogous but more far-reaching solution for the similar problem of the 1960s:

> The scheme, in short, is that central banks of the *major currencies*, with treasury support, undertake to buy *and hold* each others' currencies during crises of confidence, when they are under speculative attack ... [A]s their defense departments collaborate for defense, so should central banks and treasuries of the responsible countries ... collaborate ... to preserve monetary stability in the face of de-stabilizing speculation.[35]

In 1961, by contrast to 1936, Charlie proposed starting with "Belgium, Canada, France, Germany, Italy, the Netherlands, Switzerland, the United Kingdom and the United States," perhaps adding in Sweden and Japan later, which is more or less the grouping that would soon come to be known as the G10. And he proposed that central banks hold the currency they bought not just for twenty-four hours but until the crisis was over, which risked realizing losses. That's why treasuries had to be involved, because central bank losses would have to be compensated.

In effect, Charlie was proposing to make explicit and visible what was already implicit but hidden, namely central bank cooperation, as part of a broader agenda of "sharing" the burden of leadership. He was under no illusion that it would be easy: "There are difficulties of sharing. The process requires a deep-seated sense of social and political cohesion. But it is a necessity."[36] The sense of cohesion that already joined central bankers, on account of their regular technical interaction, needed to be nurtured more broadly between political bodies. As a sometime central banker himself, Charlie knew what was possible, and optimistically imagined that regular interaction would produce the necessary cohesion, given time.

In sum, in contrast to Triffin who wanted to replace the dollar with a proper international currency, Charlie in effect proposed to internationalize the dollar, or rather to recognize that in a world of integrated

---

[35] Kindleberger (1966, 102), my emphasis.
[36] Kindleberger (1966, 94).

142

money markets the dollar was already in fact internationalized. Importantly, however, that internationalization was only really as yet at the level of the G10, not elsewhere. Thus, Charlie insisted, in further contrast to Triffin, that the problems of the developing world were of an entirely different nature. Developing countries needed resources not liquidity, which is to say long-term capital flows not short-term capital flows. To the extent that they genuinely wanted to increase their liquid balances, they could already do so by borrowing long-term and holding the proceeds on deposit rather than spending them; no new international apparatus was needed for that.

These differences from Triffin on policy stemmed from deeper differences in how the two understood money. Charlie, as we have seen, saw the international monetary system as emerging from a process of historical evolution driven by practitioner solutions to successive empirical problems, whereas Triffin imagined a possible top-down or "constitutional" process in which experts like himself deduced an optimal system and then imposed it by fiat (treaty) on the rest of the world. A second difference: Charlie was loathe to spend time and energy negotiating formal legal agreements outlining explicit contractual obligations in a world that was rapidly changing in ways that were likely to require flexibility and creativity in response to problems that no one could reasonably anticipate ahead of time. Again, Triffin was the reverse. Perhaps these differences reflect American versus European sensibilities, or perhaps they reflect a central-banker versus an academic perspective.[37] The important point is that such differences were sufficient in themselves to prevent any meeting of the minds.

Underneath these matters of culture and style there was an even deeper difference in terms of the basic economics. Triffin, like most economists of his generation, viewed the international economy through the (Keynesian) lens of the national income and product accounts and the (monetarist) lens of the equation of exchange. As a Keynesian, Triffin was concerned to support domestic aggregate demand as a way of supporting domestic employment and was always trying to find ways to keep balance of payments problems from interfering with that objective. As a monetarist, he was

---

[37] In his memoir Coombs notably references the "university economists ... distaste and distrust of informally negotiated credit facilities" (1976, 189).

further concerned in the longer run to ensure that the world money supply grew in line with world trade at some appropriate rate, say 3–5 percent, in order to avoid both deflation and inflation.

Charlie, by contrast, always saw the balance of payments constraint as a matter of clearing and settlement, and he worried that many proposals for international monetary reform (including Triffin's) would be "likely to subvert the balance of payments discipline which is so needed and so hard to provide."[38] For Charlie, persistent payment deficits reflect a structural problem that needs correction not accommodation, and they are a real problem not a liquidity problem, which is to say a problem requiring real structural change in the countries affected not international monetary reform in the world as a whole. So much for Triffin's Keynesian short run; what about his monetarist long run? Says Charlie: "The quantity theory of money has no greater validity internationally than domestically, and in the latter connection I regard its validity as small."[39] For him, the key to long-run stability was not the steady and regular increase of the quantity of world liquidity by a world central bank, but rather the elasticity of short-term private capital markets, expanding to accommodate short-term deficits and then contracting again when deficits turn to surpluses. Trend increase of world liquidity is the endogenous consequence of this fluctuation, not the exogenous regulator of it.

This difference on the basic economics was perhaps not so immediately visible in 1961, maybe not even to Charlie himself, as his attention naturally focused on the concrete policy proposals under consideration. In 1961, he seems to have thought (hoped) that his own concrete policy proposal for an updated Tripartite Agreement would carry the day, emanating as it did from concrete banking and central banking practice. We hear that optimism in his March 1965 testimony to Congress, in his exchange with Senator Proxmire:

Mr. Kindleberger: Many of my colleagues are terrified at the thought of collaboration of central bankers superseding economic sovereignty and

---

[38] Kindleberger (1966, 100).
[39] Kindleberger (1966, 109).

so on. I think they are technicians and this is the kind of problem they can handle easily . . .

Senator Proxmire: This is a very relaxing and reassuring answer . . .[40]

As in 1959, when he had initially given testimony to the Congress on this matter, Charlie seems to be thinking that illusory concerns, once their illusory nature has been pointed out, will simply pass away. In the event, however, one concern that was not illusory proved decisive, both in the United States and elsewhere, namely the political challenge of "sharing." On the one hand, internationalization of the dollar meant that other countries needed to adapt their domestic monetary policy to conditions in the single world market, which is to say the dollar market. On the other hand, internationalization of the dollar meant that the United States itself would have to take account of world conditions, not just domestic conditions, in setting dollar interest rates. Neither one of these was an easy sell. Perhaps it could be said that Triffin, a European at heart, notwithstanding his naturalized citizenship, was grappling mainly with the former whereas Charlie, as an American, focused his attention on the latter.

In a prescient 1963 memo prepared for the US Treasury, Charlie explicitly raised the matter:

In a world crisscrossed by broad channels through which capital flows, it may be necessary to abandon or greatly modify national independence of monetary policy (just as the Federal Reserve districts have done). This is a cost, but I judge it less than the benefit . . . New York is becoming a world capital center where borrowers sell bonds and investors buy them – borrowers and investors from all over the world. The dependence of the world on United States dollar deposits – directly and via the Euro-dollar market – is healthy for the world payments system, even though it involves some cost for this country. So is the two-way dependence on the capital market. This is financial integration of the Free World, or primarily of the Atlantic Partnership. It is desirable, not a pathological condition to be overcome.[41]

---

[40] Page 382, "Balance of Payments – 1965." Hearing before a Subcommittee of the Committee on Banking and Currency. 89th Congress, 1st Session, Mar. 1965.

[41] Kindleberger (1966, 85, 87).

Given their subsequent behavior, one imagines that many if not most of Charlie's interlocutors at the Treasury weighed the costs and benefits differently. Writing in retrospect, Charlie lists the history of US capital controls imposed by those interlocutors: "the Interest Equalization Tax [of 1963] which broke up the development of an international capital market in New York and drove it to the Euro-market; ... the Gore amendment applying the tax to bank loans; ... the Voluntary Credit Restraint Program of February 1965; ... the Mandatory Program of January 1, 1968."[42] Every one of these controls was instituted as a reaction to perceived or actual European threat to cash in their dollar balances for gold. The ultimate effect, however, was to dismantle the emerging dollar system. These were policy decisions made by politicians, but encouraged by irresponsible economists whose faith in their models was greater than their understanding of the operations of the system.

Charlie's optimism circa 1965 shifted over the years to frustration, desperation, and ultimately resignation. But he did not stop fighting until it seemed clear that the battle was well and truly lost. One venue for that fight was President Johnson's Advisory Committee on International Monetary Arrangements, for which Charlie produced a number of memos, to no discernible effect.[43] In the end, realizing the direction that things were moving, he was willing to endorse creation of a new artificial Currency Reserve Unit (CRU) as a way of supporting the international role of the dollar, swayed by Alvin Hansen's argument that the world was not ready to accept a purely fiat dollar, which made it necessary to devise some mechanism for augmenting apparent gold reserves.[44] In the event, however, the Currency Reserve Unit morphed into the IMF's Special Drawing Rights and got allocated to all the members of the IMF, not just the United States. Instead of backstopping the emerging global dollar system, the SDR instead served to perpetuate the Bretton Woods myth, even as the Bretton Woods system was collapsing.

---

[42] Kindleberger (1970b, 6).
[43] KPMD, Box 3, Folder "Treasury Dept 1967–1969," "Issues and Positions in International Monetary Arrangements," July 26, 1965. See Ch. 5, n. 40.
[44] Hansen (1965).

The failure of Charlie's foray into the policy process seems to have taught him the lesson that he needed to be engaging the policy economists behind the scenes, not so much the visible policymakers. In any event, that's what we see him doing in "Balance-of-Payments Deficits and the International Market for Liquidity" (1965), which he offers as the lead chapter of the 1966 book.[45] Going now beyond his critique of Triffin, his central positive message is that the United States had in fact been operating as an international financial intermediary with respect to Europe, borrowing short term and lending long term, so satisfying the liquidity preference of Europe's borrowers who wanted long-term funding and also of Europe's lenders who wanted to hold their funds in liquid form. European financial institutions might conceivably one day do some of this themselves, though economies of scale would likely still give the United States the edge, allowing Europeans to borrow at lower rates and lend at higher rates than would be possible within Europe, given European liquidity preferences.

The point is that the United States was providing a valuable service to Europe, which unfortunately European policymakers persisted in understanding instead as some kind of exploitation, pointing to sustained US payment deficits funded by burgeoning European central bank dollar balances. Once one views these data through the lens of international financial intermediation, however, the dollar balances are revealed not as short-run capital flows but rather as long-run accumulation of needed monetary reserves, and the deficits disappear: "Below a certain point – which shifts with time, the unfolding of events, and opinion – lending long and borrowing short [as US], or vice versa [as Europe], is merely trading in liquidity. Beyond it, the long lender is overdoing it and the short lender has the right to become increasingly nervous."[46]

Thus, from Charlie's point of view, there was no trade-deficit problem. The fact that Washington policymakers perceived one stemmed merely from the way the Department of Commerce was reporting balance of payments statistics, obscuring rather than illuminating the actual situation.

---

[45] Charlie subsequently wrote a second version of this paper for the *Journal of Political Economy*, under the title "Measuring Equilibrium in the Balance of Payments," and it is this second version that he includes in his 2000 *Retrospective*. See Chapter 7 for a fuller account.

[46] Kindleberger (1966, 24).

Responding to these faulty measurements rather than to reality, short lenders were becoming nervous over a phantom. The solution was not to put up obstacles in the way of valuable international financial intermediation, but rather simply to change the accounting in order to provide policymakers with a more accurate picture of the situation. An international financial center needs a different balance of payments account than other countries in order to take proper account of its role as financial intermediary.

Having done his best to convince policymakers and now also policy economists behind the scenes, there is a sense that Charlie felt he was more or less done, and anyway he was eager to move on to other things. But first, he felt a final obligation to lay his views before the public. That is the origin of the famous 1966 *Economist* article, "The Dollar and World Liquidity: A Minority View," coauthored with Walter Salant and Emile Despres. His highly unusual step of recruiting these coauthors, and publishing in the financial press, seems to have been an attempt to make it harder for his target audience to ignore what he now explicitly recognized was a "minority view." But it seems also to have been an attempt to recruit some help with the ongoing public policy battle so that he could scale back his own involvement. Perhaps he would have better luck than Williams had had twenty years before with his own "minority view" testimony to Congress; it was worth a try.

If the plan was to turn the job of policy advocacy over to Despres, it didn't work. After the article was published, Despres took a temporary position at the Brookings Institution (Salant's home base) and produced two quite extensive bits of Congressional testimony.[47] But in March 1968 (coincident with the collapse of the London Gold Pool, an attempt to channel central bank cooperation for international monetary stabilization), Despres suffered a stroke, which meant that he was simply in no condition to respond to Nixon's devaluation of the dollar on August 15, 1971, except by authorizing publication of his past works in *International Economic Reform* (1973). And by the time that book came out, the Smithsonian Agreement had already collapsed, ushering in the world's experiment with floating exchange rates. Despres' untimely stroke, and then premature death in April 1973, provide context for understanding Charlie's continuing engagement with monetary matters after 1966 as

---

[47] Reproduced in Despres (1973, chs. 15 and 16).

recorded in the essays collected in *International Money* (1981). Instead of the last thing he wrote before turning to other matters, the 1966 *Economist* essay served as the sketch of an argument he would spend the subsequent decade fleshing out in multiple dimensions.

The minority position that Charlie embraced in 1966 was actually – or so he claimed – a return to tried and true principles, but it is important not to misunderstand. The principles he has in mind are definitely not the classic specie-flow mechanism of Hume which shaped so much of academic thinking, but rather the principles of practical banking. His position was a minority one in the economics profession, which is to say in academia, but it arose out of the practical business of banking, and in particular central banking, in which world it was just common sense. Charlie always insisted that economists, like lawyers, "are the high priests of society that provide a ritualistic justification for what practical men unselfconsciously do."[48] That's what he himself had been trying to do in his earlier *Dollar Shortage* (1950), which mounted an economic defense of the Marshall Plan. Here in 1966, we see him mounting an economic defense of the larger "dollar system" that had grown up after.

So far as Charlie could see, the actions of practical men had by 1966 moved quite far toward creating an integrated international monetary and financial system, a single money market and a single capital market, all of it denominated in a single unit of account: the US dollar. No one had planned it, least of all the economists, and most practical bankers saw only the bit of the system with which they routinely interacted, not the system as a whole. For lack of understanding, policymakers had repeatedly tried to kill this emerging dollar system with capital controls, but the fungibility of money kept finding a way around. Charlie's contribution in 1966 was to make the system as a whole visible, as a way of trying to forestall misguided attempts to kill it off.

The central idea of the *Economist* essay is that the United States needs to be understood as the financial center of this newly integrated international monetary and financial system. Most important was the operation of the international capital market, located largely in New York,

---

[48] Kindleberger (1981a, 285). Here he follows Arnold (1937). See also Kindleberger (1950, 6; 2000a, 70; 1970a, 53).

where foreigners meet one another as both borrowers and lenders. This marketplace had been key to the recovery of Europe and was now becoming key to the development of the periphery: "In my judgment, the economists have underrated the contribution to economic development of an international capital market."[49]

In addition, the United States was also the center of the international money market, the place where deficit countries settled with surplus countries. Foreign deposits in New York banks served as the means of this international settlement, and in doing so played a crucial role in facilitating the growth of international trade, allowing countries to mismatch their international earnings and expenditures temporarily, and to absorb any present imbalance by drawing down or building up their liquid balances. In effect, international short-term capital flows took place on the balance sheets of New York banks, which expanded and contracted their balance sheets as needed.

Originally, both capital and money markets had grown up in New York, but over time both had also begun developing natural extensions abroad, in Europe and especially in London, in the so-called Eurobond and Eurodollar markets. Indeed, the misguided capital controls imposed by US policymakers had only encouraged these offshore extensions where foreigners borrowed and lent among themselves in dollars, both at long term and at short term. The onshore markets nevertheless remained critically important for absorbing any net borrowing or lending, specifically net borrowing long and net lending short. For Charlie, and for the United States, this was the crucial point.

In absorbing the net dollar borrowing and dollar lending of the rest of the world, the United States was in effect operating as an international financial intermediary:

This financial intermediation performs two functions: it supplies loans and investment funds to foreign enterprises which have to pay more domestically to borrow long-term money and which cannot get the amounts they want at any price, and it supplies liquidity to foreign asset-holders, who receive less for

[49]   Kindleberger (1981a, 321).

placing their short-term deposits at home. Essentially, this is a trade in liquidity, which is profitable to both sides.[50]

A central consequence of this international financial intermediation was the integration of world capital and money markets into a single market. The price of money in this market then served as the world price around which all other subsidiary markets arranged themselves.

In operating as bank for the world, the United States thus supported the development of the global dollar system more generally. People choose to use dollars not because anyone forces them, but because they seek access to the liquidity of dollar-denominated money and capital markets. As a consequence of that choice, New York was now doing for the broader world what it had previously done for the United States more narrowly, namely knitting the nation's disparate geographical areas into a single integrated money and capital market. Economically speaking, it seemed obvious to Charlie that this was a good thing, just as good for the world as it had earlier been for the United States more narrowly. Without such intermediation, there would be less trade and less investment, less economic activity and less economic growth.

In sum, for Charlie the dollar was just a "key currency" (as John H. Williams) or a "vehicle currency" (as Robert Roosa): "International currencies are not all of equal value as units of account, standards of deferred payment and media of exchange. They stand in relationship to one another not as full equals, but in a hierarchical arrangement of ascending utility as international money."[51] For him, this hierarchy was not imposed from above, but rather arose from economies of scale that favor a single international money and from the decentralized choices of myriad market participants who chose the dollar rather than some other contender. That's how it looked to Charlie.

That's not, however, how it looked to many others, both outside and inside the United States, both economists and noneconomists. Whatever the origin of the hierarchy, the fact that the dollar sat on top was a problem. The global role of the dollar placed the United States in a position of responsibility and authority that US and non-US sovereigns

---

[50] Kindleberger (1981a, 43).
[51] Kindleberger (1981a, 27).

both came to resent, for different reasons. Thus, even *The Economist*, while essentially accepting Charlie's bank-of-the-world analytical frame, viewed his article as an assertion of American primacy, and specifically of dollar primacy – "the new nationalism." The United States may be a bank, so the editors wrote, but banks need to be mindful of the interest of their depositors lest they be subject to runs as anxious depositors shift their funds into better money, in this case gold at the promised parity of $35 an ounce. For *The Economist*, Charlie's rather cavalier attitude toward that promised parity – "let the gold go" – was a crucial sticking point.[52]

One imagines that Charlie expected better from *The Economist*, heir to the tradition of Walter Bagehot whose 1873 *Lombard Street* had served to crystallize the doctrine of lender of last resort for a time when the pound sterling served the world as international money. Viewing the matter from the vantage point of the United States, Charlie understood the problem as the failure of the United States to take responsibility for the international role that had been thrust upon it. So he was somewhat taken aback when *The Economist* interpreted his essay as a symptom, even an encouragement, of exactly that US irresponsibility. What did Charlie have in mind when he said "let the gold go"?

It is certainly true that Charlie was willing, even eager, to contemplate partial or complete demonetization of gold by the United States – "widening the margin around parity at which it buys and sells gold, reducing the price at which it buys gold, and otherwise depriving gold of its present unlimited convertibility into dollars."[53] But the reason was that the dollar, not gold, had *already* become the world's standard of value. In Charlie's view, any depreciation of the dollar against gold would inevitably be followed by similar depreciation of all other currencies, so leaving exchange rates unchanged. From this point of view, a "run" on the dollar was essentially pointless, since there was no better money into which to run. It was only the myth of gold, a myth that had unfortunately been given substance by central bankers in such misbegotten initiatives as

---

[52] In fact, Charlie's position was moderate compared to Despres, who explicitly urged unilateral demonetization of gold (1973, ch. 15).

[53] Kindleberger (1981a, 50).

the Gold Pool, that gave speculators the idea of shifting between dollars and gold in the first place.

For Charlie, the way to avoid destabilizing speculation was to eliminate convertibility altogether, and to operate a pure exchange standard, embracing de jure the system that had long been in place de facto. Yes, US gold reserves had been run down even as US short-term liabilities to the rest of the world had grown. Nevertheless, so far as Charlie was concerned, the dollar was strong not weak, and the measure of its strength was the continuing expansion of foreign deposits to the tune of $1.5 to $2 billion a year, in line with the expansion of the world economy. The market was demanding this expansion of liquidity, and the US financial system was responding by supplying it endogenously.

Even more, the system had shown itself able to supply not only the trend demand but also the occasional crisis demand as well. To that end, the central bank swap lines formally established in March 1961 by the BIS had already proven to be a serviceable lender of last resort for the pound sterling and could be expected to do so as well for other currencies as needed, including potentially the dollar: "The great merit of the Basel agreement, and the crucial feature of an international central bank, is the availability of unlimited amounts of assistance through rediscounting in a period of crisis."[54]

The response of *The Economist* was disappointing but also extremely instructive, drawing Charlie's attention to the political as well as the economic dimensions of the dollar problem. As he would later summarize: "Benevolent despotism is the best form of government because it permits us all not to pay the price of eternal vigilance. The difficulty is to keep it benevolent, or viewed as such." Charlie's proposed answer to that difficulty was to internationalize the institutions for managing the dollar. Subsequent to the 1966 *Economist* essay, he would urge formal representation of the rest of the world in the Fed's governing apparatus, specifically the creation of an Atlantic Open-Market Committee. And even that he would view as merely a stepping stone to an eventual proper world

[54] Kindleberger (1981a, 28). Coombs (1976, ch. 5) traces the evolution from 1961 of what he calls "The Federal Reserve Swap Network," as first line of defense for the Bretton Woods fixed exchange rate system.

central bank, perhaps a repurposed Bank for International Settlements, which would implement world monetary policy by means of open market operations in the offshore Eurodollar market.[55]

In this way, Charlie's urging of de jure adoption of the de facto dollar system should be seen not so much as some kind of "new nationalism," but rather more reasonably as a new kind of internationalism, the first step toward shifting responsibility for management of international money from a national to a genuinely international central bank: "With a world [central] bank, money would be issued through buying bonds or rediscounting obligations, at market rates. A country which temporarily had too much money could lend it to another which was short, as commercial banks in the USA lend Federal funds back and forth in a private market."[56] Even without a proper world central bank, the Eurodollar market was already growing up to serve that function; the political problem was that the persistence of the Bretton Woods myth made that reality hard to see.

For Charlie, the problem with the Bretton Woods frame was that, however functional it might have been for the world of 1944, the world had moved on and the forces that had produced a changed reality seemed quite certain to continue driving reality even farther away in the years to come: "I do not know, but this is where major forces in trade, transport, communications, capital movements, foreign exchange, and especially the international corporation are pushing."[57] Significantly, Charlie wrote these words not in 1966, but three years later at an academic conference he organized with the political scientist Andrew Shonfield, in an attempt to find common ground between American cosmopolitans such as himself and European regionalists such as Shonfield. In effect, the conference was an academic analogue of the 1933 World Economic Conference where John H. Williams had tried to broker a key-currency deal between the major world central banks, only to be shot down by his own President Roosevelt. Fatefully, the proceeds of the 1969 academic conference would be published in 1971, the very year that President Nixon unilaterally

---

[55] Kindleberger (1981a; 316, 107, 102, 109, 325–6).
[56] Kindleberger (1981a, 73).
[57] Kindleberger (1981a, 328).

devalued the dollar against gold, thereby bringing the Bretton Woods era to an end. History may not repeat, but it does seem to rhyme.

In 1966, however, Charlie thought it was still possible to avert disaster. Similarly, in 1969: "Demonetization [of gold] is nonetheless inevitable. The basis of national money is national credit. We approach the day when the basis of international money is international credit."[58] Even as late as 1970, Charlie could write: "I forecast that the world is moving toward internationalized control of a national money, with gold demonetized."[59] It was in this spirit that he rapidly produced his third textbook effort, *Power and Money: The Economics of International Politics and the Politics of International Economics* (1970). The problem with the dollar standard was that the dollar was increasingly the offshore Eurodollar, hence an unmanaged standard, and the central political problem was to find a way to bring that new offshore dollar under collective management.[60] Unfortunately, "discussion of the politics of the subject is handicapped by lack of agreement on the economics."[61] Most distressingly, politicians seemed now to be flirting with flexible exchange rates as a possible panacea, a policy "which solves a political problem but creates an economic one."[62]

From this point of view, Nixon's unilateral devaluation in August 1971 struck Charlie as nothing less than a crime: the Crime of 1971, he called it. The proximate cause was loose monetary policy in the United States (for election reasons) combined with tight monetary policy in Germany (for inflation reasons), which combination led to large capital flows from the United States to Germany – the dreaded hot money. Writing in 1972, after the December 1971 Smithsonian Agreement which had established new parities, but before that agreement had collapsed, Charlie asked: "With the devaluation of the dollar in 1971, and the adoption of the wider band, there is a question whether there is any international money today." By 1976, Charlie was prepared to concede defeat: "The dollar is finished as international money."[63]

---

[58] Kindleberger (1981a, 103).
[59] Kindleberger (1981a, 84).
[60] Kindleberger (1970a, 210).
[61] Kindleberger (1970a, 196).
[62] Kindleberger (1970a, 224).
[63] Kindleberger (1981a, 10, 314).

CHAPTER 7

Among Economists

In academic life, slow cooking works better than the microwave.[1]

Charlie's life as an academic had begun, fatefully, with an academic dispute. Four years younger than Charlie, Arthur Bloomfield had been a student of Jacob Viner at the University of Chicago, writing his dissertation on "International Capital Movements and the American Balance of Payments: 1929–40." In 1941, following Charlie's own career path, Bloomfield joined the Research Department of the New York Fed, rising in 1947 to the position of Chief of the Balance of Payments Division. Having met Charlie at the Fed briefly in 1938 when he was choosing his dissertation topic, Bloomfield renewed the contact after the war, reaching out for comment on his book manuscript *Capital Imports and the American Balance of Payments, 1934–1939*, which was eventually published with the added subtitle "A Study in Abnormal Capital Transfers"[2] – "abnormal" because they were inconsistent with the classical theory Bloomfield had been taught by Viner.

Bloomfield's request came in July 1948, and Charlie welcomed it as a chance to re-engage with academic research in preparation for his imminent re-entry to academic life. He was himself at that time already working on *The Dollar Shortage*. Subsequently, he would review Bloomfield's book in *Political Science Quarterly*, and Bloomfield would review Charlie's book in the *Review of Economics and Statistics*.[3] The context for these dueling reviews, however, was an earlier exchange in the pages of the *American Economic Review*.

---

[1] Kindleberger (1991a, 154).
[2] KPMD, Box 1, Folder "Bloomfield, Arthur, 1948–87." Bloomfield (1950).
[3] Kindleberger (1950), Bloomfield (1952).

Charlie went first, provoked by a footnote in Bloomfield's manuscript that purported to identify a serious error in Charlie's 1943 "International Monetary Stabilization," which, as we have seen, had sketched the intellectual agenda that Charlie would take up as an academic (Chapter 5). The offending passage concerns the chronic world shortage of dollars, which Charlie attributes to elastic demand by the rest of the world for imports from the United States, but relatively inelastic demand by the United States for imports from outside. Over time, rising US income thus leads to an increase in US imports, which increases income in the rest of the world, "most of which in turn is spent for imports from [the US]. *This rise in imports may be larger than the increase in exports which prompted it,* with the result that the original stimulus to the favorable balance of trade in [the rest of the world] eventually produces an unfavorable balance."[4]

After publication, the emphasized passage had become mildly infamous in academic circles. Charlie remembers: "it was a common occurrence during the portion of the war I spent in Washington to be stopped on the street by fellow economists and to be told that my argument had been demolished by their graduate students."[5] Apparently professors were using the offending passage to test their students' understanding of standard economic models, which uniformly predict that an exogenous increase in exports will always improve the balance of payments. Indeed, once at the Fed, Bloomfield himself had prepared a memo pointing out the error, which argument then found its way into a published textbook, which textbook further cited Charlie's future colleague Paul Samuelson: "So long as some fraction of income at every stage is leaking into domestic savings, a new dollar of exports will never be able to lift income by enough to call forth a full dollar of new imports."[6] Charlie's attention having been brought to the matter, he decided it was time to answer his critics.

His main defense was simple: "the position taken conforms to the real world if not to the mechanics of the most popular economic models."[7] In the 1943 article, he had been talking about the various dimensions of

---

[4] Kindleberger (1966, 255), my emphasis.
[5] Kindleberger (1949a, 491).
[6] Enke and Salera (1947, 599–606).
[7] Kindleberger (1949a, 491).

structural disequilibrium that the world would likely confront after the war and criticizing the adequacy of various proposals for tackling them, unorthodox as well as orthodox. His critics, however, were talking about the properties of formal economic models, and, from their point of view, the question was what features of the real world Charlie saw outside his window that were missing from those textbook models. In an attempt to meet his critics on their own ground, Charlie pointed to the possible role of so-called "induced investment" for some countries, especially developing countries, which may respond dynamically to a surge in exports by building new capacity to such an extent that imports rise by more than the initial export surge. An empirical example of such is the case of Argentina during the interwar period.

Bloomfield's response is telling. While accepting the formal logic of Charlie's defense, he objects that it is based on "additional" and "special" assumptions, and hence represents a particular case rather than a general one: "Unless some such additional assumptions are postulated, the theoretical presumption must be that an increase in a country's exports will typically result in only a smaller, or at best an equal, increase [in its imports]." Charlie's rejoinder is equally telling: "I cannot, however, accept the proposition that, because more theoretical models have been built by scholars with a tendency to undercompensate than with the opposite tendency, there is a strong argument in favor of the prevalence of this tendency [in the real world]."[8]

This disjuncture between the real world and the most popular theoretical models was a problem that Charlie had encountered repeatedly in his former life in government service, but in that world practical concerns had always trumped theoretical niceties. Because Bloomfield was writing from the New York Fed, one imagines that Charlie expected him to be similarly motivated by practical concerns and was therefore somewhat surprised to discover that the influence of academic culture loomed so large in Bloomfield's mind. Here, and not for the first time, Charlie was confronting what he would come to view as the besetting sin of academia, namely the "fallacy of misplaced concreteness." Because academics do not engage directly on a daily basis with the actual world, always so full of

---

[8]   Bloomfield (1949, 971), Kindleberger (1949a, 975).

complexity and ambiguity, they tend to drift into viewing the artificial world of economic theory, always so reassuringly simple and clear, as the central object of attention, more concrete than the actual world itself. Subsequently in 1958, Bloomfield would shift from the Fed to academia, once again following Charlie's own career trajectory, and Charlie would come to appreciate Bloomfield's work on the historical experience of the pre-1914 gold standard. But in 1969, when Bloomfield was asked to survey "Trends in International Economics," he focused entirely on advances in formal theory, in striking contrast with Charlie's own survey five years earlier which had been organized around four current issues or problems.[9] Further, Bloomfield's survey made no mention of Charlie's own work on international financial intermediation, or indeed any other empirical or policy work. One imagines that that slight was on Charlie's mind when, in 1985, he was invited to write something for a symposium in honor of Bloomfield. For the occasion, he made a point of offering an essay titled "The Functioning of Financial Centers: Britain in the Nineteenth Century, the United States since 1945," which used the frame of international financial intermediation to draw comparisons between the pre-1914 gold standard (Bloomfield's focus) and the present operation of the dollar system (Charlie's focus). He made a further point of starting the essay with a reference to their "brief dispute in an initial encounter in 1949. I have the memory that I won the early argument, but doubtless he feels equally sure that he did."[10]

The early tussle with Bloomfield established the pattern. Throughout his academic career, Charlie would chafe repeatedly against the methodological strictures of academic economics, strictures he references on the very first page of his autobiography: "I am an old-fashioned economist, who finished his training in the 1930s, spent twelve years in banks, the military and government, and in starting to teach in 1948 made the conscious and perhaps mistaken decision not to undertake the daunting task of retraining in modern analytical, largely mathematical, techniques."[11] As we have seen, Charlie's intellectual formation was in

---

[9] Bloomfield (1969). Compare Kindleberger (1965a).
[10] Kindleberger (1985b, 7).
[11] Kindleberger (1991a, 1).

prewar American institutionalism, heavily empirical and favoring inductive methods, whereas postwar academic fashion instead increasingly
favored a hypothetico-deductive method, involving formal model building, both mathematical and statistical. In 1948 this new fashion was barely
getting started, but over the coming decades the MIT department would
take a leading role in pioneering it.[12] Engaging economists on their own
ground, as Charlie had done with Bloomfield, would thus become
increasingly difficult for him as the years went on.

At first this difficulty did not bother Charlie very much, convinced as
he was that the policy process was in the end driven not by academic
disputation, but rather by practical men solving practical problems, and
in particular by the anonymous junior staffers in government agencies
who do all the work. In the academy, however, this was very much
a minority view. Most academic economists, following Keynes, believed
that "Practical men, who believe themselves to be quite exempt from any
intellectual influences, are usually the slaves of some defunct economist.
Madmen in authority, who hear voices in the air, are distilling their frenzy
from some academic scribbler of a few years back."[13] In this way of
thinking, academic disputation is the first step toward capturing the
minds of the practical men in authority. Indeed, the postwar Keynesian
revolution in economic policy had arguably sprung quite directly from
Keynes' own scribbling, and his example infected an entire generation of
economists with the idea that their own scribblings might possibly change
the world. Mere academic disputation came to seem high stakes.

In 1948, however, all that lay in the future, especially so in international economics, which remained very much of a backwater, following
the rest of economics with a lag; this gave Charlie some considerable
room to maneuver for a while. Private capital markets were more or less
shut down in most developed countries, which were still recovering from
the exigencies of war and the financial overhang of war finance. Cross-
border capital flows, both long term and short term, were also shut down,
and practically no government had any interest in reviving them, given
their apparent role in exacerbating instability in the interwar period. The

[12] Weintraub (2014).
[13] Keynes (1936, 383).

focus at Bretton Woods in 1944, by both Keynes for the UK and White for the United States, had instead been on providing machinery to enable each country separately to implement its own program of national stabilization. International economics thus came into the picture only because of concern that balance of payments problems might constrain such programs. As we have seen, the Marshall Plan solved that problem in the developed world for a few years, and then Cold War and Korean War spending for a few more, until 1958 when Europe returned to convertibility.

In the underdeveloped world, however, and in particular in Latin America, balance of payments problems were rife, even as economic development ambition was blossoming. As the United States focused on Europe, it left a vacuum elsewhere, and so that's where the newly established IMF found its most immediate purpose. In the underdeveloped world, "fundamental disequilibrium" was a recurring phenomenon, giving license for exchange rate adjustments under the IMF's Articles of Agreement. But in each specific case the practical question always was: how much to devalue, and what other measures might also be needed to ensure success? Under Edward M. Bernstein, Director of the Research Department from 1946 to 1958, a multipronged approach emerged from this practical experience, combining the "elasticity approach" of the prewar literature with the more Keynes-inflected "absorption approach" developed largely in-house, and also what came to be called the "monetary approach to the balance of payments."[14]

Quantitative work using data and formal mathematical modelling was central to the work of the IMF's Research Department. Sidney S. Alexander (1952) was the first to formalize the absorption approach, and Jacques Polak (1957) was the first to formalize the monetary approach; but in both cases, it should be emphasized, the papers emerged from practical experience in the field, brought back to the Research Department in Washington, DC, and distilled by a process of internal debate among multiple authors. These seminal papers were thus products of the institution as much as they were of the individual authors, much like the work product and process of most central banks. The key

[14] De Vries (1987, 30), IMF (1977).

point is that, at the IMF, international economics got its start from the practical problems of the underdeveloped world.

Watching all of this from his new perch at MIT, Charlie would have recognized Alexander's absorption approach as a version of what he himself had been attempting in his 1937 dissertation. And Alexander himself would have been a known quantity since he had served during the War as Director of Research at the OSS. No doubt both were factors in the decision to bring Alexander to MIT in 1956, where he would remain until retirement.

Polak's monetary approach would also have been recognizable to Charlie, given his own preferred payments approach to international economics. Polak's model built on the distinction between money of external origin and money of domestic origin that Robert Triffin had brought to the IMF back in 1946, but it was Polak and others who turned it into a practically usable policy framework. Importantly, and notwithstanding the emphasis on money supply, the IMF approach was by no means monetarist.[15] Indeed, the whole point was to emphasize how the money supply in these countries was fundamentally an endogenous variable, rising and falling with the inflow and outflow of foreign reserves, as well as the expansion and contraction of domestic credit. The emphasis on these monetary magnitudes was partly an accommodation to data availability, but it worked because countries in the underdeveloped world were typically quite underdeveloped financially as well. Bank credit was essentially the only financial instrument, and given the lack of international capital flows, changes in official foreign reserves of the central bank were essentially the only means of settling international payments. Further, in many of these countries, the fiscal Treasury was effectively conjoined with the monetary central bank, so IMF field investigations typically involved working with both, advising how to avoid balance of payments crises by controlling both domestic spending and credit.

In the case of the monetary approach, there was no need for MIT to recruit anybody since they already had Charlie. Instead, the flow went the other way as Robert Mundell, one of Charlie's first PhD students,

<hr>

[15] De Vries (1987, 30).

graduating in 1956, spent two years at the IMF (1961–3). His dissertation had been pure trade theory, nothing at all on money, but he had taken a guided reading course from Charlie that would have provided him with a basic understanding of the relevant literature on international money. And Charlie had helped Mundell to get the IMF job, no doubt remembering the importance of his own early stints at the Fed and BIS.[16] Indeed, there are echoes of Charlie's 1939 "Speculation and Forward Exchange" in the paper Mundell wrote jointly with Fleming at the end of his IMF sojourn, "Official Intervention on the Forward Exchange Market: A Simplified Analysis." Notably, the paper builds explicitly on the work of Charles Coombs at the New York Fed, whose 1976 memoir Charlie would later review glowingly.[17]

The point to emphasize in all of this is not only that postwar thinking about international money had its origins in the world of central bank and IMF practitioners, but also that that thinking then spilled over into academic circles at MIT through contacts such as Alexander and Mundell. Although Charlie always favored the Williams key-currency approach and so opposed elevation of the IMF into a global central bank, he quite definitely recognized the usefulness of the institution for fleshing out the periphery of the emerging global dollar system. Indeed, in his review of the official history of the IMF, Charlie went so far as to analogize the Fund's structural adjustment programs to the Marshall Plan – both programs used outside funding to support a program of structural change – and to praise the "Darwinian fashion" in which the Fund developed over time to meet changing circumstances.[18] He does not mention (but it is relevant) that the author of the official history, Margaret Garritsen de Vries, was herself an MIT PhD, graduating in 1946 with a thesis that she wrote under Paul Samuelson on the management of Federal debt in the postwar period. Charlie's arrival two years later thus merely continued and solidified an IMF–MIT cross-fertilization that predated him.

---

[16] Boughton (2003, 3).
[17] Fleming and Mundell (1964). Footnote 1 cites Coombs (1963). Kindleberger (1977c).
[18] Kindleberger (1988b).

All of this cross-fertilization on international money operated largely under the radar, however. More visibly, MIT was building itself into a center for academic discourse focused primarily on national economic stabilization. In 1948, that discourse was organized around the simple Keynesian fiscal multiplier model, which understood domestic output as driven by aggregate demand, broken down into aggregate consumption, investment, and government spending. From the point of view of this model, international economics enters the picture merely as exports (an external source of demand) and imports (an external leakage of demand), which is to say the balance on current account. An exogenous increase in exports increases domestic income directly and also indirectly because the higher income increases consumption spending, while some of the increase leaks abroad in the form of increased imports. This, it will be noted, is exactly the frame of the 1949 Bloomfield–Kindleberger debate. The important point to note is that money enters the picture nowhere.

The reason for this initial neglect of money in the national economics discourse can be traced to US wartime practice of using the central bank to support the price of government bond debt, both short term and long term. In effect, the central bank balance sheet and hence the money supply simply absorbed any excess supply or demand of government bonds at the fixed policy price, expanding or contracting respectively, and this practice continued well after the war. Only in 1951 in the famous Fed–Treasury Accord did the Fed wrest control of short-term interest rates from the Treasury and begin to use that control for stabilization purposes.

Importantly, the initial academic response to that 1951 institutional change came not from MIT but rather from the University of Chicago – specifically from Milton Friedman and his students, whose emphasis on monetary policy rather than fiscal policy mounted an assault on the emerging Keynesian mainstream view. Even before the Accord, Friedman (1946) had mounted a sustained attack on Oskar Lange's crypto-Keynesian *Price Flexibility and Employment* (1944) and had proposed "A Monetary and Fiscal Framework for Economic Stability" (1948) as his alternative. Subsequently, the students in Friedman's Workshop on Money and Banking produced *Studies in the Quantity Theory of Money* (1956), and

Friedman's lead essay for the volume, "The Quantity Theory: A Restatement," provided the analytical foundation for his subsequent manifesto *A Program for Monetary Stability* (1959). The empirical foundation of the monetarist edifice, *A Monetary History of the United States* (1963) coauthored with Anna Schwartz, followed soon after. Suffice it to say, in the field of money Chicago got a very big jump on MIT.[19]

The central figure in MIT's response to Friedman was Franco Modigliani, who joined MIT in 1962 after visiting for a year in 1960, and began producing a stream of papers on the monetary transmission mechanism beginning with "The Monetary Mechanism and its Interaction with Real Phenomena" (1963). MIT's choice of Modigliani was in effect an endorsement of Modigliani's own version of Keynes, which he had worked out in his PhD dissertation (under Jacob Marschak at the New School for Social Research) and published as "Liquidity Preference and the Theory of Interest and Money" (1944). This was the so-called IS–LM model, with one curve for fiscal policy denoting equilibrium in the goods market and a second for monetary policy denoting equilibrium in the money market, a model which would become central to the analytical approach that Samuelson would promote as the "neoclassical synthesis," starting with the 1955 edition of his best-selling textbook.[20]

Just so, armed with this model, in 1961 MIT went to Washington to join the Kennedy administration: Paul Samuelson as unofficial advisor to the President himself and Bob Solow as senior economist at the Council of Economic Advisors. Meanwhile, back home at MIT, Modigliani took charge of developing the monetary sector of the Fed–MIT–Penn (FMP) model, the first large-scale econometric model of the United States – basically a fleshed-out version of the two-curve IS–LM model, calibrated to past data. The way the model worked, monetary policy set the short-term rate of interest, which then got translated into a long-term rate by a term structure equation and into a risky rate through an equity pricing

---

[19] This paragraph and the next are taken from Mehrling (2014, 178, 185–187) with minimal edits. See the original for a story of "MIT and Money" that focuses on the national discourse rather than, as here, international money.

[20] Giraud (2014, 149).

equation. These capital market rates then entered expenditure equations in the "real" sector of the model.

Throughout the 1960s, this same IS–LM model organized the debate between the Keynesians at MIT and the monetarists at the University of Chicago. One point of contention was the slopes of the two curves, which in the model determine the relative efficacy of fiscal and monetary policy. Another point of contention was the movement of the curves over time, which in the model determines how quickly the economy converges to long-run full-employment equilibrium. For our purposes, the important thing is not these points of contention, but rather the points of agreement. Keynesians and monetarists both had much the same model of the economy, and for both groups the monetary side of that model was a matter of money supply and money demand, with the money supply taken to be exogenously fixed by the central bank.

As a sometime student of Willis, that was not at all how Charlie thought about money. Further, as against the emerging national macroeconomic orthodoxy at MIT, Charlie's message, in effect, was that in the emerging international world of integrated money and financial markets the very notion of purely domestic monetary policy was an illusion. In his view, the US money rate of interest established the level for the entire world, not just for the United States, and foreign central banks merely established spreads around that level. In this sense, foreign central banks were to the Federal Reserve System as the regional Federal Reserve Banks were to the New York Fed inside the United States. The implication of this point of view was that US monetary policy was de facto international monetary policy, and foreign monetary policy was only about managing the balance of payments, not domestic economic stabilization: "One market implies one price, which implies one money and one monetary policy."[21]

The economists didn't want to hear that at all, and even less so their political masters. No sovereign wants to be told that monetary sovereignty is a myth: "Sovereignty is the last asset to be pawned."[22] The spirit of the age, crystallized at Bretton Woods, was that each country was to look after

---

[21] Kindleberger (1981a, 106, 324).
[22] Kindleberger (1981a, 327).

its own aggregate income and employment, trading goods and services with the rest of the world as needed, but strictly controlling all capital flows, both short-term and long-term. In this way, the balance of payments should be driven by the balance of trade, perhaps fluctuating over time, but with exports tracking imports on average over time. The world was not one integrated market, but rather many separate national markets, economic islands engaging with each other at arm's length. And the job of the economist was not to advise how best to manage the world system as a whole, but rather to advise the domestic sovereign how best to maximize income and employment on his own island.

Toward that national stabilization goal, initially the IS–LM frame merely took over the foreign trade multiplier analysis from the original nonmonetary Keynesian model, embedding it now into the IS curve. Domestic money entered the model through the LM curve, but international money still entered nowhere. Obviously this was unsatisfactory, and so a generation of academics set to work, eventually adding a third curve that described equilibrium in the foreign exchange market, so extending the IS–LM model to what became known as the IS–LM–BP model (BP for balance of payments). Significantly, Robert Mundell played a central role in this, starting with some papers he published during the IMF years, reworked as chapters in *International Economics* (1968).[23] In 1976, Mundell's student Rudiger Dornbusch, by then himself a professor at MIT, would dub the IS–LM–BP model "Mundell–Fleming" and popularize it in his 1980 textbook *Open Economy Macroeconomics.*[24] The inclusion of Fleming was meant to acknowledge the contribution of Fleming's 1962 paper produced independently from Mundell's, also at the IMF. Says Boughton, official historian of the IMF: "What has become known vernacularly as the Mundell-Fleming model is essentially Fleming's equations with Mundell's policy analysis."[25]

We will have occasion to delve into this account of the development of the standard model a bit later, but for the Kindleberger story it makes more sense to start earlier, with the work of Egon Sohmen, another

---

[23] Mundell (1961, 1963), Mundell (1968, ch. 15, 18).
[24] Young and Darity (2004).
[25] Fleming (1962), Boughton (2003, 3).

student of Charlie's who graduated in 1958. Sohmen's thesis, published as *Flexible Exchange Rates; Theory and Controversy* (1961), subsequently served as a foundation stone for academic discourse as the fixed exchange rate system that had been established at Bretton Woods came under stress and increasingly academic economists saw flexible exchange rates as a possible solution.

Milton Friedman had opened the subject way back in 1953 with his essay "The Case for Flexible Exchange Rates." As a monetarist, Friedman imagined a world in which each country independently controls its own domestic price level by controlling its own money supply. The problem then emerges that if monetary policies in different countries are not coordinated, they will likely be incompatible with a fixed exchange rate system; the currency of the country with the higher rate of inflation will tend to depreciate. The solution to the problem was flexible exchange rates, a policy which thus emerges as the necessary international component of the monetarist policy agenda that Friedman promoted at the national level. Over time this logic, coming as it did from a national macroeconomic perspective, would make increasing sense to the Keynesians as well. Flexible exchange rates came to seem like a way to increase the autonomy of governments seeking to control domestic employment and inflation.

In advocating for flexible exchange rates, Sohmen made common cause with Friedman, but his larger intellectual frame was always more Charlie than Milton. Like Charlie, Sohmen's ideal system was always a single world currency, and he always emphasized short-term capital flows, not reserve flows, as the key mechanism for absorbing temporary imbalances. Just so, under the gold standard, exchange rates had fluctuated within a narrow band around mint parity, as stabilizing short-term capital flows absorbed imbalances rather than gold flows: "The gold standard is the perfect example for the effectiveness of stabilizing speculation."[26] The attempt at Bretton Woods to establish a fixed exchange rate system, with the dollar convertible into gold at $35/oz. and with every other currency convertible into the dollar, was an attempt to create an approximation to a world currency system, at least for the world of commodity trade.

---

[26] Sohmen (1969, 79).

The fatal flaw of the Bretton Woods system, however, was price stickiness; not only wages, but especially output prices due to widespread monopoly. The result was that, over time, price levels in different countries drifted away from each other, causing some currencies to become overvalued and others undervalued. The resulting payment imbalances then eventually exhausted the capacity of short-term capital flows and reserve flows, leading to more serious intervention in the form of tariffs and capital controls, all in an ultimately futile attempt to defend the fixed exchange rate. And all the while, speculators were placing their bets, attracted by the prospect of imminent devaluation or revaluation, forcing central banks to engage in ever more heroic measures only eventually to capitulate, shifting the exchange rate discontinuously and then holding fast to the new rate until the same problem emerged again. In this way, according to Sohmen, the Bretton Woods fixed exchange system had turned out in practice to be the enemy of free trade in goods and capital. The solution was to abandon the fixed exchange rate system and embrace flexible rates instead.

What Sohmen imagined as an alternative was a system where the exchange rate drifts gradually, to keep the price systems of different countries in alignment, while temporary imbalances are absorbed by short-term capital flows. In such a system, interest rates move to facilitate absorption of temporary imbalances, while exchange rates move to facilitate absorption of permanent imbalances. The workability of this ideal system, however, clearly depends on whether speculation is stabilizing, as it apparently was under the gold standard, or destabilizing, as it arguably was in the interwar period. Sohmen's book was therefore largely focused on the question of stability, starting with the simple world of commodity trade. Will depreciation improve the balance of payments or make it worse? Put another way, starting from a position of trade balance, is the equilibrium stable or unstable?

Sohmen's first venture into academic publication, while still a graduate student, had involved an argument that, even if the initial equilibrium is unstable, there are always other stable equilibria above and below the unstable one. So, if you experience instability, the trick is to seek out one of the stable equilibria instead. This argument found favor with Milton Friedman, who had asserted something similar in a footnote to his 1953 article, and so Sohmen's article found its way into the *Journal of Political Economy* in 1957. Subsequently, however, the article would come under attack by Jagdish Bhagwati and Harry Johnson in the *Economic Journal*, which provoked Sohmen to "Comment" and Bhagwati-Johnson to "Rejoinder."[27] Unwittingly, Sohmen had wandered into the battle between the monetarists and the Keynesians that was then heating up, but there are echoes here also of the Bloomfield–Kindleberger academic–practitioner debate. As Kindleberger, Sohmen would fight on his critic's ground, even as his main defense was empirical realism.

In fact, the issue of stability in a pure trade model was only a preliminary to the main argument in Sohmen's thesis, which was about stability in a world of capital flows. In a flexible exchange rate world, international trade involves exposure to exchange rate risk, and the question arises whether forward exchange markets can be relied upon to hedge that risk. Sohmen said yes, while Charlie said no, and more or less the whole case for flexible exchange rates rides on that answer. On principle, following the example of his own thesis advisor Angell, Charlie did not require that Sohmen agree with him, and he passed the thesis anyway. But they continued to debate the issue periodically in multiple venues up to and even after Sohmen's premature death.

In the volume Charlie edited to honor Sohmen posthumously, his own chapter, "Myths and Realities of Forward – Exchange Markets," leads with three myths supported by Sohmen:

Myth 1. Forward markets take exchange risk out of floating exchanges.

Myth 2. Broad and efficient forward markets will spring into existence under floating exchanges.

Myth 3. With forward-exchange markets, monetary authorities need no foreign exchange reserves; they can sell foreign exchange forward and roll maturing contracts over, ad infinitum.[28]

In Charlie's view, the ideal that Sohmen imagined as an alternative to Bretton Woods was simply not going to work in practice the way that he imagined it would in theory. Against Sohmen, Charlie urged that

---

[27] Sohmen (1957), Bhagwati and Johnson (1960), Sohmen (1961b), Bhagwati and Johnson (1961).

[28] Chipman and Kindleberger (1980, ch. 8).

a flexible exchange rate system was likely to inhibit the growth of world trade and probably dry up long-term cross-border capital flows more or less completely, as exchange rates got whipsawed by destabilizing specu-lation – shades of the 1930s. In the event, as we shall see, both men were wrong. For now, the important thing to appreciate is that both Sohmen and Charlie were in the minority among academic economists, since they were both centrally concerned with the international system as a whole, whereas most everyone else was thinking just about national economic policy. For everyone else, Keynesians and monetarists both, flexible exchange rates seemed like an extra degree of freedom for national policy, which could only be a good thing.

Just so, as we have seen, Franco Modigliani had been hired at MIT to expand the macroeconomic stabilization toolkit from fiscal policy to include also monetary policy. Unemployment and inflation were the targets he was trying to hit, so his interest in international money was largely about preserving space for an activist domestic monetary policy agenda. We see him doing exactly that in his various proposals for international monetary reform, starting with "A Suggestion for Solving the International Liquidity Problem" (1966), which he coauthored with Peter Kenen, then a professor at Columbia University. More or less along Triffin lines, they proposed a new international monetary unit to be called the MIT (Medium for International Transactions) to be issued by a new MIT bank, successor to the IMF, which would have the remit to increase the supply of this new reserve asset in line with the secular increase in demand from national banking systems. For Modigliani, the big payoff from such a system was avoiding the necessity for deficit countries to adopt deflationary policy domestically; they could instead just devalue.[29]

Graduate students who were hearing one thing in Franco's class and another in Charlie's organized a debate between the two men on January 10, 1966, at 4:30 pm, cocktails and dinner to follow. Neither Charlie's *Economist* manifesto nor Franco's MIT proposal were published yet, but they were imminent. Professors were invited to the debate as well, and Bob Solow spoke up on Franco's side in favor of flexible exchange

---

[29] Modigliani and Kenen (1966, 8).

rates, earning him a riposte from Charlie that Solow would remember and recount at Charlie's eightieth birthday celebration: "The audience should keep in mind that MIT does not pay Professor Solow to think about international economics."[30] The same, of course, could have been said of Modigliani, but that didn't stop him from developing his remarks into a long memorandum for the Fed's Economic Consultants Meeting of October 20–21, 1966, explicitly attacking what he called the "CPK position," which provoked a formal reply by Charlie dated November 29th.[31]

Modigliani would go on to coauthor with a student three more versions of his international monetary reform proposal, now shifting focus to the SDR.[32] A letter from Charlie commenting on the first of these three versions survives and shows the distance between the two men as wide as ever:

> There is a fundamental monetary issue here between the school which says that money is created by the state, or by legislation or international agreement, and another which says money is created by usage … You dismiss without a hearing the case for internationalization of monetary policy to avoid the kinds of deficits and surpluses which have been so troublesome in the last few years. Your independence of domestic monetary policy is an assumed goal, not debated or debatable.[33]

Outside of MIT, the flexible rate case burgeoned as well. In 1967, Milton Friedman debated Robert Roosa, now at the Council on Foreign Relations, and the published proceedings became required reading everywhere. At Harvard's new Kennedy School of Government, Francis Bator, a 1956 MIT PhD just returned from high office in the Johnson administration, wrote for *Foreign Affairs* rejecting Charlie's proposal to "crown the dollar" (Bator's words, but without explicitly naming Charlie) and embracing instead a new kind of international money: the SDR.

---

[30] KPMD, Box 24, "Reminiscences of Charles P. Kindleberger on his Eightieth Birthday, October 12, 1990."

[31] KPMD, Box 1, "Graduate Economics Association Seminar." The Modigliani memorandum was eventually published with light revisions as Modigliani (1973).

[32] Modigliani and Askari (1971, 1973), Askari and Modigliani (1972).

[33] KPMD, Box 1, "Graduate Economics Association Seminar." CPK to FM, July 16, 1971.

Farther afield, Harry Johnson, professor at the University of Chicago, pressed "The Case for Flexible Exchange Rates, 1969" as one of thirty-eight papers published after the June 1969 Burgenstock conference titled *Approaches to Greater Flexibility of Exchange Rates.*[34] The academic bandwagon was thus rolling, well before Nixon's 1971 decision to devalue.

Only the Johnson contribution did Charlie choose to address, in "The Case for Fixed Exchange Rates, 1969," presented at a Boston Fed conference in October 1969. Charlie had in fact been trying to bring Johnson on board with his own position for some years, in a series of private letters, to no avail. (The first step in this campaign was apparently Charlie's choice of Johnson as [paid] critic of the manuscript for his 1962 *Foreign Trade and the National Economy.*) So when Milton Friedman seemed to change his position to something very close to Charlie's, he felt the wind at his back and decided to push on Johnson in public.[35] Friedman's idea was that the United States should stop buying and selling gold, eliminate all capital controls, and renounce any intervention to influence the price of the dollar, leaving other countries to choose whether to peg to the dollar, float, or whatever. The end result of all this, Friedman suggested, would be that

New York would resume its growth as the center of the capital market of the world . . . Set the dollar free, and make it clear that it will continue to be free, and the Euro-dollar market will shrivel and New York will become in the final decades of the twentieth century what London was in the final decades of the nineteenth century.[36]

Buoyed by this unexpected (monetarist) support, as he chose to interpret it, Charlie responded firmly to (Keynesian) Johnson:

The main case against flexible exchange rates is that they break up the world market. There is no one money which serves as a medium of exchange, unit of account, store of value, and standard of deferred payment . . . Under any system of flexible exchange rates, the drive to

[34] Friedman and Roosa (1967), Halm (1970), Bator (1968).
[35] Kindleberger (1981a, 84 n. 1, 182 n. 5).
[36] Friedman (1969, 365).

establish an international money is virtually inevitable ... The stable exchange rate system, in my judgment, is inherent in the evolutionary process by which barter moves to become efficient trading through the use of a single money.[37]

The Burgenstock and the Boston Fed conferences were just two of many in those years. Reviewing the published proceedings of yet another one, Charlie observed:

One new industry of the 1960s is the holding of conferences on the international monetary system by academic economists with an occasional admixture of central and commercial bankers. One need only mention in alphabetical order Algarve, Bald Peak, Bellagio, Bologna, Brookings, Burgenstock, Claremont, Chicago, Ditchley ... to make the point. The rediscovery of money in international economics, somewhat belatedly perhaps, and of Gresham's law (by Triffin) sets monetary economists in motion to the airport, papers in hand. To miss a conference is to be assigned to review the proceedings, either before publication for the university press which gets the duty, or afterward for an economic periodical.[38]

The specific conference that Charlie had been assigned to review in this case had been held in September 1966, organized by Robert Mundell with the support of Harry Johnson, both at that time professors in the economics department at the University of Chicago and coleaders of the famous International Economics Workshop. Charlie had not been in attendance (hence the assignment), but he had been at the original Bellagio conference in 1963 that launched the industry, and that had been enough for him.[39] Enough for Mundell too, and the Chicago conference was explicitly intended as an alternative to Bellagio, focusing now on "problems" in monetary theory rather than plans for monetary reform.

---

[37] Kindleberger (1981a, 174–175).
[38] Kindleberger (1971, 127), quoted also in Kindleberger (1989c).
[39] Proceedings of that early effort appear in Machlup (1964). Connell (2013) provides a useful chronicle of the continuing series of Bellagio conferences, including the shift eventually to Burgenstock with proceedings published as Halm (1970).

In Charlie's intellectual formation, as we have seen, the concrete problems of the international monetary system – the transfer problem posed by reparations in the 1920s and then the hot money problem posed by the collapse of the international monetary system in the 1930s – had provided the material from which it was the task of economists to spin new economics. It was natural, therefore, for him to draw attention to the issues he saw as currently most pressing, issues unfortunately "largely slighted" by the 1966 Chicago conference proceedings. Here are the real problems, according to Charlie:

> How, for example, to define equilibrium and disequilibrium in the balance of payments of a country with a dominant capital market; the familiar Triffin problem posed by Gresham's law with two or more reserve assets growing at different rates; international financial intermediation, its use and abuse; the viability of a system with a series of national money and capital markets of equal size and efficiency, as contrasted with a system ordered in hierarchical progression, from broader and more efficient to narrower and less efficient.[40]

Here perhaps we hear the gentle rebuke of a professor to his former student, urging him to direct his energies to the actual problems that confront us in the real world, rather than to artificial "problems" in academic theory. Charlie closes his review with a more explicit appeal: "Many of the components of an international monetary theory are contained in these pages. The coherent structure such as produced by a Friedman, Modigliani or Patinkin is still missing. The obvious candidate for producing such a grand synthesis is the man who has a theory and has produced many of the parts, Mundell himself."[41]

This was not the first time Charlie had touted Mundell. In a letter of November 3, 1964, Harry Johnson had written to enquire whether Charlie might be interested in writing a treatise for a series published by Aldine. Charlie responded by proposing instead Mundell, or Ron Jones:

> As for me, I can detect no signs of treatise-pregnancy. After I finish with European growth in the fifties (along with everybody else), I contemplate

---

[40] Kindleberger (1971, 128).
[41] Kindleberger (1971, 131).

more economic history. International trade is becoming too hairy ...
I have my doubts about whether Mundell will ever write a book – he
scarcely stops anywhere long enough to write a full-length article; but if
he would write up his stuff on money it would be good.[42]

It was perhaps partly on the strength of this recommendation that the
University of Chicago hired Mundell starting July 1965, but there are
indications that he was not initially planning to stay long. Already on
September 27, 1965, Charlie was writing to his friend Emile Despres to
inquire whether Stanford might be interested in hiring him.[43] And
Mundell himself remembers "an offer from MIT around 1966," which
he ultimately turned down in favor of staying at Chicago, where for
a while he seems to have served as an ally in Charlie's attempt to split
Johnson from Friedman on the issue of flexible exchange rates.[44]

What did Charlie like about Mundell? What he liked most was
Mundell's monetary internationalism and defense of fixed exchange
rates, which in his mind put Mundell in the same key-currency camp as
himself and John H. Williams, specifically "Mundell's conclusion that
one country must be responsible for price stabilization, but not its own
balance of payments, while the rest of the world concentrates on its
balance of payments, but ignores price stabilization."[45] Significantly,
this conclusion can be found in Mundell's 1969 paper "Toward a Better
International Monetary System," which cites a forthcoming "note" by
Charlie in the *Journal of Political Economy*, which, as editor, Mundell
would have greenlighted.[46] This "note" is mentioned as one of several
contributions to the theory of optimum currency areas, which literature
Mundell (1961) had originally got started. In fact, however, the note
turned out to be a full-length paper, "Measuring Equilibrium in the
Balance of Payments," which, moreover, Kindleberger thought enough
of to include in his final *Retrospective* (2000).

---

[42] KPMD, Box 2, "Johnson, Harry G., 1961–85," CPK to HJ, Nov. 9, 1964, and Nov. 27, 1964.
[43] KPMD, Box 2, "John Despres." CPK to ED, Sept. 27, 1965.
[44] Vane and Mulhearn (2006, 107).
[45] Kindleberger (1989c, 52).
[46] Mundell (1969, 642 and 638).

Charlie's 1969 paper reads as further thoughts on his 1965 paper criticizing the accounting conventions that had given rise to unwarranted policy concern about US deficits, which he had reprinted as the first chapter in *Europe and the Dollar* (1966). The most significant additional material in the new paper addresses the question of how, given the inadequacy of existing accounting structures, one could in practice detect whether a country such as the United States was in trouble or not. Charlie's answer addresses both liquidity and solvency. As a bank, the United States did need to keep an eye on its reserve balance. In the short run, reserve drain could be made up by borrowing the reserves back from wherever they went, if not from private short-term capital markets then using public liquidity swaps between central banks. Sustained reserve drain, however, would be a different matter, requiring more substantial intervention. Further, the United States also needed to keep an eye on its net worth, most importantly by paying attention to the balance between earnings on its foreign assets and payments on its foreign liabilities. A positive balance, which the United States most definitely enjoyed, showed that there was nothing to worry about on that score, at least not yet.

In context, Mundell's 1969 paper can thus be read as a complement to Charlie's – indeed, even as a kind of follow-up to Despres–Kindleberger–Salant (1966). Put simply, Mundell's "Better International Monetary System" is nothing less than the DKS global dollar system. Says Mundell:

> Without hardly anybody noticing it, the gold exchange standard in its old form was dead, and the dollar exchange standard had taken its place ... a system in which the United States took on a new role of world banker, not just in the sense of being a key currency center, nor the provider of a reserve money and the main settlement currency, but as a world banker in the more comprehensive sense of guiding the monetary policy of the world.[47]

This certainly looks like Mundell breaking with Chicago and joining instead with Kindleberger. Even more, this looks like Mundell trying on the role that Emile Despres had been unable to fulfill, namely taking Charlie's place when Congressional testimony was needed. Indeed,

---

[47] Mundell (1969, 631).

a footnote tells us that the paper is a revised version of testimony Mundell gave on September 9, 1968, at Hearings on "Next Steps in International Monetary Reform" for the Sub-Committee on International Exchange and Payments of the Joint Economic Committee, chaired by Senator Proxmire. This particular experiment would not be repeated, but the important thing is that it was tried. In 1969 Mundell and Kindleberger were making common cause in defense of the dollar system.

Mundell remained very much his own man, however, and subsequently took things in his own direction, most notably in his 1969 advocacy for a European currency, an idea which Charlie for a long time viewed as an incorrect extension of the key-currency approach.[48] For Charlie the optimal currency area was the world, not a region; each European currency should be fixed to the dollar, creating in effect an international money, rather than fixed to each other and floating against the dollar and in doing so breaking the world into separate trading regions. Thirty years later, on the eve of the creation of the euro (the eve also of Mundell's Nobel Prize), Mundell would host an international conference in Kindleberger's honor on the theme "The Euro as Stabilizer in the International Economic System." Charlie, now ninety years old, offered his musings on "A New Bi-Polarity?," by which he meant the possibility that a declining United States might make common cause with a rising Europe. As Charlie saw it, that common cause would take the form of stabilizing the dollar–euro exchange rate in normal times, but also shared responsibility for global lender of last resort.

To recap, back in 1969, notwithstanding academic enthusiasm for flexible exchange rates, Charlie had hopes that the dollar system could be saved. His was still a minority view, but with Friedman and Mundell apparently on his side, he no longer felt as lonely as three years earlier, when he had just Despres and Salant. Unfortunately, it soon became apparent that neither Friedman nor Mundell were as firmly on his side as he imagined. Friedman made this abundantly clear in his vigorous "Discussion" of Charlie's Boston Fed paper, reiterating his 1953 case for flexible rates, now putting even more emphasis on the dependably stabilizing role of speculation and emphatically rejecting any idea that

---

[48]   Mundell (1973).

global money needs to be managed. For Charlie, central bankers were always watching and waiting, prepared to intervene in order to prevent destabilizing speculation from wreaking havoc. For Friedman, it was the central banks themselves who were the source of havoc, in their misbegotten attempts to manipulate the money supply in order to stabilize economic fluctuations. No meeting of the minds there.[49]

Mundell's advocacy for a European currency meant that he also was not so firmly on Charlie's side. At first it seemed largely a matter of political judgment, Mundell taking the view that the best way forward given Nixon's monetary irresponsibility was for Europe to go its own way collectively, perhaps eventually pegging the common currency to the dollar (as also the Japanese yen) to form a world currency he called the Jeurodollar. But then Mundell published his own version of world monetarism and went on to embrace supply-side economics in partnership with Arthur Laffer. Charlie rejected all of it.[50]

No doubt these were disappointments, but as always the important thing for Charlie was not to win the academic dispute but rather to communicate the correct view to the authorities charged with managing the system. The authorities at the Fed were no problem, but it soon became clear that the new Nixon administration was not listening to the Fed. In 1971, John Connally, newly appointed Secretary of the Treasury, told the world that "The dollar is our currency, but your problem" and proceeded to remove the dollar from the gold standard.[51] This, according to Charlie, was the Crime of 1971.

After the fact, Charlie would come to appreciate that Connally was in fact responding to a sudden deterioration in the trade account, not so much to the sloshing of hot money as he thought at the time, and hence he would take a more forgiving stance toward the decision to devalue. The United States had become adjusted to a pattern of dynamic comparative advantage, a concept Charlie attributed to John H. Williams, that was breaking down in 1970, and the result was a serious balance of

---

[49] See also Friedman (1953, 176 n. 9) casting aspersions on Nurkse, and Johnson (1973, 8) on central bankers more generally, both references cited in Kindleberger (1981a, 204 n. 4).

[50] Mundell (1971), Kindleberger (1982, 56–57).

[51] Coombs (1976, 219).

payments problem, no longer just an accounting illusion.[52] Whatever the reason for the 1971 devaluation, the important thing was that the academic advocates of floating rates got what they wanted, and the world embarked on an experiment to see whether these theories worked in practice. Charlie's attempt to stem the tide had failed.

Meanwhile the success of Mundell's 1966 Chicago conference had spawned a legion of imitators, and a range of subnetworks all over the world, generously funded by foundations happy to jump on the bandwagon. For the floating rate academics it must have seemed like the Keynes dream come true, their scribblings now on the verge of being incised on the pages of monetary history. Jet-setting Johnson took the lead, moving between his appointments at both the University of Chicago and the London School of Economics, playing a key role in keeping the subnetworks all moving in the same direction.

After 1971, this activity only intensified, organized now increasingly around Johnson's own thinking, "disseminated, and intellectually enforced, through the networks" as he said, and published eventually as *The Monetary Approach to the Balance of Payments* (1976).[53] Johnson continued to treat Mundell as cofounder of the monetary approach, even though after 1971 Mundell separated himself from Johnson, starting his own series of periodic conferences at his villa in Santa Colomba, Italy, focused more on international commercial banking leaders than on academics.

Charlie meanwhile kept his distance from it all:

No enforcer has successfully worked on me, and [unlike Johnson] I permit myself the indulgence of believing that markets mostly work but occasionally, like intellectuals, are caught up in the coils of fashion and euphoria ...

There is something to be said for scholars staying in their studies and classrooms, rather than jetting compulsively around the world, hastily scribbling an overdue paper on the plane, skimming the other papers the night before they are presented ... In the international field enough is as good as a feast, as my old chairman used to say. No, it's better. There are

---

[52] Kindleberger (1981a, 141, 186), Williams (1929).
[53] Johnson (1981, 89), Frenkel and Johnson (1976).

strongly diminishing returns to conferring, and at the personal level they are frequently negative.[54]

Instead of wasting his time in the academic fray, Charlie simply watched from the sidelines, waiting for the "coils of fashion and euphoria" to burn themselves out.

By 1976 he was ready to draw "Lessons of Floating Exchange Rates." He and Sohmen had both been wrong: "Initiation of flexible exchange rates was not succeeded by a drying-up of capital movements [as Charlie had anticipated], or by capital movements only in a stabilizing direction [as Sohmen had anticipated]."[55] Instead, a big surprise for Charlie, capital flows, both long term and short term, had continued even as behind the scenes central bank cooperation had worked to mitigate the worst of destabilizing speculation, even managing to recycle the surpluses caused by the (first) oil shock.

The continuation of capital flows in the face of flexible exchange rates counted as a remarkable success in Charlie's eyes, but a remarkable failure for advocates of floating rates since it meant that the shift to floating had failed to separate domestic capital markets as intended. Notwithstanding floating rates, there was still one world capital market and one world money market, and both were dollar markets: "With flexible exchange rates and capital movements, independent monetary policies are compromised."[56]

The central problem now was that this global market was fundamentally unmanaged, basically because the Nixon administration was acting irresponsibly in its own perceived national interest rather than taking responsibility for managing the global system, and because without the United States on board no one else could do it. Instead, each country was on its own, more or less the situation analyzed by the IS–LM–BP model, which rose to prominence on the back of this entirely unsatisfactory state of affairs. Central bank cooperation behind the scenes had kept the

---

[54] KPMD, Box 25, "The Economic Review as a Literary Art Form." Unpublished "Comment" on Johnson "The Role of Networks of Economists in International Monetary Reform." The last section of this passage also appears in Kindleberger (1989c, 48).

[55] Kindleberger (1981a, 189).

[56] Kindleberger (1981a, 201). Compare Rey (2018).

system from collapsing, but continuing irresponsibility of the United States had led to increasing inflation worldwide.

In 1976, Charlie was gloomy, let down by precisely the policy practitioners that he had depended upon to do the practical thing. His frame of course came from war time experience, when the whole country was pulling together for a common goal and the best and the brightest migrated into public service to do their part. The Nixon years were different. But Charlie should have remembered his own long-held view that there are inherent evolutionary forces that lead from instability to stability. In time, Paul Volcker, Chairman of the Federal Reserve from 1979 to 1987, would channel those forces to tame domestic inflation and then to restore international monetary stability. In Charlie's retrospective view, the 1985 Plaza Accord was the crowning achievement of those years, pointing the way forward to a reconstructed global dollar system. But it would take a decade to get there.

Reviewing Harry Johnson's *On Economics and Society* (1975), Charlie pulled no punches: "The collection shows the strengths and weaknesses of the compulsion which has driven Johnson in economics. His forte is exposition, and pursuing economic analysis to its conclusions, but the initial ideas are often those of others."[57] The same could be said of the 1976 volume *Monetary Approach to the Balance of Payments*, in which case the initial ideas were Mundell's and so in part Charlie's as well. We have seen how Charlie was sympathetic to the original IMF version of the monetary approach in the hands of Polak and his practitioner colleagues, working on problems of the periphery. The question was how to develop the approach for the rather different problems of the core, where financial markets are fully developed and integrated cross-border. In that regard, Charlie viewed the Mundell–Johnson academic version of the monetary approach as a big disappointment.[58]

Writing in 1976, Charlie expresses that disappointment: "Only the monetarist approach potentially allows for complete treatment of capital

---

[57] Kindleberger (1976a, 271).

[58] See Polak (2002) for a retrospective that draws a sharp contrast between the IMF's practitioner version and Johnson's academic version of the monetary approach.

flows, but its practitioners for the most part abstract from these and assume that changes in real [money] balances affect changes in expenditure rather than those in assets or liabilities, i.e., result from changing consumption and/or investment and not [from changing] wealth or the composition of wealth."[59] A few pages later: "A major advantage of the monetarist approach is that it permits adjustment through capital movements ... Real balances can be restored not by changes in expenditure, but by reductions in wealth, that is restoring real balances by portfolio adjustment, by selling off foreign assets or incurring liabilities to foreigners."[60]

One problem with the academic monetary approach was thus its excessively narrow focus on money supply and money demand, ignoring all the other financial markets that are available for adjustment. After he retired, Charlie would go even farther in emphasizing this point. In his mind, the supply and demand frame for the analysis of money, a frame taken over from the closed economy IS–LM model, was itself the problem. For Charlie, it will be recalled, short-term capital movements ideally play a balance-wheel function, expanding and contracting endogenously to facilitate temporary imbalances: "Most of us adjust our holdings of money to our streams of income and spending, not income and spending to some rigid demand for money. And one can always lend a monetary surplus or borrow to make up a deficiency, without changing output or spending."[61]

> It is hard for all but true believers to put much credence in the monetary theory of balance-of-payments adjustment, and for two reasons. In the first place, the theory runs counter to economic common sense and intuition. Instead of money serving as a buffer stock to offset temporary disequilibria between income and expenditure, as in conventional economic reasoning, income and expenditure are varied to maintain a wanted stock of money. The intuitive model is stood on its head. Secondly, the theory ignores the function of the banking system in providing liquidity in the form of

---

[59] Kindleberger (1981a, 195). In this reprinted version, the original "i.e." was replaced with "that is," presumably by some editor, which garbles the meaning a bit. I have restored the original.
[60] Kindleberger (1981a, 198). See also Kindleberger (1982, 54).
[61] Kindleberger (1984c, 299).

money . . . If a country wants more money, to use an anthropomorphism, it indulges in international financial intermediation, borrowing long and lending short, acquiring by the latter process foreign-exchange reserves which serve as the basis for an increase in the domestic money stock.[62]

Here, as always, Charlie insists that money is ultimately an entry on the balance sheet of some bank or central bank somewhere, an inside not an outside phenomenon when viewed from the perspective of the world as a whole. Recovery of private markets, both money markets and capital markets, and then integration of those markets across the face of the world, had produced a system with a certain logic of its own, while economists had developed a class of models with a certain logic of *its* own. By 1976, Rudiger Dornbusch had replaced Charlie at MIT, as open economy macroeconomics had already replaced the cosmopolitan view Charlie had tried to bring to international economics. Neither developments in the world nor developments in economics had turned out the way Charlie had hoped, but it was a relief to no longer have responsibility for either and to be allowed instead to immerse himself in his new passion: economic history.

---

[62] Kindleberger (1982, 54–55).

III

HISTORICAL ECONOMIST, 1976–2003

CHAPTER 8

Independence

Anything can happen and often does. The day of positive economics, useful for prediction, is still some distance away.[1]

Why economic history?

Coming to academia directly from the State Department, as he did, Charlie brought with him a sense that economics and politics were inextricably intertwined. He had loved his time at State: "It has been remarked that the Department of State is the only government department without constituents, which is to say that it is under the disability of attempting to serve the general, rather than an individual interest."[2] As he left Washington, the Department had just finished negotiating the Havana Charter that established the International Trade Organization, a new international organization which, along with the World Bank, Charlie viewed as "the only hope for the ultimate restoration of world economic order."[3]

In the event, of course, individual interest won out, as Congress refused to ratify the Charter. Not for the first or last time, politics threw up obstacles to universalistic solutions. But Charlie refused to despair. In the longer run, so he chose to believe, Darwinian evolution driven by economic logic tends to find a way. "In economics, the worldwide is efficient. In social questions, small is beautiful ... The world is more and more cosmopolitan."[4] A committed internationalist, Charlie always felt himself to be standing on the side of history; academia was for him

[1] Kindleberger (1985c, 152).
[2] Kindleberger (1955b, 438).
[3] Kindleberger (1949b, 242).
[4] Kindleberger (1977b, 557, 560).

simply an alternative venue for serving the general interest, job security enabling him to take the long view.

In the short run, however, the noise of politics quite typically drowns out the trend of history, as multifarious individual interests push this way and that at multifarious levels of society. Indeed, the complexity of the political process means that a scientific understanding of the system as a whole is probably quite impossible, much less the identification of a small number of causes responsible for any given ultimate effect. Here is the reason that the "true believer" finds so much traction, in politics and also in economics, simply because the true scholar finds so little. But that is no reason for the scholar to desist; curiosity is the thing to cultivate, not certainty. "Is economics a science, or is it, like law, merely an aid to advocacy?"[5] Having narrowly escaped his ordained fate as a lawyer, as an academic Charlie embraced a life of scholarship and resisted all temptation to join the political fray.

Thankfully for the scholar, the economic system is more amenable to scientific understanding than the political, but that is not to say that economists do not regularly make a hash of it. In this respect, a recurring hobbyhorse for Charlie throughout his career was the tendency of economists to use partial equilibrium methods for general equilibrium problems, such as the balance of payments and exchange rates.[6] In the real world, everything depends on everything else, and viewing that real world through the lens of a model in which some things are taken as exogenous can seriously mislead. Sometimes the balance of payments is driven mostly by the current account, and sometimes mostly by the capital account, so no single partial model will fit all cases. The art of economics is knowing which to choose when.

A second, more specific hobbyhorse was the tendency of economists to neglect money and banking or, perhaps worse, to bring money into the picture through a simplistic monetarist account. Shortly after his arrival at MIT, Charlie singled out Henry Wallich for high praise as an exception to what was already becoming the rule, "a reminder of money and banking theory which is undeservedly going into neglect."[7] Looking back thirty

---

[5] Kindleberger (1976b, 300).
[6] Kindleberger (1957b).
[7] Kindleberger (1952a, 95).

years later: "The difficulty lies in the narrowness of the IS-LM analysis . . . The basic difficulty is that, except for Hyman Minsky, modern economists have thrown away the Adam Smith, John Stuart Mill, Alfred Marshall, Dennis Robertson, Ralph Hawtrey analysis of credit instability"; "The monetarist approach in the short run is intuitively ridiculous . . . In the short run money needs are balanced not through changes in spending but through borrowing or repaying debts."[8]

A final hobbyhorse was the tendency of economists to view economies other than their own through an analytical lens refined for the case they know best. Just so, by holding up their own economies as comparison, economists in the advanced industrialized world draw attention to the wide range of things that are missing from developing economies and then recommend attacking that wide range all at once. "Balanced growth" is typically favored over so-called "unbalanced growth" simply because of a priori analytical deformation rather than as the result of any sustained engagement with the facts on the ground. By contrast, Charlie insisted that the beginning of wisdom is the admission that no one knows much about economic development, and then "concentrating on the smallest number of priority blocks to a cumulative and self-sustaining process of economic development indigenous to the local setting."[9]

It was these three hobbyhorses that led Charlie bit by bit, over his years in academia, away from economics proper and toward a greater appreciation of the work of economic historians, specifically those engaged in what he called the "old economic history" by contrast with the self-proclaimed new economic history (so-called "cliometrics"), which was more or less just standard econometrics using old data. Reviewing an early contribution in the latter vein by young Jeffrey Williamson, Charlie chastised: "Anything can happen, and generally does. When it reminds us of this, history is useful indeed."[10] In the former vein, Charlie's heroes were instead scholars such as Alexander Gerschenkron, "the doyen of economic history in the United States, widely informed, deeply read, subtle, urbane, and full of zest," and

---

[8]   Kindleberger (1981b, 1586; 1980a, 820).
[9]   Kindleberger (1952b, 392).
[10]   Kindleberger (1965c, 55). Williamson (1978) would return the favor in his review of Kindleberger (1978a).

Stephen Schuker, "old fashioned economic history at its best, carpentered with the skill of a cabinet maker from snippets of information from books, articles, and especially diplomatic and banking archives."[11] When Charlie made his shift into economic history, it was with these examples in mind.

In fact, not only Gerschenkron's style but also his specific theme of the advantage of economic backwardness would become a kind of loose agenda for Charlie's own researches. Late starters in economic development, says Gerschenkron, cannot depend on the efforts of their own indigenous entrepreneurs, but are forced instead to rely on banking to supercharge their development efforts. Such was the case in France with the Crédit Mobilier, an example that subsequently spread to Germany and across Europe. And the really late starters, such as Russia and much of the present developing world, are forced to go even farther by relying on the state to mount a kind of forced march development.[12] This theme – banking and the state as the two prime movers of financial history – runs through all of Charlie's mature work as an economic historian.

I say "economic historian," but more correctly I should say "historical economist" since Charlie always insisted on the distinction. Even as he was clearly inspired by the work of proper historians and very much appreciated their embrace of him as a member of the tribe, he was always an economist first, and he embraced history quite explicitly as a strategy for improving economics: "We can improve economic analysis, I believe, by testing its models against the facts in a variety of contexts, where the conditions in other economies furnish the counterfactual to a single case from which it is dangerous to generalize."[13] Most importantly, by revealing the limitations of particular economic models, comparative history would, so he hoped, insert a little humility into the economics profession: "The improvement in economic analysis comes when a priori notions favoring monetarism, flexible exchange rates, world monetarism, supply-side economics, international financial intermediation, and the like are tested against historical episodes";[14] "It is my considered opinion, as well as my passionate conviction,

---

[11] Kindleberger (1963b, 362; 1977a, 843).
[12] Gerschenkron (1962).
[13] Kindleberger (1978a, 3).
[14] Kindleberger (1982, 63–64).

that economics needs history – perhaps even more than history needs economics."[15]

But this somewhat negative and critical agenda was always only the first step for him, a kind of ground-clearing exercise preliminary to a deeper and more positive agenda to follow. Having stripped economics of its hubristic overreach, what remained would be solid foundations on which the profession could reliably build – general economic laws more than specific economic models: "A search for uniformities in history, or the elaboration of economic 'stories', strikes me as a vital complement to, and, for one whose professional formation took place in the 1930s, *even a substitute for*, high-powered theory, mathematical modelling and statistical testing."[16]

At MIT, these might well have been read as fighting words, MIT being the very epitome of high-powered theory, mathematical modelling, and statistical testing. But Charlie was too much the inveterate team player for that. Observe that "complement" acknowledges the central position of the standard MIT approach, and "substitute" is explicitly framed as his own personal choice, not a competitor for the hearts and minds of the MIT graduate students. Only after his retirement in 1976 would Charlie actively promote comparative economic history as an alternative for others: "It is in the nature of man to evangelize, to urge others to behave as he does, and I am no exception."[17] That's from *Economic Response* (1978), in which he presents six examples of the kind of comparative history approach he favors, four of which he would reprint in his 2000 *Retrospective* as an indication of the importance he attached to this work.[18]

Two years later, in his Mattioli Lectures of May 1980 (belatedly published as *Economic Laws and Economic History* [1989]), Charlie offered his own selection of fundamental economic laws:

[M]y interest is in better theory in the sense of more useful, more general and more relevant theories, and the discarding of that which is merely elegant but has no bearing on how people behave in an economy ... The

---

[15] Kindleberger (1978a, 241).
[16] Kindleberger (1985c, 4), my emphasis.
[17] Kindleberger (1978a, 241).
[18] This is the book he dedicated to "AJ and UW," which refers to Aunt Jen and Uncle Will Walker.

object of the exercise is to discuss a few laws deeply rooted in observed reality that have powerful explanatory power for some, but not for all economic history, to show that eclecticism rather than an all-encompassing system of interpretation is the wiser attitude to bring to the study of the economic past.[19]

Here, in these four lectures, we find the nearest that Charlie ever came to a general economic treatise. The first lecture, on Engel's Law, is really about the theory of economic development, emphasizing its inherently unbalanced nature. The second, on the Iron Law of Wages, extends his earlier embrace of the Lewis model as a framework for thinking about economic growth. The third, on Gresham's Law, brings money into the picture: "With two or more monies, we are subject to the instability of Gresham's law. Any attempt to limit ourselves to one money is likely to be thwarted by the market's need for different monies for different purposes and its capacity to create them." And the final lecture, on the Law of One Price, takes as its theme the tendency for market expansion and integration, in commodity markets and also money and capital markets, with the result that the increasingly single world market implies a single world price. The central challenge in such a world is political: "while the optimum scale of economic activity is getting larger and larger, the optimum social scale appears to be shrinking."[20] It is the same challenge Charlie had brought with him into academia back in 1948: universalism versus individual interest, and long-run economics versus short-run politics.

It is against this background that we must read Charlie's three major works of economic history: *The World in Depression* (1973), *Manias, Panics, and Crashes* (1978), and *A Financial History of Western Europe* (1984). The latter two are explicitly works of comparative economic history, written as exemplars of the method he now wished publically to evangelize, but we can read the first in that frame as well. Written starting in fall 1969 and finished in spring 1971, it is perhaps significant that he took on the project more or less at the very moment of his abortive defense of fixed exchange rates at the Boston Fed conference in October 1969. Taken together, this trilogy can be read as Charlie's attempt to use history to improve economic

---

[19]   Kindleberger (1989a, ix, xi).
[20]   Kindleberger (1989a, 63, 87).

analysis specifically on international money, and also specifically as a substitute for existing high-powered theory, mathematical modeling, and statistical testing in his chosen field of specialty.

The World in Depression, 1929–1939 (hereafter *WID*) is many things, but first and foremost it is an attempt to improve economic analysis by testing the monetarist model against a variety of facts in different contexts. Indeed, chapter 7 of Milton Friedman and Anna Jacobson Schwartz's *A Monetary History of the United States, 1867–1960* (1963), wherein they propose a monetarist explanation of what they call "The Great Contraction, 1929–33," serves as a kind of stalking horse for the entire book. Already on the second page of the introduction, Charlie is taking off the gloves: "Friedman's explanation of the 1929 worldwide great depression is national, monetary, related to a policy decision. It is uni-causal. In my judgement it is wrong."[21]

At MIT, of course, attacking monetarism was no danger – quite the reverse. Indeed, one imagines that such an attack might well have served as helpful cover for Charlie's evident deviation from the standard MIT methodological commitments. In due time, his book attracted a scathing review by Anna J. Schwartz herself in the pages of the *Journal of Political Economy*, more or less a badge of honor for an MIT man: "Some friends thought I should have replied to the review. Absolutely not. Let the market decide."[22] And so it did. Subsequently, a second revised and enlarged edition was published in 1986, and in 2013 the original edition was reissued on its fortieth anniversary.

When the book was first published, economist reviewers bemoaned the lack of analytical apparatus (while historian reviewers regretted the lack of any new facts). Perhaps remembering those critical responses, economic historians J. Bradford DeLong and Barry Eichengreen, in their introduction to the 40th Anniversary Edition, propose an implicit analytical framework in the work of Hyman Minsky: "The Minsky paradigm emphasizing the possibility of self-reinforcing booms and busts is the implicit organizing framework of *The World in Depression*. It comes to the

---

[21] Kindleberger (2013, 20).
[22] Schwartz (1975), Kindleberger (1991a, 179, 205).

fore in all its explicit glory in Kindleberger's subsequent book and summary statement of the approach, *Manias, Panics, and Crashes.*[23]

But in *WID* Charlie never cites Minsky, neither in the 1973 original nor in the 1986 second edition. Indeed, he seems not even to have known of Minsky in 1973 – though certainly he did by the time of the second edition, and yet still chose not to cite him. Deepening the puzzle, it is certainly true that Minsky figures centrally in the 1978 *Manias, Panics, and Crashes*, although not quite for the purpose that DeLong and Eichengreen suggest, as we will see. Even more, it is also true that Charlie promoted Minsky explicitly in his role as coeditor of a conference volume *Financial Crises, Theory, History and Policy* (1982), for which Minsky offered the lead paper. So why no mention in the 1986 revision of *WID*?

We find the answer in Charlie's comment on Minsky's contribution to an October 1981 MIT seminar on "Banking and Industry in the Inter-war Period":

> Minsky's model (1984) of the impact of the credit system on the prices of financial assets, and their repercussions back on banking, credit and income, is much richer than the simple monetary model. *It is none the less limited, as Minsky indicates:* it is limited to the United States; there are no capital movements, no exchange rates, no international commodity prices, nor even any impact of price changes on bank liquidity for domestic commodities; all assets are financial. In combination, these limitations mean that Minsky is not interested in the communication of the collapse of stock-market prices to commodity markets between September and December 1929, or in the further pressure on United States, German and gold-bloc prices from the depreciation of sterling in September 1931.[24]

This "communication" in 1929 and "further pressure" in 1931 were, as we shall see, central to Kindleberger's own understanding of the Depression at the world level, whereas Minsky's analytical lens had been quite specifically developed instead to illuminate postwar business cycles within the United States. Minsky and Kindleberger were thus certainly fellow travelers, both of them discontent with the standard

---

[23] DeLong and Eichengreen (2013, 6).
[24] Kindleberger (1985c, 301–302), my emphasis.

analytical frameworks, and both looking to forge their own alternative. But we seriously underestimate Kindleberger if we see him merely as an international extension or adaptation of Minsky.

Instead, if we want to understand *WID*, we need to read it in the context of Charlie's own intellectual development as the work of a man trying to understand the events of his own formative years, bringing to bear his subsequent life experience as a central banker as well as twenty years of teaching. Charlie himself suggests as much in his autobiographical reminiscences published in his preface to the book.[25] But I would go further to suggest, as well, the importance of Charlie's wartime experience as an intelligence analyst. His method in the book is recognizably more or less exactly that of an intelligence analyst, combing through an enormous volume of field reports in order to form his own synthetic view of the overall state of play, the telling detail often revealing the underlying structure better than the mass of official statistics. And I would also suggest the importance of his immediate postwar experience at the Department of State, working on reconstruction first of Germany and then of Europe more generally. Intimately involved as he had been in these experiences of the United States shouldering responsibility when no one else could, he was especially attuned to the consequences of its failure to do so in 1929.

"The main lesson of the interwar years," Charlie states in the concluding pages of *WID*, is that "for the world economy to be stabilized, there has to be a stabilizer, one stabilizer." In the first edition of the book, he emphasizes three particular dimensions of stabilization: "(a) maintaining a relatively open market for distress goods; (b) providing counter-cyclical long-term lending; and (c) discounting in crisis."[26] In the third of these, we hear the central banker, acutely aware of lender-of-last-resort responsibility in times of liquidity crisis. But in the first two we also see the sadder

---

[25] Kindleberger (2013, 16). In the second edition, he adds two additional paragraphs of reminiscence that were "cut out at the last minute on the basis of advice from a colleague that I now regard as misguided" (1986a, xv). The offending paragraphs are the second and third, pp. xvii–xviii, concerning a two week stint he spent in March 1928 as a runner for a Wall Street brokerage house.

[26] Kindleberger (1973, 304, 292). See also Kindleberger (1987b, 58), and Chapter 4 n. 39.

and wiser central banker, having learned from experience that mere liquidity provision only buys time and does nothing much to address underlying imbalances in (a) commodity markets and (b) capital markets. Indeed, imbalances in both of these markets were, so Charlie had argued earlier in the book, exactly the challenge faced by the Bank of England starting in 1929, a challenge that ultimately proved too much for it to handle: "In 1929, 1930, and 1931 Britain could not act as a stabilizer, and the United States would not."[27] The result was the collapse of the international monetary system.

"By way of apology," says Charlie in the self-deprecating way of the WASP, "I find the key to why the depression was so wide, so deep, and so long in my specialty, the international monetary mechanism. This should surprise no one." The biographical truth, of course, is more or less the opposite since, as we have seen, he chose the international monetary mechanism as his specialty precisely because of his life experience with the depression. In this respect, it is significant that he dedicates the book to the memory of his father, "who struggled with great courage against a physical handicap, and against the Great Depression."[28] This book was personal to him, perhaps the most personal thing he ever wrote, not excluding his autobiography. Written as Charlie was on his way out of a department and a profession where increasingly he found himself "on its fringes," the book seems originally to have been conceived as a culminating academic achievement, a kind of completion of the intellectual journey he had begun in 1929, and continued at Columbia 1933–6 and the New York Fed 1936–9. When he mentions economists at the Fed "producing proposals for an ultimate demonetization of gold, and suggestions of taxes and other devices to contain hot money," he is talking about himself (see Chapter 3).[29]

---

[27] Kindleberger (1986, 290).
[28] Kindleberger (1973, 305, 292, 18). It is perhaps significant that he includes in the index an entry for S. Murgatroyd, just as he had done in the 1937 thesis to reference the dates of his engagement and marriage, but there seems to be a typo. In the 1973 book, page 261 references the 1936 Tripartite Agreement (his engagement) but the 1937 increase in reserve requirements (his marriage) is referenced on page 266 not 253.
[29] Kindleberger (1973, 270).

Written before the breakdown of Bretton Woods, when Charlie still believed that the dollar system could be made to work, *WID* was only published after the shift to flexible exchange rates, with all the ensuing instability. Although finished in spring 1971, the book's publication was delayed until 1973, so Charlie tells us, because the German publisher did not want the English original to come out before the German translation. Quite by accident, the timing turned out to be perfect, as readers looking to understand the instability of the new world found obvious analogy with the instability of the 1930s. Charlie seemed to have been prescient, anticipating the future that lay ahead and warning of its danger. The result was that, instead of being the culmination of his academic career, the book opened the possibility of a new chapter, which Charlie characteristically grabbed with both hands.

Just so, soon after the book's publication, we see Charlie making room for a new life chapter in his decision to turn over his two successful textbooks to others, Peter Lindert taking *International Economics* and Bruce Herrick taking *Economic Development*. (Lindert's Cornell dissertation on pre-World War I key currencies had caught Charlie's attention, as did also Herrick's MIT dissertation on the Chilean development experience.[30]) And we see him developing his chops for the new adventure in the essays in *Economic Response* and the lectures in *Economic Laws*, as mentioned above. The comparative historical method he promoted in these books is exactly the method he would use subsequently for his own specialty, first in *Manias, Panics, and Crashes* and then finally in *The Financial History of Western Europe*. In the event, it was this latter book, not *WID*, that would become his culminating academic achievement.

The 1986 revision of *WID*, Charlie says, was his idea not the publisher's. In context, we can imagine that he wanted to draw the attention of readers of his subsequent books back to the first. The revised edition explicitly responds to critics of the first, both monetarist and Keynesian, but the central narrative remains unchanged. In the first edition, Friedman's monetarism was the main target; in the second edition,

[30] Lindert (1969), Herrick (1966).

standard Keynesianism in the person of his own student Peter Temin gets equal treatment for its wrong-headed uni-causal frame.[31]

> My real purpose, related to the foregoing, is, I suppose, an evangelical one. I have failed to persuade large numbers of scholars . . . Other themes of the original book have been ignored rather than refuted. These include the importance of the liquidity squeeze caused by the stock market collapse of October 1929 for commodity prices, which dropped worldwide by 12 to 20 percent in the year from August 1929 to August 1930; the importance of irreversible price declines for bank failures; the deflationary impact on the United States, Germany, and the gold bloc of the sharp depreciation of the pound sterling (causing appreciation of the dollar, the Reichsmark, and the gold currencies) by 30 percent from September to December 1931.[32]

The themes ignored by his monetarist and Keynesian critics, it will be recognized, are exactly the themes that were ignored by Minsky. Here, however, the main difficulty, as he explicitly notes, is the unwillingness of his monetarist and Keynesian critics to venture outside the bounds of the standard IS–LM model, not a difficulty suffered by Minsky. Importantly, these themes were not ignored by contemporaneous observers: "the conventional wisdom of the period was not as wrong as most economists believe in its concern with the dangers of speculation, the necessity to raise prices, the desirability of lowering tariffs, and the need to stabilize exchange rates."[33] Who is he talking about? Readers knowledgeable about Charlie's life will note his appreciative references to Ralph Robey, James Angell, and John H. Williams.

---

[31] Kindleberger (1986a, 5). Taking this criticism apparently to heart, Temin (1989) subsequently moved considerably in Charlie's direction, addressing specifically Charlie's emphasis on commodity prices in 1929 and the devaluation of sterling in 1931 (Temin 1989, 55, 75). But the focus remains on the policy response in individual countries and not on the dynamics of the international system.

[32] Kindleberger (1986a, xiv).

[33] Kindleberger (1986a, 11). This is not an isolated quotation. Also: "the conventional wisdom was, in this judgment, correct" (p. 72); "it is hard to avoid the conclusion that there is something to the conventional wisdom" (p. 116); "there is much to be said for the conventional wisdom of the period" (p. 136); "Contemporaneous conventional wisdom in the early 1930s thought falling commodity and asset prices important" (p. 169).

Charlie's objective in *WID* is thus quite explicitly to use the historical experience of the Great Depression to cast doubt on the generality of monetarist and Keynesian orthodoxy and also to make room for alternative views, specifically a reconsidered version of the conventional wisdom of his youth. The analytical essence of the alternative he favored, however, remained substantially underdeveloped in the first edition, which may be why readers missed it, and it is only quite briefly signaled by additions to the second edition. In the latter, for example, we find one added paragraph on the importance of commodity dealer finance (p. 113) and two added pages on what he now explicitly terms the "ratchet" theory of interaction between exchange rate instability and worldwide deflation (pp. 226, 294). Both of these themes he would develop at greater length elsewhere;[34] but apparently he decided not to overburden the 1986 revision with them, so leaving the impression that he was merely offering a backward-looking defense of his own teachers.

The biggest substantive change in the second edition was in its conclusion, where the original three stabilizing functions are now extended to five, and printed as a numbered list:[35]

(1) Maintaining a relatively open market for distress goods;
(2) Providing countercyclical, or at least stable, long-term lending;
(3) Policing a relatively stable system of exchange rates;
(4) Ensuring the coordination of macroeconomic policies;
(5) Acting as a lender of last resort by discounting or otherwise providing liquidity in financial crisis.

The new stabilizing functions are (3) and (4), added by Charlie to take account of the experience with flexible exchange rates in the years after the first edition. The world had for a while embraced flexible exchange rates as a way to avoid the necessity of macroeconomic policy coordination, but experience showed that goal to have been illusory. Under the gold standard of the nineteenth century, exchange stability and macroeconomic coordination had been implicit; to the extent that the Bank of England took responsibility for managing the gold standard, both were

---

[34] Kindleberger (1999, ch. 1; 1990, ch. 13).
[35] Kindleberger (1986a, 289).

implicitly part of the Bank's more general responsibility for stabilization. Under an alternative standard, whether a revived dollar standard or something else, that responsibility would need to be made explicit, and that's why Charlie added to his list.

The other changes to the list are small edits to (2) and (5), which reflect the evolution of Charlie's thinking about long-term capital flows. While retaining his observation that the sterling system worked in part because of stabilizing countercyclical capital flows and that the dollar system failed in part because of destabilizing procyclical capital flows, he now sees merely stable capital flows as maybe the best that can be achieved, business investment and public investment both taking a long view independent of the cycle. Further, now lacking the prospective support of countercyclical capital flows, he understandably sees the need to embrace a wider range of liquidity measures, not just the discount window.

None of these edits changed the basic thrust of the argument. The updated conclusions merely ensure that busy generals who jump to the end of the intelligence analyst's report get what they need for the decisions they have to make. The important question in Charlie's mind remained that of who exactly those busy generals would be: Americans if the future is a revived dollar system, some other nationality if not, but ideally the leadership of a newly empowered set of international institutions, "a world central bank, a world capital market, and an effective General Agreement on Tariffs and Trade."[36] This last, because it would require cession of economic sovereignty, was perhaps the least likely in the short run, but nonetheless worth working toward. Economics and politics remain, as always, inextricably intertwined.

The narrative of *WID* is straightforward. The first chapters set the scene. The heritage of war, Charlie says, posed a problem of excess production, which put incipient downward pressure on commodity prices, but that could have been managed if macroeconomic stability had been preserved. Unfortunately, a further heritage of war was the unresolved business of reparations and war debts, plus postwar overvaluation of the pound and undervaluation of the French franc, all of which

---

[36] Kindleberger (1986a, 305).

stood in the way of sustained international lending.[37] With the private market mechanism for absorbing shocks thus blocked, it would be up to policymakers to act, and, when they didn't, the result was disaster.

The role of the stock market boom and crash was to reveal this underlying vulnerability. First the boom undermined long-term capital movement, reversing needed capital outflows and instead drawing in capital from all over the world, and especially from London. Subsequent credit squeeze, as foreign lenders withdrew short-term credit against stock market collateral (so-called "call money"), then caused the stock market crash of 1929. The real problem came as that credit squeeze was subsequently "communicated" to commodity markets, as banks withdrew their finance of burgeoning inventories built up in the boom years, forcing liquidation. To its credit, the New York Fed made some effort to meet the liquidity crisis, albeit thwarted somewhat by resistance from the Board of Governors, and for a while it looked like the economy might be recovering. But by then the commodity price decline had already internationalized the crisis, as developing countries dependent on commodity exports, typically unable to borrow to fill their export earnings gap, cut back on imports and devalued. The Fed's halting efforts did not even begin to reach that dimension of the crisis and so it kept rolling, initially in the periphery but ultimately reaching the core, where short-term borrowing had for a while sustained imports in the face of reduced export earning.

The key to the second stage of the crisis was the subsequent collapse of long-term capital flows as a consequence of credit-quality deterioration, which made it impossible for the core to refinance their cumulated short-term borrowing. The resulting balance of payments problems hit first Austria, then Germany, and finally Great Britain. Given the centrality of sterling in the international monetary system, Britain's devaluation in September 1931 dealt a further deflationary shock to the world, since it amounted to an involuntary appreciation of other currencies, which hit the United States especially hard since the gold bloc responded by converting dollars into gold. Note that this is not so much a story of contagion from one country to another as it is a story of how a common

---

[37] Kindleberger (1973, 295).

international shock affected different countries differently, depending on their own particular financial and political context.[38] The result was that commodity prices fell farther, with the consequence of widespread bank failure as farmers defaulted on their loans. The Depression, which had begun with a liquidity squeeze potentially controllable by timely lender-of-last-resort intervention, was now beyond the capacity of central banking to stem. Breakdown of the international monetary system meant breakdown of international trade, retreat to currency blocs, and inefficient national production.

In 1933, no less a figure than Keynes attempted to put a brave face on matters by publically embracing so-called "National Self-Sufficiency" and, after Roosevelt torpedoed the 1933 World Economic Conference, that became the credo of the United States as well.[39] What followed was the era of "hot money" as speculators sought safe haven first in one and then another currency. Only in 1936, with the Tripartite Agreement, was there the beginning of an attempt to put the international monetary system back together again, but war preparations meant that it came to nothing much.

That's the story Charlie tells in *WID*, and it is compelling enough in its own right. But he does not just want to understand the depression. Equally important, he wants to use that understanding as a test of standard economic models, specifically monetarism. Friedman and Schwartz of course blamed the whole thing on mistaken Fed monetary policy, specifically deliberate contraction of the money supply. Charlie's main counterargument concerns the timing of changes in the money supply relative to changes in prices:

> Monetarists may be interested in contemplating a quotation from the *Federal Reserve Bulletin* of June 1938, p. 437: "The events of 1929 taught us that the absence of any rise in prices did not prove that no crisis was pending. 1937 has taught us that an abundant supply of gold and a cheap money policy do not prevent prices from falling."[40]

---

[38] Ferguson and Temin (2003) usefully flesh out the details of the German case.
[39] Keynes (1933).
[40] Kindleberger (1973, 272 n. 11; 1986a, 271). In both editions, the page reference is incorrectly given as p. 437, instead of p. 456. Further, the quoted passage is actually

More generally, Charlie suggests that the world Depression was so wide, so deep, and so long not because of mistaken policy intervention, but rather because of market instability that overwhelmed the capacity of policymakers to act. The key to the disaster was not any inherent instability of markets, but rather the overwhelming of policymakers; and that happened because the two shocks, in 1929 and 1931, came at a delicate moment when the system was in transition from sterling to the dollar and from Great Britain to the United States as leader of the international monetary system. In Charlie's view, the shocks to the system, even as large as they were, could have been stemmed by timely and vigorous intervention, but that would have required leadership for which the United States was unprepared. Importantly, mere central bank cooperation would not have been enough.[41]

In all of this, we see Charlie looking at the world through the eyes of a sometime central banker – a lens shared by essentially none of his economist colleagues, Keynesians no more than monetarists. Instead, they looked at the world through the lens of their models. Referencing the first phase of the Depression, Charlie insists: "There is no way in which these price declines can be connected with a mechanism that goes through either the quantity theory of money, since money aggregates barely changed at all, or through Keynesian effects on spending by consumers, with or without wealth in consumption functions"; "It cannot be contended that Keynesian analysis explains the 1930s any better than monetarism"; "No monetarist or Keynesian model can account for such precipitous declines … A point on which I insist, but one neglected by virtually all other observers, is that the decline in stock prices was communicated to commodity prices through the banking system."[42]

And yet his economist colleagues remained unconvinced. The reason, so Charlie came to believe, was that there was no place in their models for

---

from the 8th *Annual Report* of the Bank of International Settlements (where it can be found on p. 11), from which an extensive excerpt is reprinted in the Fed's *Bulletin*. The sentiment expressed is thus not the Fed's alone, but rather that of the entire world central banking community more generally.

[41] This, despite Charlie's abiding respect and affection for his former brothers-in-arms at the New York Fed, as noted in Clarke (1967) and Coombs (1976). On the latter, see his glowing review (Kindleberger 1977c) and Kindleberger (1978b, 204–205).

[42] Kindleberger (1985c, 269, 290, 303).

the mechanisms on which he insisted: "The empty debate between [monetarists] Friedman and Schwartz and [Keynesian] Temin ... focuses on a model with no international capital movements, no commodity prices, no prices of financial assets."[43] Faced with the incomprehension of his economist colleagues, Charlie seems to have come to the conclusion that he needed a model in order to beat a model. That's why, when Martin Mayer brought his attention to the Minsky model, he decided to take it up, and subject it to the same "testing against the facts in a variety of contexts." That's what *Manias, Panics, and Crashes* is all about. As in *WID*, Charlie states his conclusion up front: "The general validity of the Minsky model will be established in the chapters that follow."[44]

In *Economic Response*, introducing a long list of potential topics ripe for comparative economic history treatment, Charlie notes that the list "omits a discussion of financial crises on which I am currently engaged, as I have no interest in encouraging competition."[45] He is talking about *Manias, Panics, and Crashes: A History of Financial Crises* (hereafter *MPC*) published in the same year, dedicated "To the MIT Old Guard of the 1940s ... in gratitude for support and friendship." The Great Depression is only one of the historical cases he discusses – actually two, as he distinguishes 1929 and 1931 – as he treats also essentially all examples he could find reaching back to 1720. We can understand *MPC* thus as an attempt to extend the analysis of *WID* in both time and space in a search for a possible regular historical pattern. The titles of the core chapters of the book (chs. 3–7) report the pattern that Charlie found: "Speculative Manias," "Fueling the Flames: Monetary Expansion," "The Emergence of Swindles," "The Critical Stage," and "International Propagation."

The pattern is this: Some kind of "displacement" gets the thing going initially; the ensuing "mania" is then a speculative bubble fueled by credit expansion, with "financial distress" emerging at the peak; followed possibly by "panic," in which the bubble bursts and credit contracts. The monetary dimension of the process comes from the fact that typically

---

[43] Kindleberger (1985c, 303).
[44] Kindleberger (1978b, 20).
[45] Kindleberger (1978a, 10).

some of the credit expansion involves creation of money substitutes, and typically the panic then involves a flight from speculative assets and the new forms of money into money proper issued by a central bank. On the bright side, it is this feature of financial crisis that offers the central bank the opportunity to allay the panic by timely and forceful lender-of-last-resort intervention.

Writing in 1978, after the breakdown of Bretton Woods and in the midst of the unhappy experience with flexible exchange rates, Charlie was particularly interested in the international dimension of financial crises, so much so that he explicitly limited his historical cases on that basis. Given the willful destruction of Bretton Woods by the United States, there was a real question regarding whether there was any international lender of last resort. Public statements by Henry Reuss, Chairman of the House Banking and Currency Committee, and Arthur F. Burns, Chairman of the Board of Governors of the Federal Reserve System, suggested that the United States might be unwilling to serve, just as it had been in 1931: "The danger is that they mean what they say, and that in a future crisis, as in 1931, countries and international organizations will try to shrug the responsibility of international stability off onto others."[46]

It will be observed that, in this account of the central argument of *MPC*, I have yet to mention Minsky. The reason is that Charlie himself is at pains to insist that the pattern he finds in these historical examples is not so much a validation of the *specifics* of the Minsky model, but more generally a vindication of an entire tradition of economic thought, "held by many economists prior to 1940, that has unaccountably slipped into disrepute during the Keynesian revolution and then monetarist counter-revolution. A notable up-to-date exception is Hyman Minsky."[47] Even Charlie's much-admired mentor Alvin Hansen comes in for criticism on this score, insofar as it was his influential promulgation of the Keynesian revolution that dismissed the earlier generation's emphasis on the instability of credit: "A study of manias, bubbles, crashes, panics, and the lender of last resort helps us to move from classical thesis

---

[46] Kindleberger (1978b, 208, 226).
[47] Kindleberger (1978b, 72).

through revisionist antithesis [such as Hansen] to a more balanced synthesis. Or so I claim."[48]

From this perspective, the attraction of the Minsky model is not only that it dresses old wisdom in modern garb, but also that it represents one step on the road toward a more balanced synthesis, albeit not the last step. Minsky's scathing review of Peter Temin's 1976 *Did Monetary Forces Cause the Great Depression?* would have revealed to Charlie that Minsky was a fellow traveler, discontent with both monetarist and Keynesian orthodoxy.[49] Says Charlie, "Neglect of the instability of credit began by and large with the depression of the 1930s, with the Currency and Banking Schools converted into monetarists and Keynesians." What is needed is not the ongoing "dialectical symbiosis" in which these two warring schools were presently locked, but rather a dialectical synthesis. Charlie offers his own: "Our conclusion is that money supply should be fixed over the long run but be elastic during the short run crisis."[50]

In the end, Charlie thus presents his own work *not* as a heterodox alternative to standard Keynesian or monetarist theory, as Minsky did, but rather as a complement to them: "The Keynesian and Friedmanite schools, along with most modern macroeconomic theories that synthesize them, are perhaps not so much wrong as incomplete."[51] Some people think markets work well all the time, and others that they work terribly most of the time. Charlie took a middle position: "Markets generally work, but occasionally they break down. When they do, they require government intervention to provide the public good of stability."[52]

For Charlie, Minsky is thus useful primarily because he is a "lineal descendant" of the older classical model, generalizing its insights "in modern terms," but only to that extent.[53] He is careful to distance himself from Minsky's notion that the modern US financial system is "unstable, fragile, and prone to crisis," as well as "his emphasis on the fragility of the

---

[48] Kindleberger (1978b, 70, 13).
[49] Minsky (1976).
[50] Kindleberger (1978b, 70, 55, 12).
[51] Kindleberger (1978b, 23).
[52] Kindleberger (1978b, 15, 21, 8, 15, 220, 6).
[53] Kindleberger (1978b, 15, 21).

monetary system and its propensity to disaster": "We need not take seriously novelists like Erdman, nor accept uncritically the predictions of Minsky." This last is apparently a reference to Paul Erdman, who started his successful career writing financial thrillers with his 1976 publication *The Crash of '79.*

Charlie is further always careful to distance himself from the "pessimistic, even lugubrious" side of Minsky, and not just because Charlie himself was basically an optimistic and cheerful personality.[54] The more fundamental reason comes down to his belief that lender of last resort not only can stay a panic, but also that general awareness of the lender-of-last-resort function can even prevent panics and so forestall crises, allowing speculation to die out gradually rather than necessarily ending in a catastrophic collapse. In his view, dependable lender-of-last-resort backstop at the domestic level is the reason that domestic panics have become much less common. And uncertainty about lender of last resort at the international level is the reason that international panics have become more common.[55]

For Charlie, Minsky goes too far in emphasizing inherent fragility, but it is important to appreciate that in other respects Charlie thought that Minsky did not go far enough. Emphasizing business credit from banks within the United States, Minsky's model was intended quite narrowly to be a financial model of the US business cycle. By contrast, Charlie's interest is mainly in the financial crisis that sometimes comes at the peak of a business cycle, and he is interested in all kinds of financial crises, especially those with international dimensions. Further, and importantly, he is interested in the instability of credit quite generally, not just business and bank credit: "Before banks had evolved, and afterward, additional means of payment to fund a speculative mania were available in the virtually infinitely expansible nature of personal credit."[56]

The mechanism of instability that Charlie emphasizes is also different. Whereas Minsky emphasizes positive feedbacks between business spending on investment and subsequent expansion of aggregate income and

---

[54] Kindleberger (1978b, 15).
[55] Kindleberger (1978b, 215–220).
[56] Kindleberger (1978b, 16).

business profit, Charlie puts his emphasis squarely on speculative price bubbles and on positive feedbacks in prices that reinforce both mania on the upside and panic on the downside, which is to say that he is interested in capital gains and losses, not operating profits from business. For Charlie, it is the asymmetric response to price changes that accounts for changes in aggregate income; nothing ensures that the response of those who benefit from price change will net out against the response of those who are hurt. Destabilizing speculation is his central theme, resulting in "over-trading" at the top and requiring lender of last resort when the bubble bursts.

To be sure, Charlie does sometimes allow himself to get swept up in the human drama of financial crisis, as well as the inevitable psychological element of that drama. Just so, the swindles he describes so lovingly in chapter 5 of *MPC* are, he insists, "demand-determined," which is to say that in the grip of mania the demand for swindles brings forth its own supply. Such is the human condition. Nevertheless, having had his fun, Charlie is also careful to insist that financial crisis remains essentially an economic phenomenon. The important positive feedbacks occur in the mechanics of the credit system, which have their own logic, quite separate from the dopamine feedback that overcomes individual speculators.

What about the present prospects for crisis? Writing in 1978, Charlie insists that the "Minsky model" fits very well the unstable market for foreign exchange in the flexible exchange rate world and also the burgeoning market for developing country debt. Will these be the next financial crises? Charlie won't say: "I do not forecast world economic collapse, because I think that our profession of economics does not know the dynamics of the system well enough to do so."[57] Uncertainty about whether the United States will act when needed as international lender of last resort, however, certainly suggests that financial crisis will remain, in the words of his chapter 1 title, "A Hardy Perennial," as would Charlie's historical account of past financial crises. He himself published three more editions of *MPC*, each one updated with new crises. After Charlie's death, Robert Aliber took over for three more editions, and as of this writing an eighth edition is anticipated in 2022, now with Robert McCauley (a student of Charlie's from 1978) taking the reins. A hardy perennial indeed.

[57] Kindleberger (1978b, 220).

Chef d'Oeuvre

A competent military officer is a generalist who can solve all kinds of problems.[1]

The whole point of *MPC* was to bring attention to a neglected line of economic thought that had focused on the instability of credit. But that was just the first step. Charlie's larger ambition was to use his new comparative historical method to test economic theory in his own specialty more generally, with the aim of establishing foundations on which a more adequate understanding of the international monetary system could be built. This is the explicit goal of his next book, *A Financial History of Western Europe* (hereafter *FHWE*), though almost all readers seem to have missed it. In the first paragraph of the introduction, he states quite plainly the objective of the book: "ranging economic theories against the facts of history and, if possible, *deriving theories from accumulated fact.*"[2]

In Charlie's mind, this book was to be his culminating treatise on international money, and, if we want to understand it, that is how we must attempt to read it. After the fact, Charlie realized that the project was "perhaps excessively ambitious" and so perhaps less successful than he had hoped.[3] Reviewers of the book who read it merely as a reference work of economic history can thus be forgiven. Even so, there is a reason that Charlie called this book his "chef d'oeuvre." Reading the book through

---

[1] Kindleberger (1991a, 70).
[2] Kindleberger (1984a, 1), my emphasis. The dedication, "To SMK once more, after forty-five years, with feeling," explicitly links this book with his first.
[3] "Economist Development," p. 18. KPMD Box 19, "The Economist and the Academy."

Charlie's eyes, in the context of all his previous output, perhaps we can synthesize and reconstruct what he was trying to do.

The book had its origin, so Charlie tells us, in lecture notes for a course he taught only twice: first at the University of Texas at Austin in Spring 1979, and second at MIT in Fall 1980. At Austin, in effect he was taking up the challenge of his wartime buddy Walt Rostow, who had claimed that there was no proper monetary theory prior to 1914 because money and finance were entirely passive until then, not the prime movers of economic events that they would later become.[4] Charlie finds, quite to the contrary, a rich mine of materials produced in and concerning exactly that pre-1914 period, which materials he uses to derive the theory that he then uses to understand post-1914. I say "finds," but in fact Charlie had been teaching European economic history regularly for years and was already familiar with much of the material. What is new is his ambition to use that historical material explicitly to test the limitations of existing theories (i.e., monetarist and Keynesian theories) and to derive new, more robust ones.

The Gerschenkronian themes of banking and the state, now renamed "Finance" and "War Finance," are the prime movers of Charlie's narrative, and a central theme throughout is finance as "an independent force for good or ill": "War is a hothouse and places enormous strain on resources, which finance is used to mobilize. Financial innovation occurs in wartime." The innovation that he has in mind concerns institutional change: "New men, new ways of doing things threatened the old." Not for nothing does he give his old teacher Wesley Clair Mitchell pride of place in the epigram to the first chapter. Says Mitchell: "Cannot economic history be organized most effectively around the evolution of pecuniary history?" Mitchell's empiricism, as founder and research director of the National Bureau of Economics Research, had been quantitative and statistical. Charlie's own empiricism was otherwise, as he says: "it is not my style, and statistics do not on most aspects of the subject go back far."[5] Instead, comparative economic history was Charlie's way of carrying on

---

[4] See extended quote of Rostow (1978) at Kindleberger (1984a, 3).
[5] Kindleberger (1984a, 3, 5, 8, 1, xvii).

the American institutionalist tradition, improving on his teachers, as all good students do.

Banking and the state are the prime movers of Charlie's financial history, but puzzlingly the book is not mostly arranged as a chronological narrative. An appendix to the introductory chapter offers us four "chronologies" – War, Monetary Events, Banking Landmarks, and Financial Events – but that's just a list of dates with no connecting narrative. What follows are three parts (totaling 285 pages), which treat "Money," "Banking," and "Finance," respectively. The purpose of this unexpected organization, apparently, is to derive theory from accumulated fact in each of these three areas. The final two parts (totaling 175 pages) then treat "The Interwar Period" and "After World War II." The point of these parts is to use the derived theory to make sense of the financial events of Charlie's own life – incredible events that he himself had witnessed and had struggled to make sense of contemporaneously.

Regarding "Money," the story Charlie tells in Part One "is one of continuous innovation" driven by persistent shortage of metallic currency. One driver of this shortage was trade with the East, for a long time a sink for precious metals of all kinds; another driver was war. Historically, financial innovation was the answer to shortage, most importantly the bill of exchange, followed by deposit banking, and then the bank note. Each of these, Charlie emphasizes, was an innovation by merchants themselves to meet their own immediately pressing need, and in each case the innovation was some kind of credit instrument to substitute for the shortage of metal: "The point to be emphasized is that when a market lacks money sufficient for its needs it takes steps to correct the deficiency."[6]

The bill of exchange came first, Charlie explains, as a way of shifting clearing balances at one medieval fair into the future and to the next fair, rather than insisting on settlement in metallic currency.[7] The essential quality of money is thus revealed to be means of payment: a means of exchange for buying goods today and a store of value for settling payments promised in the future.[8] Metallic currency serves both functions,

[6] Kindleberger (1984a, 24).
[7] Kindleberger (1984a, 36–41).
[8] Kindleberger (1984a, 19).

of course, and we can therefore consider bills of exchange as a means of economizing on the use of that currency by permitting a small amount of currency to facilitate a larger amount of trade. Alternatively, and perhaps more helpfully, we can consider the bill of exchange as just a new form of money, invented by merchants in order to facilitate mutually beneficial trade that would otherwise be prevented by the shortage of currency. As a substitute for coin, the bill of exchange came first, but, the general principle having been established, it was followed in due course by bank deposits and then bank notes.[9]

Pushing in the opposite direction, the same shortage of metallic currency quite regularly gave rise to various measures by state actors to safeguard the metallic supply and even to augment it through deliberate export promotion policy, measures that collectively came to be known as "mercantilism." Similar mercantilist impulses show up throughout subsequent history: in the Bullion Report of 1810, in the Currency School thinking that informed the English Bank Act of 1844, and, indeed, in modern world monetarism as espoused by Arthur Laffer and Robert Mundell. Thus, from the very beginning monetary debate proceeded with "expansionists" on the one side and "contractionists" on the other. The debate between the Keynesians and the monetarists is just the most recent iteration of this perennial debate, and like previous iterations it also reflects the reality of continuous (private) financial innovation posed against continuous (public) opposition to that innovation.[10]

For Charlie, Gresham's Law provides a way to push beyond this perennial dialectical opposition to a higher-level synthesis. Yes, shortage of money regularly gives rise to new forms of money, but this solution creates a new problem since inevitably users compare the new with the old and then shift from one to the other in anticipation of changes in their relative price, causing instability that calls for management: "The problem is virtually insoluble: two or more monies are needed to perform different tasks, but two or more monies are unstable." Charlie's account of bimetallism revolves around precisely this instability: "Instead of the mint price stabilizing the market price, the market price, responding to

---

[9] Kindleberger (1984a, 50).
[10] Kindleberger (1984a, 8).

changes largely in supplies of precious metals, has destabilized the mint price through the workings of Gresham's Law."[11]

In historical practice, the problem of bimetallism was solved by demonetization of silver and adoption of the gold standard as the single international money. Inevitably, once silver was out of the way, the market then proceeded to create bank money as a new second money: a promise to pay gold instead of gold itself. Meanwhile, states pushed toward a universal money in this international monetary conference and that one, but the effort led nowhere.[12] Instead, what emerged from the Darwinian process of financial evolution was the sterling standard, which used sterling credit as the international currency of commerce.

Under the sterling standard, the destabilizing dynamic of two monies still operated, but crucially now under the management of the Bank of England: "The gold standard was, in effect, a sterling standard, managed and operated by the Bank of England at the center ... Management was required because the market will respond to market restriction, if it gets the bit between its teeth, by creating more money."[13] Charlie ends Part One of *FHWE* with an account of how that system worked:

> The Bank of England set the level of world interest rates, which accounts for the fact that national interest rates moved up and down together, while other countries had power only over a narrow differential between the domestic level and the world rate. With sterling bills traded worldwide, serving as a close substitute for money in foreign countries, and their interest rate manipulated in London, the gold standard was a sterling system.[14]

Here, in the establishment of the sterling standard, as at so many turning points in monetary history, we see an example of what Charlie considers to be "a critical point of monetary theory": "the difference between the Knapp state theory of money (that money is what the state declares it to be and designates as legal tender for debts public and private), and nominalism (that money is what the market uses to fulfill

---

[11] Kindleberger (1984a, 6, 56).
[12] Kindleberger (1984a, 65–68).
[13] Kindleberger (1984a, 68–69).
[14] Kindleberger (1984a, 70).

the purposes of money). States may propose, but markets dispose."[15] In Charlie's view, financial innovations typically arise to meet the needs of the users of money, not from deliberate design by higher political authorities. Indeed, markets quite regularly reject or find ways around deliberate designs. Just so, the Bank Act of 1844 tried to control the money supply by creating a Bank of Issue that had to hold gold against any increase in bank note issue. But the result was just expanded use of bank deposits as a substitute for notes, and that set the stage for the worldwide sterling standard managed by the discount policy of the Bank of England.

In addition to his positive objective to derive useful theory from accumulated fact, Charlie was of course also interested in clearing out nonuseful theories – what he calls "myths." There were a lot of them: the idea that the origin of banking was goldsmiths rather than merchants; the notion that barter historically evolved into the money economy and then the credit economy, whereas in fact all three coexisted from medieval times; and especially the idea that changes in the general level of prices can be traced to prior changes in the quantity of money (i.e., the quantity theory of money) instead of, as is more usually the case, the reverse. Regarding the latter, Charlie emphasizes that war particularly has been a common driver of prices and the search for gold and silver in the Americas more plausibly a result of high prices than a cause of them.[16]

An especially persistent myth, which therefore merits repeated dismissal in Charlie's account, is the classic specie-flow mechanism posited by Hume (and beloved by economists ever since), which claims that gold flows cause price-level adjustments that equilibrate trade. To the contrary, so Charlie insists, the persistent drain of specie to the East caused no such price-level adjustment, neither deflation in the West nor inflation in the East, and indeed the drain persisted as a continuous strain without noticeable sign of adjustment because of persistent hoarding in the East. The enthusiasm for the specie-flow mechanism by present-day

---

[15] Kindleberger (1984a, 22).

[16] Kindleberger (1984a, 35, 51; 21, 45; 24). On the latter point, Vilar (1976) is his primary source, referenced repeatedly.

world monetarists thus has no basis in historical fact: "Gold movements respond more readily and more frequently to capital flows induced directly by discount rate changes than to changes in price levels and trade balances."[17]

Building on Part One, the central theme of Part Two "Banking" is Gerschenkron's historical hypothesis about the importance of banking for economic development in the moderately backward countries of Europe, by comparison to England. By the time Charlie was writing, Gerschenkron's famous essay of 1952 (published as the lead essay in Gerschenkron 1962) had sparked considerable historical literature by his numerous students and others treating individual cases. It is this literature that provides Charlie with ample hay for processing in Part Two.

The case of Britain, the earliest industrializer, is the paradigm against which all late developers are compared, and accordingly Charlie is at pains to trace the natural history of financial development in that case as a baseline for comparison. War, not any exigency of economic development, was the trigger for Britain's financial revolution, specifically the creation of the Bank of England, and Britain's subsequent repeated success in war against larger opponents traces directly to the success of that financial revolution. By contrast, the subsequent evolution of the British banking system more generally was largely a story of trial and error by market participants that proceeded over centuries; complete financial integration within the country was not achieved until the twentieth century. For Charlie, the central institutional features of the system that emerged from that evolutionary process establish the general rule; one might even say that a theory of banking emerges from all this accumulated fact.

Charlie sketches the outlines of this theory in two pages at the beginning of Part Two. Most important is the evolution from mere deposit banks to "lending banks which actually create deposits or money," since it is that alchemy (my word, not his) that Gerschenkron's late developers purportedly harness for their purposes. Further, the hierarchical geography of banking, in particular the rise of financial centers such as

---

[17] Kindleberger (1984a, 24, 68).

London and the subsequent spread of banking networks to the hinterlands, was not imposed from above, but rather emerged as a natural outcome of trial and error by multiple individual bankers. And finally, the hybrid (my word again) character of the central bank, which functions at the same time as both "the government bank and a bankers' bank with responsibility for monetary policy," emerged from lived experience, as also the role for a lender of last resort and the ultimate location of that role at the Bank of England.[18]

In the British case, banking was mostly connected to commerce, not industry, because the capital needed at the dawn of the Industrial Revolution was small and typically quite easily met by available private family resources. Indeed, in the British case, most banks had their origin in commercial activity, as successful merchants discovered that banking offered an easier and more stable life. The elasticity of bank credit provided essential grease for the wheels of commerce and also the essential mechanism for lender of last resort in times of crisis. The main problem was that understanding of how the system worked lagged behind institutional evolution, a case in point being Lord Overstone who, in the controversy over the Bank Act of 1844, wrote "with the assurance that characterizes many monetarists."[19] (Echoes here of the Depres–Kindleberger–Salant "minority view" of the dollar system.)

By comparison to Britain, the financial development of France lagged for almost a century, even after the establishment of the Crédit Mobilier by the Pereire brothers.[20] Why so? In Charlie's view, it is a case in the first place of premature financial innovation, specifically the banking machinations of John Law in the Mississippi bubble, which "set back the course of banking and bank notes in France more than a century." But it wasn't just him. The innovation of the French assignats to finance the French Revolution, based on land seized from the church, "embedded paranoia about paper money and banks."[21] It was in this context that Saint-Simonianism arose, including

---

[18] Kindleberger (1984a, 73). In other work, I have identified these same three ideas – alchemy, hierarchy, and hybridity – in addition to the instability which Charlie treats in Part One, as the four reasons that money is "difficult" (Mehrling 2017).

[19] Kindleberger (1984a, 85).

[20] Kindleberger (1984a, 113–115).

[21] Kindleberger (1984a, 96, 99).

the idea of using money creation as a strategy for fostering industrial development, but nothing much came of it until the establishment of the Crédit Mobilier, the bank that Gerschenkron singled out as the paradigmatic investment bank later copied by Germany and others. Charlie reads the record differently. It is true that the Crédit Mobilier was a large force in *public* finance, lending for railroads and other public works, not only in France, but also abroad. But it did very little lending to industry, and on that score does not really support the Gerschenkron thesis.[22] Charlie concludes that "France lagged a hundred years behind Britain in money, banking and finance, and that this was both a reflection and a cause of its economic retardation."[23]

According to Charlie, it is Germany, characterized by "particularly close relationships that ran between the great banks and large-scale industry," that best fits the Gerschenkron thesis: "The history that took several hundred years in Britain was telescoped into sixty-five in Germany."[24] What particularly interests Charlie about the German case, however, is the way that banking and the sped-up industrialization that it financed was for a long time held back by lack of monetary unification within the country, which in turn was held back by lack of political unification. Indeed, the whole industrialization process only got started in earnest after 1871, political unification having come in the course of successful war against France. There is a lesson here, so Charlie suggests, for those in contemporary Europe who hope to use monetary integration as a lever to force political integration.[25] History suggests that the reverse order is more typical.

Banking experience in Italy and Spain provides two more negative cases for the Gerschenkron thesis. Banking development there most certainly was in both cases, much of it introduced from France and Germany, but it led to no industrial breakthrough. Instead, "Italy and Spain are seen as 'colonized' by foreign banking by the time of the nineteenth century, as contrasted with institutions that grew up out of

---

[22] Kindleberger (1984a, 109).
[23] Kindleberger (1984a, 115).
[24] Kindleberger (1984a, 129, 212).
[25] Kindleberger (1984a, 117).

local initiatives." "In Spain, and to some extent in Italy, economic development was in fact set back a generation. Banks were needed, but so was an adequate socio-political matrix of laws, regulation and custom in which they operated, and appropriate government policies."[26]

Having thus dispatched with Gerschenkron in Part Two, Charlie's central theme in Part Three – "Finance" – is instead his own alternative historical thesis, which revolves around the centrality of financial booms and busts: "financial crises [which] have tended to appear at roughly ten-year intervals for the last 400 years or so."[27] An important mechanism involved in these crises, according to Charlie, is the international flow of capital, the central role of which has quite typically been overlooked by local historians specialized in the history of their own individual countries. The final chapter of this Part (chapter 15: "Financial Crises") reads as the culminating statement of theory derived from accumulated fact, not only of Part Three but also of the preceding parts as well. It is this theory that Charlie will use as his framework for making sense of the post-World War I chronology that follows.

As in *MPC*, Charlie emphasizes that booms typically begin with some "displacement," which "can be monetary or real." He credits the concept to Minsky, but in fact Minsky never used it; it is pure Kindleberger and, indeed, the central organizing concept for the entire Part Three:[28] "The displacement that gets the most attention in these pages is war and the end of war. War both cuts off old connections in trade and finance, and is likely to require the fashioning of new."[29] In particular, war has often been the impetus for foreign borrowing, which opens channels that remain after the war is over (ch. 12). It is these new channels that bring the boom, as initial trickle subsequently widens the channel to enable eventual flood: "The consequence of limited horizons that change

---

[26] Kindleberger (1984a, 74).

[27] Kindleberger (1984a, 269).

[28] Kindleberger cites Minsky (1982) but neither the word nor the concept appears in that chapter. Elsewhere he speaks of the "stages of a financial crisis, worked out by Hyman Minsky with a small assist from me" (1988a, 110). In his paper for Minsky's festschrift, he thanks Martin Mayer for bringing his attention to Minsky, "who got me to think about instability in financial markets" (1995, 131). On Minsky himself, see Mehrling (1999) and Neilson (2019).

[29] Kindleberger (1984a, 270–271).

discontinuously is that capital flows take place in deep channels (the same is true of migration). Unlike water flowing evenly over a broad surface, capital moves like water in sluices or conduits, ignoring or bypassing better opportunities on occasion, because of the high cost of obtaining information about them."[30]

War cuts new channels, and so too often does the end of war, when the victor imposes an indemnity on the loser (Ch. 13). The Franco-Prussian indemnity of 1871, perhaps the paradigmatic case, receives especially loving treatment:[31] "Money payment of the indemnity was accomplished, of course, by recycling."[32] France borrowed the money to pay Germany, in part from its own citizens but also from foreign (including German) sub-scribers to the loan. One consequence of this borrowing was new channels for foreign lending and borrowing that then got used for other purposes.

War and the end of war are not the only sources of displacement, but whatever the source, the important point is the way that initial displace-ment subsequently plays out in speculative booms, and the way these booms spread internationally by means of capital movements from coun-try to country. Subsequent distress and then crisis propagate similarly: "Euphoria and speculative excess are characterized by a rush out of money, including credit that the system monetizes on the way up, into securities, commodities, land, or whatever, bidding up their prices. After distress of long or short duration, the process is reversed, and the move-ment starts out of real assets or securities into money."[33]

At the moment of crisis, a desperate search begins for a lender of last resort – "some source of cash to ease the liquidation of assets before prices fall to ruinous levels" – and quite typically one is found to engage the symptoms of the immediate crisis. The problem comes from the fact that, due to international capital flows, booms and busts are quite typically international; "The question arises as to a lender of last resort between nations." Usually, the reigning world financial center can be relied upon to take on that task, but that just raises

---

[30] Kindleberger (1984a, 219).
[31] Kindleberger (1984a, 239–250).
[32] Kindleberger (1984a, 249).
[33] Kindleberger (1984a, 275).

a further question: "Who helps the center when it gets into trouble?" Historically, central bank cooperation has been the answer.[34]

Prior to 1700, the world lacked a lender of last resort, but it also largely lacked the credit mechanism that made such a lender necessary. After 1700, the credit mechanism and the lender of last resort grew up together, assurance of the latter being the enabler of the former. Most economists view the lender of last resort as a source of moral hazard and hence a cause of instability, excessive credit expansion being encouraged by assurance of central bank backstop. Not Charlie. He saw instead encouragement and support of entrepreneurial risk, essential for economic growth. In his view, economic development depends on the credit mechanism and would be (was in fact before 1700) stifled in a world with no lender of last resort. Instability of credit is, in this way of thinking, part of the price we pay for economic development, and so too the necessity for management of that instability by a lender of last resort.

Charlie's story about the relationship between finance and economic development can thus be seen as an attempt to improve on Gerschenkron. In Charlie's account, the emphasis is not on degrees of backwardness in different *individual* countries, but rather on communication *between* countries, and on the international spread of information, institutions, and capital. For Charlie, financial development plays a central role in economic development, but the process is much more bottom-up, unplanned, and international than Gerschenkron allows. And it also typically works itself out in booms and busts.

A central puzzle remains: Why this recurrence? Don't people learn from past experience? Charlie's answer, drawn from the historical record, emphasizes the dynamic between informed insiders and uninformed outsiders. Each boom involves mobilization of a new crew of outsiders, who are left holding the bag when insiders liquidate. The a priori view of Milton Friedman that destabilizing speculation is theoretically impossible is thus disproven both historically and theoretically: "Each individual may be rational, expecting to sell out before the collapse, but the fallacy of composition assures that not all can be."[35]

---

[34] Kindleberger (1984a, 277, 280, 281).
[35] Kindleberger (1984a, 272–273).

The purpose of Parts One through Three was to glean lessons from history that can help us to understand our own time, which is to say the time experienced by Charlie himself. Born in 1910, he had come to consciousness in the aftermath of World War I, and it is that experience that he wants retrospectively to understand in Part Four. From the point of view of the preceding parts, the most important thing to appreciate is that World War constituted monetary displacement on a scale never before seen in world history. Subsequent euphoria, distress, and crisis were therefore to be expected, along the general lines sketched in chapter 15, but this time would be different. This time there were multiple domestic displacements, each one transmitted internationally by capital flows and together acting to produce boom–bust on a scale never before seen. All of this was to be expected, but the exact course of events remained to be determined, in part by political forces different in each country and in part by the ability to mount an effective international lender of last resort operation, never before tested at such a scale.

The monetary displacement came from the war finance of the Allies, and also from postwar reparation charges to Germany. At the war's origin, Germany apparently imagined a quick war that would be financed by a subsequent indemnity to be imposed on France, along the lines of the 1871 resolution of the Franco-Prussian War. In the event, however, what Germany got was a long war, and it was France, along with the Allies, that got the chance to impose an indemnity on Germany. France naturally imagined that the indemnity would be recycled, along the lines of 1871: "Germany would issue bonds to be bought by Americans with monies then turned over to reparation claimants. Real reparations would be paid by Germany when and if she paid off the bonds."[36] That's not what happened, of course, but Charlie's frame for understanding what in fact did happen is clearly an imagination of how that counterfactual might have played out.

The first step of the counterfactual would have been to come up with a number for reparations that was acceptable to both the Allies and to Germany. Only then could Germany mount the necessary borrowing operation. Subsequently, just as France had experienced a boom in the

---

[36] Kindleberger (1984a, 300).

aftermath of the 1871 indemnity, one might have expected a similar boom in Germany post-reparations. A second step of the counterfactual would have been settlement of inter-Allied war debts, mostly owed to the United States by the UK and France, again possibly involving some recycling, but more likely considerable outright forgiveness since, after all, the Allies had been on the same side, with the UK and France providing the bulk of the human sacrifice.

The important point to appreciate is that, financially speaking, these two steps were deeply linked. Greater German reparations would have enabled greater payment of inter-Allied debts, and, contrariwise, greater forgiveness of inter-Allied debts would have made room for imposition of a less Carthaginian peace on Germany. Financially speaking, there was a deal to be made, but in the event the politicians were not able to find their way to it. The result was boom and bust on a world scale.

Charlie asks "could the Germans have paid reparations in the amount of the May 1921 ultimatum if they had loyally tried to? The answer is probably no."[37] As a result, we never even got past the first step of the possible solution. Why not? One reason is simply that the May 1921 number catered more to the domestic politics of the victorious Allies than to financial reality. But even had saner heads prevailed, there was still the problem of "loyally tried to." Simply put, in Germany the politics were never there to accept an indemnity. Charlie points to "the socio-political condition of the German peoples, unwilling to bear the burdens of war, reparations, or supporting their compatriots in the Ruhr by explicit sharing decisions, but rather printing money and letting the fates decide the outcome."[38] The contrast here is with the French indemnity of 1871, where political leaders were able to rally the country to pay because that was the only way they would get Alsace back from the Germans. Not so the Germans. When France occupied the Ruhr in an attempt to move things along, it only intensified Germany's resolve to resist.

But the Germans were not the only problem. Strikingly, Charlie lays considerable blame at the feet of the Allied economists, most prominent

---

[37] Kindleberger (1984a, 305).
[38] Kindleberger (1984a, 325).

among them the young John Maynard Keynes, who failed to apply the appropriate recycling analytical framework. (He was not the only one. Academic debate quite generally focused on real transfer, i.e., the famous debate between Keynes and Ohlin, which misses the point.) In this regard, Keynes' 1919 account of the Versailles Peace Conference, *Economic Consequences of the Peace*, "changed the course of history." For one, it "encouraged the Germans to resist paying reparations." And for two, it "helped the Republicans in the United States to defeat American ratification of the Versailles Treaty and keep the United States out of the League of Nations."[39] In this way, in both Germany and the United States, it was politics that blocked the two main steps on a possible road to financial settlement. To their eternal shame, economists facilitated that blockage rather than helping to break it down.

Charlie posits June 1922 as the fateful turning point, when hope for a possible rational financial settlement finally gave way. Until that time, German monetary inflation and deutschemark depreciation had been moderated by short-term capital inflows as speculators sought to profit from what they supposed to be temporary disequilibrium. After June, however, the stabilizing inflows stopped and destabilizing outflows began to dominate as speculators joined German authorities in selling deutschemarks for whatever the market would bear, driving down the exchange rate and sparking the hyperinflation that would destroy the currency within the next year. In this process, notably prices rose first, and the German money supply followed after – exactly the opposite of the monetarist quantity theory of money.

Why did Keynes write as he did? Maybe he was a bit pro-German, but probably more important was his concern for the postwar fate of the City, the prewar financial center of the world in London. Removal of Germany as a trade competitor had sparked hopes of postwar British revival, which had led to a little postwar boom–bust, but in the longer run the prewar sterling system was clearly threatened by an emergent dollar; New York bankers had made no secret of their ambition to take the place of London bankers: "Churchill does not quite use the expression 'dollar standard' as a replacement for sterling and gold. The words can be

---

[39] Kindleberger (1984a, 299).

found, however, in the *Tract on Monetary Reform* (Keynes 1924, p. 215). Britain was conscious of the approach of the end of an era and was striving to stave it off."[40]

For Britain, everything else followed from that misbegotten ambition: the return to gold at the (overvalued) prewar parity, and also the attempt to reinstate the prewar managed gold standard system in which the world interest rate was set by the Bank of England. In that ambition, moreover, Britain found itself substantially on its own as the United States refused to help, neither in Brussels 1920 nor in Genoa 1922. The sterling–gold exchange system that emerged from these efforts was thus an artificial construct from the beginning, imposed from above rather than emergent from market practice, and consequently it proved fragile. Charlie points to a July 1927 meeting on Long Island as a final attempt to organize central bank cooperation, too little too late: "Central bank cooperation, never deeply rooted, wilted *even before* the hot sun of 1929, and the torrid blasts of 1931."[41]

The core problem in all of this, in Charlie's mind, was lack of leadership, and for this he places the blame squarely at the feet of the United States. Refusal to lead on reparations gave free rein to greedy and vengeful voices in Europe, and refusal even to discuss inter-Allied debt settlement gave European negotiators little room to maneuver even if they had wanted to. In the event, Keynes' 1919 description of the Americans as "easily gulled" provided ample cover for Congressional intransigence,[42] and the end result was an impossible situation for the international monetary system.

One bright point in this sorry tale: the speculative attack on the French currency had been successfully contained for a time by determined central bank lender-of-last-resort intervention (ch. 19), demonstrating what might have been possible more generally had there been the necessary leadership. Destabilizing speculation (as in Germany after June 1922) is not inevitable if authorities are willing to intervene to reverse expectation: "To keep speculators' expectations reversed in the

---

[40] Kindleberger (1984a, 300, 341).
[41] Kindleberger (1984a, 332, 344–345), my emphasis.
[42] Kindleberger (1984a, 308).

longer run, however, the authorities must adopt effective means of monetary and fiscal stabilization. This may be more than the average set of politicians may be able to accomplish in a given socio-political state."[43]

The politicians having failed to lead in the immediate postwar settlement, it was left to the bankers to cobble something together, and this they proceeded to do. Just so, the Dawes Plan of 1924 can be understood as an "initial recycling operation," showing the world a possible way forward, and for a while it worked. If anything it was *too* successful: "oversubscribed eleven times. It marked a discontinuity in American foreign lending," the beginning of a foreign lending boom that would end in tears. The Young Plan, put in place April 1930, can be understood as a second tranche of this recycling plan, but by then it was too late. Instead, Hoover's Moratorium and the German Standstill Agreement, both of 1931, halted both reparations and inter-Allied debt payments, temporary measures soon made permanent.

The boom over, now comes the bust, and here we see Charlie retracing the history he had recounted in *World in Depression*. As early as 1928, the US stock market boom had brought an end to the foreign lending boom that had been launched by the Dawes Plan, leaving short-term capital flows to fill the gap until the Young Plan could be put together. Realizing that the stock market boom was being driven by speculation financed by short-term borrowing from abroad, New York bankers prepared to lend into the inevitable collapse by withdrawing credit elsewhere. But the resulting credit crunch forced commodity dealers to liquidate their inventories, driving world commodity prices down: the first step in the Great Depression.[44] Falling prices undermined balance sheets, first of firms and then of banks, marking the beginning of the distress phase of the financial cycle.

In the event, the Fed made some attempt to stem the collapse, but it was not nearly enough, and when hot money brought gold outflow the Fed reversed itself, raising the discount rate. "This is another case where

---

[43] Kindleberger (1984a, 355).
[44] This is the same argument Charlie had made in *WID*. One thing that is new here is his recognition that his argument "fit easily into the Hawtrey mold of *Currency and Credit* (1919)" (Kindleberger (1984a, 364).

institutional inhibitions would have been swept aside if there had existed coherent leadership and cohesive followership."[45] As earlier, the United States would not lead, and so Britain was left to soldier on as best it could until it could no longer. Significantly, sterling depreciation in 1931 was not followed by Deutschemark depreciation – memory of hyperinflation stood in the way of rational economic response – exacerbating the international transmission of deflation.

For the United States, the turning point in the depression came from Roosevelt's decision in advance of the 1933 World Economic Conference to devalue the dollar. In response, finally prices began to rise, and by mid-1933 "the corner of the depression had been turned." But only for the United States, not for anyone else. Given the failure to agree on currency stabilization, "successive depreciation of the pound sterling, the yen, the dollar and the gold bloc were each excessive and communicated over-valuation and deflation to the rest of the system."[46] The Tripartite Agreement of September 1936 did little to stem this tide, serving mainly as cover for French devaluation. But it did mark a minor triumph for the key-currency approach, which had been championed by the New York Fed since the 1920s as a viable alternative to the doomed sterling–gold exchange standard.

Against this background, Part Five of *FHWE* reads as a kind of auto-biographical culmination, though without any explicit marker of Charlie's own contributions to the momentous events he records. WASP reticence, no doubt, which unfortunately also functions to obscure somewhat the analytical frame that Charlie uses to make sense of these events. The important point to keep in mind is that the postwar financial history of Western Europe is intertwined with Charlie's own life. Just so, as Chief of the Division of German and Austrian Affairs (GA), Charlie had an inside view of the challenge of reconstructing Germany after the war (chapter 22). He is speaking, therefore, in part of his own life project when he says: "I regard the German monetary reform of 1948 as one of the great feats of social engineering of all time."[47] Further, as staffer for

---

[45] Kindleberger (1984a, 381).
[46] Kindleberger (1984a, 384, 399).
[47] Kindleberger (1984a, 418).

negotiation of the Anglo-American Loan, and executive secretary of the committee that prepared the Marshall Plan legislation, he similarly had an inside view of the role played by the United States in the reconstruction of Europe more generally (chapter 23). And finally, as professor at MIT, he had watched with paternal interest the evolution of the European monetary system, as individual currencies first returned to convertibility, and then, after Nixon abandoned US leadership of the dollar system, as Europe took the first steps toward monetary union and the creation of a common currency potentially rivaling the dollar. All of these world-historical events are, for Charlie, personal.

Even more, he views them all through the analytical lens he had spent a lifetime honing. Other writers on postwar economic history typically follow the hopeful thread of the purported multilateralism that originated at Bretton Woods – "the worldwide approach" as Charlie calls it – but that is emphatically not his tale. He follows instead the key-currency line that insists on the inherently hierarchical character of international money. From this point of view, the postwar financial history of Western Europe is mainly about how the various individual European currencies, as well as the joint European efforts in the direction of monetary union, fit in with the evolution of the global dollar system.

Further, whereas other economists quite typically adopt a monetarist frame, Charlie emphatically does not. Signaling his deviation, he now explicitly quotes Harvard economist Gottfried Haberler as chief expositor of the erroneous economist's view, in 1948, that reconstruction required nothing more than "stop the inflation and adjust the exchange rate." To the contrary, "believers in dollar shortage [such as Charlie himself] followed the banking school in insisting that the balance-of-payments deficit had structural origins."[48]

Finally, whereas other economists (and, even more so, political scientists) quite typically adopt a nationalist or regionalist frame, Charlie consistently takes the point of view of the world system as a whole, transcending both the national interest of his own United States and the regional interest of the Europeans whose actions he is recounting. As an economist, he always viewed the optimum currency area as the entire

---

[48] Kindleberger (1984a, 436).

world and the particularist sovereignty claims of individual nation-states as the biggest obstacle to construction of this economic ideal.

Viewing postwar financial history through this lens, the story Charlie tells in Part Five is essentially one of governments proposing and markets disposing. Crucially, in the immediate postwar period, markets were in no condition to dispose much of anything. The choice was social engineering or barbarism. In Germany, in particular, money was simply not functioning: "city dwellers would trek individually to the countryside at the weekend, carrying books, lamps, appliances, and the like to barter for potatoes brought back to the city in passenger trains in kilo lots in rucksacks." The 1948 German monetary reform fixed all that, in a supreme act of government; "only government can provide the public good of stable money, although it is evident that it does not always do so." Those, such as Milton Friedman, who retrospectively cite the German monetary reform as a victory of market forces over government get the history exactly backward, and the economics as well; "Monetary reform is not something that can be left to the market to work out."[49]

For Charlie, the real question was why, in this case, government was able to provide that public good, which would prove so hard to provide in later decades. The answer is social and political conditions: "the vacuum of power interests [inside Germany], and the assertion of responsibility by the occupying powers [outside Germany], made it possible for reasonable policies to be adopted." Note the word "reasonable." We are dealing here with engineering, not science; with the practical craft of building bridges that don't fall down, not with the academic abstraction of a frictionless market. And it is the very special social and political conditions of the postwar period that allowed implementation of this reasonable approach, specifically the willingness of the United States to lead, and the willingness of Germany to follow. Neither of these conditions could be taken for granted. Unwillingness to lead could easily have been justified by the economist's creed that no leadership was necessary, and unwillingness to follow could easily have been justified by the nationalist's creed that money is no business of the occupying powers since sovereignty is inviolable. Suffice it to say that the preconditions for the

---

[49] Kindleberger (1984a, 415, 416).

1948 monetary reform were special. Government proposed, the market disposed, and the result was *Wirtschaftswunder* (economic miracle).[50]

In other places, and at other times, the results of government proposing were more mixed, as Charlie's subsequent history recounts. Just so, the Lend-Lease arrangement for Allied war finance, signed August 1941 before the US official declaration of war, represents US leadership and practical learning from the disaster of war finance in World War I. But the precipitous end of Lend-Lease in spring 1945, more or less simultaneous with German surrender, represents a near-disastrous failure of US leadership, repaired partially by the 1946 Anglo-American Loan, which then failed instead for lack of followership.[51] Subsequently, the Marshall Plan got both leadership and followership more or less right, and the result was European recovery.

At the same time, however, the Marshall Plan's enthusiasm for European integration, an artifact of America's desire to create a Cold War bulwark against the Soviet Union, made less economic sense and, indeed, planted seeds for subsequent trouble. The European Payments Union (EPU), created to facilitate multilateral clearing and to overcome the inefficiency of dollar hoarding within Europe, might well have posed an obstacle to European integration with the rest of the world. Fortunately, former European colonies were included indirectly in the EPU, with the United States covering the overall deficit with the rest of the world, so de facto the EPU was a world not a regional clearing system. Similarly fortunate, "the swap network that developed in Basel after March 1961 as a lender of last resort was worldwide rather than European."[52]

Unfortunately, the apparent success of the EPU created the impression that monetary union might serve as an initial step (and also subsequent leverage) toward eventual political union, rather than as an eventual culmination to be achieved only *after* political union. Against this, Charlie insists that what apparent integration was actually achieved within Europe was mostly a result of each individual European country integrating with the larger world economy, and in particular with the dollar system: "Things equal to

---

[50] Kindleberger (1984a, 415).
[51] Kindleberger (1984a, 426).
[52] Kindleberger (1984a, 452).

the same thing are equal to each other, but they are not necessarily integrated." The rise of the Eurodollar and Eurobond markets, after 1971, created an offshore dollar system (markets disposing) that served this equalizing function, even as European politicians flirted with ideas of a Europe-wide currency (government proposing) as replacement for the dollar.[53]

We have seen in previous chapters (6, 7, and 8) how Charlie hoped that Europe might grab the reins of leadership left flapping in the wind by Nixon's abdication. Unfortunately, the subsequent history of Europe's monetary reform efforts dashed those hopes. Significantly, Charlie ends the book with these words: "I conclude that the EMU [the Werner Plan] has failed, and that the EMS promises little advance over the EMU to solve the European monetary problem, *or to provide a European monetary substitute for the failing dollar*, needed to undergird world economic stability." Governments may propose, but markets dispose. "The European and the world systems will limp along for some time. Ultimately, new hierarchical arrangements will emerge."[54]

Indeed, even as he was writing, the seeds of a new hierarchical arrangement were already sprouting, in the form of the offshore Eurodollar and Eurobond markets. As mentioned, Charlie noticed both of these developments, but he saw them mainly as vehicles for equalizing asset prices within Europe, rather than as the seed of a new globalized dollar system, as they turned out to be.[55] The second edition of *FHWE*, published in 1993, offers a more rosy forecast for European monetary union, presumably on the basis that the 1992 Maastricht agreement had put in place sufficient political union to make monetary union a realistic possibility. But Charlie is no more hopeful about the future of the dollar, notwithstanding the habits of G7 cooperation that continued even after the breakdown of Bretton Woods (e.g., the 1985 Plaza Accord, and the 1987 Louvre Accord). "The safest prediction is that there will be another transitional period, like that between the world wars, after which a new continental or national leadership will emerge."[56]

---

[53] Kindleberger (1984a, 448, 449–453). See also Kindleberger (1969c).
[54] Kindleberger (1984a, 463, my emphasis).
[55] McCauley (2020), Schenk (2020).
[56] Kindleberger (1993, 457).

Chef d'oeuvre? It must be admitted that in *FHWE* Charlie's reach quite definitely exceeded his grasp. There was simply too much material, and his stated ambition to derive more adequate theory from it all thus remained largely unrealized. Furthermore, because of this, even his more modest objective to reveal the inadequacy of existing a priori theories, monetarist and Keynesian alike, also remained largely unrealized. It takes a theory to beat a theory.

Although *FWHE* thus doesn't really deliver as a stand-alone book, when we read it against the corpus of Charlie's previous work, as we have been trying to do, it makes more sense. I have emphasized that Charlie viewed the world as a central banker, not so much as an economist, and that this way of thinking began early, under the influence of H. P. Willis in his first graduate years (Chapter 2). Charlie came to regret his juvenile enthusiasm for Willis' policy views on the Depression – the problem was not inflation, but rather deflation, and the real bills doctrine underestimated the need for active monetary management – and that regret likely blinded him to the far-reaching influence of this formative intellectual experience. But it need not blind us.

As we have seen, Charlie's insistence in his thesis on viewing short-term capital flows, not gold, as the principal means of international settlement builds on an analogy with the US experience with bankers' balances. This comes from Willis, and is the foundation of everything that followed, in particular Charlie's lifelong insistence on understanding the balance of payments as essentially a matter of settlement in the international payments system, a point of view reinforced by his years at the Fed and the BIS (Chapter 3). In this regard, Charlie was from the very beginning thinking like a central banker, not an economist.

We have further seen how, once he shifted to academia, he used this distinctive approach as the analytical framework for his textbook *International Economics*, and then later also as the framework for his "minority view" understanding of how the dollar system worked (Chapter 6). Short-term capital flows, he came to understand, were not just ways of absorbing temporary surpluses and deficits, but even more the key mechanism for supplying the international demand for dollar reserve balances. The US "deficit" was just a byproduct of international financial intermediation, with the United States serving as a bank. Further, in the absence of a world central bank, the system of central bank swap lines, cobbled together by the BIS in 1961, was the essential mechanism for central bank cooperation in defense of the dollar system.

If the payments approach is thus the analytical core of Charlie's thinking, the centrality of the dealer function, that is, market-making for profit, is a critical second but more emergent element. We can trace this element too back to early days, not so much the thesis but rather "Speculation and Forward Exchange" (1939), the article he wrote to make sense of the pattern of exchange rates during the Tripartite Agreement period. Covered interest parity arbitrage by speculators kept sterling and the dollar in line with each other, but not any other currency because the markets required for arbitrage were shut down; no market-makers, no markets. Similarly, in the immediate postwar period, given continuing lack of markets, the BIS substituted its gold swap facility, in effect making markets between inconvertible European currencies until, after the move to convertibility, private speculators stepped in and the BIS was able to shift instead to using its swap facility to backstop those private markets.

For a long time, the importance of the dealer function in Charlie's thought was limited to foreign exchange markets, and, as a consequence, it is not so obviously an element distinct from the underlying payments frame. Here perhaps Charlie was in part unconsciously channeling Willis' unease with the emerging new understanding of liquidity as "shiftability," an understanding which implies that liquidity depends on dealers standing ready to absorb excess demand or supply. Indeed, we see that unease explicitly in Charlie's concern, expressed in the *10th Annual Report* of the BIS, that central banks are being asked to play the role of "shifter of last resort."[57]

A more obvious reason for the limited role of the dealer function in Charlie's early thinking was of course the limited role of dealers themselves under conditions of Depression and War. Capital markets, both short term and long term, were more or less shut down. and indeed largely remained so in the immediate postwar period. Only gradually did they get put back together again, first domestically and then internationally, the

---

[57] See Chapter 3, n. 25.

Eurodollar and Eurobond markets coming into their own only after the breakdown of Bretton Woods.

This explains why it is only in *World in Depression* that the dealer function finally emerges as a clearly separate element, centrally important for understanding the link between the US stock market crash and the subsequent persistent fall of commodity prices. Commodity prices are made by dealers, who absorb temporary excess supply into their own inventories, and these inventories need to be financed, which means that disruption of finance can force liquidation of inventories at fire-sale prices. Similarly, the collapse of long-term capital flows was really about the collapse of international capital markets, which is to say the absence of profit-seeking dealers willing to use their own balance sheets to support new bond issues.

Both of these ideas – banking as a payments system and banking as a dealer system – came together in Charlie's *MPC* understanding of financial crises as essentially liquidity crises, arising from the inability of borrowers to make promised payments combined with a further inability to postpone those payments to some future time. Lender of last resort can put a floor on this kind of crisis precisely because the liabilities of the lender are means of payment for everyone else. At the international level, however, the central challenge is that there is no world central bank whose liabilities can serve that function, while the ability of national central banks to cooperate toward that end is limited by national political constraints. Viewed in this light, *FHWE* is essentially a story of the Darwinian coevolution of an integrated world market with an international lender of last resort, a world market for commodities and also for capital, both short term and long term. As such, it is essentially a story of financial development in support of economic development, both processes advancing together in Darwinian evolutionary fashion by means of boom and bust – a story that continues to this day.

Thinking of Charlie as an international monetary economist, one might have thought that his chef-d'oeuvre was the 1981 collection *International Money*. Certainly, that is the book that initially attracted my attention. The book is organized as a treatise, with four parts: "International Money," "International Payments," "International Capital Markets," and "Toward a New Monetary World Order." But it doesn't really deliver, remaining more "A Collection of Essays" written in the decade from 1966 to 1976, as the subtitle advertises, than a systematic treatise connecting up Charlie's disparate views on specific topics into a unified analytical structure.

As we have seen, in 1964 Harry Johnson invited Charlie to write a treatise for a series he was editing, but Charlie turned him down.[58] Instead of a treatise, he wrote the essays collected in *International Money*, which served instead as a bridge to his new life as economic historian, and hence to *FHWE*. To be sure, there is a unified analytical framework underlying it all, as I hope to have shown. But it is up to the reader to find it, and probably only readers who already share Charlie's idiosyncratic perspective, typically because of private banking or central banking experience, can feel the unity. Trained economists, who come to the book with their own preexisting theoretical frame (a priori, as Charlie would say), understandably experience the book instead as the collected musings of a mind that had missed most of the analytical advances of the postwar period, which is to say not a serious analytical contribution.

From this point of view, we can better understand why Charlie calls *FWHE* his chef d'oeuvre. On the one hand, that's simply what it felt like to him: a master work in which he was using his waning powers to pull together the threads of a life spent thinking about international money and finance. On the other hand, he seems to have been trying to draw attention to the book, his last best shot at being heard and taken seriously, by economic historians if not by economists. Note well that Charlie is not asserting that his book is better than works by others, thus carefully avoiding invidious comparison with his students and former colleagues, Nobels among them. He is simply saying that, for him, it is the best thing he ever did.

Notwithstanding all its imperfection, the book seems to have left Charlie with a sense of completion. He had done his best, holding nothing back. For a WASP, that was reason enough for pride in the outcome. Years before, when he had left his young family behind in order to take up a leadership position in the Enemy Objectives Unit in wartime London, his mother-in-law had encouraged him. It was his duty, she said, "you have it to do," and she backed it up with her own support of Sarah and the children until the war was over.[59] As we have seen, this same sense of duty subsequently led him to

---

[58] Chapter 7, n. 42.

[59] CPK to Steve Magee, Dec. 8, 1998. KPMD, Box 20. See also Kindleberger (1988a, 157).

accept leadership positions in the effort to reconstruct first Germany and then Europe (Chapter 4). It is in this context that we should understand his similar sense of personal responsibility for the well-being of the world dollar system. Here we find the bright thread that runs throughout his entire academic life, first as an international economist and then, when he could see no way to make further progress on that line, as an economic historian. He had it to do.

As readers, we may be disappointed in *FHWE*, and for our own good reasons, but Charlie was not, and for his own good reasons: "In my new métier, economic history as opposed to international economics, I find I can still work up a great deal of love."[60] Fifteen years after *FHWE*, looking back on his life's work, Charlie would reflect: "I prefer not to count myself an institutionalist, a monetarist, a Keynesian, a technologist, a demographer, a financial analyst, and the like but a jack of all trades (and master of none?)."[61] All of these were of course respectable ways of being an economist, but Charlie identified with none of them even as he dabbled in all of them. Looking through his characteristic self-deprecation, we can identify Charlie's approach to economics more objectively as that of the competent military officer referenced in the epigram to this chapter: "a generalist who can solve all kinds of problems."

If increasingly such an approach was viewed, especially by the freshest crop of technically proficient economists, as disqualification for economist status, so much the worse. In an age when academic economists increasingly built careers within specialized subfields, Charlie embraced instead synthesis and systems-level thinking. In an age when economics increasingly took the form of mathematical and statistical modelling, Charlie reinvented himself instead as a comparative economic historian. The younger generation may not have seen Charlie as very much of an economist at all, but Charlie himself always did, claiming the identity in the very title of his autobiography *The Life of an Economist*. Claiming *FHWE* as his "chef-d'oeuvre" is Charlie's way of affirming the choices he had made in his life's journey and also of asserting the continuing validity of his approach no matter what others might say.

---

[60] "Economist Development," p. 18. Unpublished talk given at Bard College, Oct. 11, 1986. KPMD Box 19, folder "The Economist and the Academy."

[61] Kindleberger (1999, 5).

CHAPTER 10

Leadership

Muddling through in Darwinian fashion is my preferred solution.[1]

The way the American Economic Association works, the president-elect is in charge of the program of the annual conference (lots of work), but then the following year mainly presides, with his main duty (actually honor) being to give the presidential address. Accordingly, Charlie would have spent a good chunk of 1984 arranging the program that ran from December 28–30 in Dallas. And then, at his leisure, he would have produced his presidential address, delivered December 29, 1985, in New York. For Charlie, the AEA presidency was an unexpected honor, but more importantly a responsibility and an opportunity for leadership. The outputs of his presidency quite definitely show him rising to the occasion.

Most noticeable in the 1984 program are the high-profile invited lectures – two of them. For the Ely lecture, Charlie invited his long-time friend and war buddy Alec Cairncross to reflect on "Economics in Theory and Practice," meaning the relationship between academia and the real world. Cairncross had spent his career in Britain shifting back and forth between the two: "between the priestly who live in clouds of theory and the lay brethren in Washington, Whitehall, and elsewhere, who do battle in the corridors of power."[2] It was a life that Charlie might have had in the United States had it not been for the McCarthy witch hunt.

For the luncheon talk to the joint session of the AEA with the American Finance Association, Charlie chose Alexandre Lamfalussy,

---

[1] Kindleberger (1988a, 12).
[2] Cairncross (1985, 1). See also Kindleberger (1995, ch. 12), prepared for the Cairncross festschrift.

General Manager of the Bank for International Settlements, who offered remarks on "The Changing Environment of Central Bank Policy." Financial fragility was his central concern, and specifically the question of whether fragility is increased or reduced by the "four interconnected evolutionary processes" he identified: the global disinflation process begun by Volcker in 1979 and still continuing; the striking internationalization of money and capital markets that was creating a single global market; the rapid pace of financial innovation, specifically interest-rate and foreign-exchange swaps for managing risk in these new global markets; and, finally, the seemingly inexorable process of deregulation. Lamfalussy concludes: "In a financially integrated world no country can isolate itself from the others, no matter what its exchange rate regime"; worryingly, this calls into question the useability of monetary policy.[3] Another life that Charlie might have had, except for the Nazi invasion of Paris that prompted his hasty departure for home.

The program itself further shows Charlie's touch, most obviously in the sessions "In Honor of Stephen H. Hymer," and "Economic History: A Necessary Though not Sufficient Condition for an Economist," the latter including both economists Kenneth Arrow and Robert Solow and economic historians Peter Temin and Paul David. Other sessions more likely proposed to him, but meeting his favor as they might not have done for a different president-elect, include "The Use and Abuse of Econometrics," "Credit and Economic Instability," and "After-Keynes Cambridge Contributions" – the latter showcasing the Cambridge England Keynesians, as opposed to the Cambridge Massachusetts Keynesians (Charlie's MIT colleagues). Organized by Hyman Minsky, the session included papers by Jan Kregel (himself a Cambridge England Keynesian), Bertram Schefold, and Roy Weintraub (a critic of the Cambridge England Keynesians).[4] An evident theme running through all of these sessions is the attempt to foster conversation between economists who more usually talk to separate audiences in separate worlds.

Regarding his own presidential address, Charlie's colleague Peter Temin advised him not to use the occasion to opine on methodological

---

[3] Lamfalussy (1985, 410).
[4] Personal communication, Roy Weintraub.

issues, and he chose to take that advice. Thus, Charlie's enthusiasm for economic history shows up not in the address, but rather in the book that came out of the economic history session, Bill Parker's *Economic History and the Modern Economist* (1986), and even more so in Charlie's own later collection of essays, *Historical Economics, Art or Science?* (1990). More on all of that below. The important point for now is that, in 1985, Charlie chose to use the most visible platform he ever had to speak instead on "International Public Goods without International Government." Here we see him at the end of his career attempting to foster conversation between economics and political science, just as he had back at the beginning with his abortive 1950 "The Distribution of Income, Political Equilibrium, and Equilibrium in the Balance of Payments."

Well aware that his audience were all economists, Charlie's pitch was in language that all trained economists understand. Standard economics warns of the possibility of market failure. Left to its own devices the market mechanism can be expected to supply an inefficiently low quantity of public goods simply because, by definition, public goods are freely available to everyone, and so no one is willing to pay for their supply. A classic example is clean air. Here is a situation where the market does not work, and that makes room for the argument that we should not use the market, but rather government. More generally, Charlie always embraced what he called a "vacuum theory of government" – namely, that government steps in to do what the market can't or doesn't do well.

The problem is that, at the international level, there is no government, and so the vacuum theory leaves open the question of how international public goods get supplied, if at all. In practice, Charlie says, the solution has generally been for one nation to step forward as "leader," taking on the task itself for whatever reason. The particular public good closest to Charlie's heart was of course provision of global money, coordination of macroeconomic policy, and stabilization of exchange rates, but the argument is general, applying to peace-keeping operations as well. In the absence of such a leader, the market can be expected to supply an inefficiently low quantity of needed public goods.

The argument is recognizably an extension of the case Charlie had made in *World in Depression* concerning the need for a stabilizer, one stabilizer. In 1931, Britain could no longer play that role, and the United States would not, and so we got world depression. Subsequently, the United States did take up that role, and, as a consequence, economic matters went better for a while, until unilateral abandonment of that leadership role by Nixon, which in Charlie's mind had raised the prospect of another depression. On that score, the important point to appreciate is that by December 1985, when Charlie gave his presidential address, he saw real reason for hope. Three months earlier, the major powers had met at the Plaza Hotel in New York City and agreed to cooperate on stabilizing the major currencies. It was only a first step, but the United States seemed finally to be willing to lead again, and the major powers seemed once again to be willing to follow. In his address, Charlie wanted not only to celebrate this new development, but also to urge further building on this promising start, which he saw as a possible pivot point in history.

The main argument in Charlie's address is about public goods because that's what he thought his audience would understand. But in fact, and notwithstanding Temin's advice, there is a methodological theme that runs throughout as well, concerning not economic history but rather political science. Charlie's target here is the "imperialism" of the Chicago school – George Stigler and Gary Becker are mentioned by name – who see economics as having nothing to learn from political science and political science as subordinate to economics. For them, as a matter of a priori theory, the market works – and it works just as well internationally as it does domestically if only government will get out of the way and let it do so, which is actually easier at the international level since there is no international government. In opposition to the Chicago School, Charlie's MIT home department had long emphasized the prevalence of various market failures, both microeconomic and macroeconomic, and hence also the general case for government intervention, but mostly the MIT line had been at the level of the nation-state, not international. Thus, we can understand Charlie's address as a challenge just as much to his MIT friends as to his Chicago opponents: How to address market failure at the international level when there is no international government?

It was also a challenge just as much to political science as it was to economics, since political scientists quite typically take the point of view of the individual nation-state, rather than the world as a whole. Stimulated by the turmoil of the 1970s, the political science community had already begun engaging Charlie's argument in *World in Depression*. Robert Keohane in particular, in his book *After Hegemony* (1984), had proposed that patterns of behavior between nation-states (so-called "regimes") that had become customary during the Bretton Woods period might be relied upon to sustain world order even after the formal collapse of Bretton Woods. In 1985 Charlie was talking mainly to the economists in front of him, but he clearly had in mind also the political scientists, who he would shortly address in a commissioned review of Keohane's book published in 1986 under the title "Hierarchy versus Inertial Cooperation." In his presidential address he foreshadows that subsequent engagement: "I am a realist when it comes to regimes."[5]

On the heels of his presidential address, invitations for subsequent addresses flooded in and Charlie was very busy for a while, flitting here and there and very much enjoying all the attention that his ideas were now getting. Significantly, he took the opportunity to reissue *World in Depression* in a revised edition (1986) and also *Manias, Panics, and Crashes* (1989).[6] In this context, it is easy to understand why Charlie welcomed the inquiry from Peter Johns of Wheatsheaf Books in England as to whether he would be interested in putting together a collection of recent papers. He had been using the abundance of speaking requests to flesh out the argument of his books in multiple directions, and so welcomed the opportunity to pull these various threads together. In the event, there would be three Wheatsheaf books.

The first one, *The International Economic Order: Essays on Financial Crisis and International Public Goods* (1988), devotes its first half to various follow-ups on *WID*, in speeches to college students, economic historians, bankers and central bankers, and in testimony to both the British House of Commons and the US Congress. The second half of the book begins with a reprint of the presidential address, continues with follow-ups addressed to different

---

[5] Kindleberger (1988a, ch. 9, 137).

[6] Also *Marshall Plan Days* (1987) and *The German Economy* (1989). *International Capital Movements* (1987) was based on the Marshall Lectures he had given at Cambridge University in Fall 1985.

audiences (political scientists, Japanese and European policymakers), and concludes with a series of earlier papers that trace the development of Charlie's thought on these matters back to 1960.

A central frame for the whole book is the Plaza Accord of September 22, 1985. In his November 13 testimony at the so-called Congressional Summit, Charlie was already signaling the importance he attached to the meeting: "Baker's initiative of September 1985, holding out the possibility of renewed American leadership in policy coordination and moving toward international monetary stability, is the way to go." Importantly, in the same testimony, he also explicitly rejected calls for more comprehensive reform, such as a new Bretton Woods: "It is a mistake to have a meeting of bodies before there is a meeting of minds."[7] The calls to which he refers had been coming largely from what today we would call the Global South: a set of proposals that had been circulating since 1974 under the name New International Economic Order. As a key-currency man, Charlie had not thought much of the multilateral façade of the original Bretton Woods, and he thought even less of the NIEO, sympathetic though he was to the goal of economic development. What the world needed was leadership, not discontents sniping from the wings.[8]

The importance of Plaza for Charlie was that the possibility of world depression that had been worrying him ever since August 1971 was now quite definitely off the table: "So long as the G-7 central banks are committed to something like the Plaza agreement or the Louvre agreement, however modified, the dollar will be supported by public authorities if private investors should experience revulsion from it. This is the lender-of-last-resort function at the international level."[9] The psychic relief of this development seems to have opened up mental space (and distance) for Charlie now to consider the period from 1971 to 1985 as history, in particular asking himself why, in the absence of an international lender of last resort, had there been no Depression? In the first half of the 1988 collection, we see him wrestling with exactly this question, using the framework of *WID* and *MPC.*

---

[7] Kindleberger (1988a, 109, 108).
[8] Kindleberger (1978c) is his most comprehensive treatment of the NIEO.
[9] Kindleberger (1988a, 10).

Using *MPC*, Charlie proposes to understand the 1971 Nixon shock as a massive "displacement," which subsequently sparked an enormous credit expansion, both domestically in the United States and internationally in the so-called Least Developed Countries (LDCs). The domestic credit boom showed up in mortgage lending (the thrifts), as well as farm and oil-patch lending, all of which eventually overdid it and fell into distress. But unlike similar problems that arose from the boom of the 1920s, distress did not become crisis; "The major difference was that in the 1980s, the FDIC and FSLIC were in place."[10] Loans failed and banks failed, but the system held because bank liabilities (deposits) were backstopped by government insurance programs.

The same could not be said of the LDC loans, however. Charlie makes a big point that the boom in LDC lending was already underway in 1971, well before the first OPEC oil shock in 1973, as a result of easy money in the United States flowing first to Europe and then looking for an outlet. What began as a trickle in 1971 would, after OPEC, become a flood, and eventually that too was overdone, resulting in distress. In fact, the tightened monetary policy under Volcker after 1979 was the most immediate trigger for that distress. For a while lending stopped as world interest rates spiked, raising the cost of funds for banks above the contracted receipts from loans, which cost the banks then passed through to borrowers at the moment of refinance. Things definitely got hairy for a while in individual cases, but again the system as a whole held. Why so?

Writing in 1982, on the heels of the Mexican debt crisis, which had been backstopped by the intervention of the US Treasury with the famous Brady bonds, Charlie judged that although there was not yet the meeting of minds necessary for an international lender of last resort, the Brady venture showed what could be done in the meanwhile: "Distress is not a time for heroics. Shorten sail and steady as she goes."[11] That is more or less what was done elsewhere as well, working-out and writing-off, and it all worked, more or less. But for Charlie the more important thing was that this experience of tough sailing had the

---

[10] Kindleberger (1988a, 89).
[11] Kindleberger (1988a, 120).

further result of finally creating the meeting of minds that made the Plaza Accord a possibility only three years later.

In short, the displacement of 1971 did not cause depression because it did not cause the collapse of the international monetary system. This surprised Charlie, who had expected long-term international capital flows to cease, with short-term flows following soon behind, as had happened in 1931. But it didn't happen. Instead of credit collapse we got credit expansion, and instead of deflation we got inflation. Significantly, Charlie sees the same ratchet effect, with exchange-rate instability causing price-level instability, operating in both the 1930s and the 1970s: "The result was structural inflation in an inflationary world ... the ratchet was the opposite of that in the deflation of the 1930s."[12] In both periods, the movement of exchange rates operated not to bring the economy back to equilibrium, but rather to drive it farther away – a prime example of the market not working. Given lack of leadership in the 1970s (as in the 1930s), for a long time there was no choice but to continue using the market, and the result was rising inflation. Plaza marked the end of all that.

The question begged by this historical account, of course, is why it took so long to get to Plaza, and that's the question that the second half of the book attempts to answer. The answer, in short, is politics. It will be recalled that, in 1971, Charlie thought that Nixon was simply making a huge blunder in economic policy, egged on by a few wrong-thinking economists. But as time went on and the world did not collapse, Charlie moved beyond this initial position, coming to see that Nixon's hand had to a large extent been forced by the actions of others, "free-riders" on US international leadership who ultimately exhausted the domestic political limits of that leadership.

For Charlie, the problem traced back at least to 1960. At that time, he had been asked to write a think piece for John J. McCloy on the future course of US economic policy, which he titled "The End of the Dominant Role of the United States and the Future of World Economic Policy."[13] Writing from Paris, where he was on sabbatical, he proposed that it was

---

[12]   Kindleberger (1988a, 60).
[13]   Appreciation of the significance of this assignment requires appreciation of the key role McCloy played, largely behind the scenes, in multiple administrations. See Bird (1992). Recall that more or less at this same time, Charlie produced his first explicit engagement with Triffin, see Chapter 6, n. 29.

time for the United States to shift from a position of dominance to one of leadership: "The United States could no longer dictate to other countries what was needed to be done in the field of economic foreign policy; it was obliged at that time to ask, not tell them."[14] In the event, Charlie's message was welcomed neither in Washington, so Charlie tells us, nor in France, where economist Francois Perroux was promoting the idea that the United States had already shifted in the opposite direction, from mere dominance to outright exploitation.

The French did not agree with Charlie, but at least they were willing to publish what he wrote, while the Americans were not, which is why his paper appeared only in French.[15] One imagines that this experience gave Charlie second thoughts about his plan at the time to re-engage with active government service, once he managed to regain his security clearance. We have seen how instead he subsequently followed the evolving drama of Europe and the dollar (Chapter 6) and then made a conscious shift into economic history with *World in Depression* (Chapter 8), in effect putting this episode behind him. But in 1971 Nixon's abdication of leadership brought the matter back up to consciousness. And a timely invitation to give the Frank D. Graham Memorial Lecture at Princeton in 1977 gave him the incentive to put his thoughts in order, not to mention a welcome chance to sit for a moment in the chair that Graham had done so much to deny him back in 1948.

Like Graham, Charlie had for a time considered the nation-state as an institution that had outlived its usefulness: "The increase in mobility produced by innovations in transport and communication during and after World War II led some of us to conclude that the nation-state was in difficulty."[16] But whereas Graham had thought the way forward was international laissez-faire, Charlie thought the way forward was to yield national sovereignty to some new form of international governance. In the event, both views got their comeuppance in the 1970s with a resurgence of nationalism, not least in the United States, and it was this development that Charlie wanted to understand.

---

[14] Kindleberger (1988a, 185).
[15] Kindleberger (1961).
[16] Kindleberger (1988a, 132).

The problem, as he came to understand it, was that whereas the optimum economic area is the entire world, the optimum political area is much smaller, in many cases smaller even than the nation-state. Politics thus quite definitely rules out any possibility of world government:

> Political scientists properly place a high value on pluralism and object to such hierarchical structures as are implicit in a gold standard managed by London or a dollar standard dominated by the United States ... But pluralism tends to underproduce vital public goods [such as global money] and to overproduce a public bad, neo-nationalism ... The free rider is the bane of pluralism, just as the imperious leader is the bane of hierarchy.[17]

The answer, so Charlie would propose in 1977, was to seek a middle ground between pluralism and hierarchy that he called "federal functionalism" – a phrase he attributed to the economist Richard Cooper. What might that look like, concretely? The book records the development of Charlie's subsequent thinking on this matter. The central problem is that effective leadership requires willing followership. Ideally, followership is voluntary, freely chosen, but the perennial temptation of free-ridership means that voluntary compliance cannot suffice. The key therefore is collective enforcement, emphasis on collective: "Despite Adam Smith and the Chicago School, profit-maximizing economies having too few dedicated leaders, with insufficient individual commitment to voluntary compliance, and collective groups unprepared to restrain their demands, will not function."[18] What is needed is a kind of club, with rules that are enforced by club members who have signed on to the same rules themselves: "Bind the members of the international community to rules of conduct, to which they agree."[19]

For individuals, the matters of voluntary compliance and also of collective enforcement are both largely about values, unwritten rules instilled in childhood and thus reinforced by an adult peer group: "More basic an

---

[17] Kindleberger (1988a, 225–226).
[18] Kindleberger (1988a, 208).
[19] Kindleberger (1988a, 193).

incentive than maximizing income and wealth is obtaining the approval of one's peers." In this vein, Charlie's critique of Keohane points out that he fails to "leave room for conscience, duty, obligation, or such old-fashioned notions as *noblesse oblige*."[20] But these of course are virtues of individuals, not nations. Also, they are perhaps the virtues to which Charlie himself aspired and that he tried to enforce in his own chosen adult peer group – but what about everyone else?

Says Charlie: "A leader, one who is responsible or responsive to need, who is answerable or answers to the demands of others, is forced to "do it" by ethical training or by circumstance of position."[21] The key point is that leadership does not necessarily depend on ethical values; it can emerge organically from "circumstance of position," as J. P. Morgan effectively took on central banking functions before there was a Fed, and as the United States eventually took on the responsibility of leadership when Britain could no longer. In both cases we see leaders rising to the occasion, responsive to need and answering the demands of others.

Leadership can emerge that way, but not followership, and therein lies the source of the inherent instability of the leadership solution: "The [leadership] system is essentially unstable, subject to entropy. Even if it is not perceived as domination, leadership is not regarded as legitimate."[22] From this point of view, the Nixon saga was not so much about Nixon abdicating leadership, and more about everyone else abdicating followership. It was the inherent instability of the leadership system that caused it to break down in 1971, and it was the subsequent experience of instability that created the possibility of reinstituting a reformed leadership system at Plaza in 1985: "Leadership to provide the public good of stability, properly regarded, misunderstood as exploitation, or sniped at by free riders, seems a poor system, but like democracy, honesty, and stable marriages, is better than the available alternatives."[23]

This, then, is the main intellectual line that Charlie was pursuing in the years after his presidential address. It is easy to imagine him

---

[20] Kindleberger (1988a, 207, 157).
[21] Kindleberger (1988a, 157).
[22] Kindleberger (1988a, 191).
[23] Kindleberger (1988a, 193).

continuing to produce work in this rich vein, using his speaking invitations to remain engaged as he watched the slow process of rebuilding the leadership system, as he hoped. But life intervened. In Fall 1986 his wife Sarah suffered a stroke, which forced Charlie to curtail his travel and then to face the prospect of moving out of his beloved Lincoln home. After sorting through and disposing of the accumulation of a lifetime, he moved with Sarah on October 3, 1989, to Brookhaven, a new assisted living facility in nearby Lexington. Significantly, Charlie's introduction to the second Wheatsheaf book, *Historical Economics, Art or Science?*, is dated November 1989, and he specifically thanks Peter Johns "for urging me to proceed with the collection." Given the disruption to his life, it is remarkable that he was able to proceed, and testament to the importance that he attached to the subject matter. Having listened to Temin regarding his presidential address, he was now determined to have his say, imagining perhaps that this would be his last substantive book.

In Charlie's mind, the book amounts to an extended argument for restoring the place of economic history in the training of young economists, "so as to bring a historical perspective to economic questions."[24] His argument is largely by example: examples of his own work as a historical economist, notably including his very first effort, "The Postwar Resurgence of the French Economy" (1963a). Such an effort, he avers, "can be undertaken only midway in an economist's development and after a firm grounding in economic theory and perhaps in an economic special field. My interest is not in producing economic historians but rather in diluting the rigor of modern technical economics through exposure to a fairly broad range of human economic experience."[25] That's what he had been trying to do in his own teaching. Now he was offering his own work as a resource for others who might be inclined to follow his lead.

As a set of examples, this second Wheatsheaf book inevitably has less thematic coherence than the first one. For our purposes, the most important chapters are those that show him building on his *Financial History of Western Europe* (1984). Just so, chapter 3, "Spenders and Hoarders: The World Distribution of Spanish American Silver, 1550–

---

[24] Kindleberger (1990, 349).
[25] Kindleberger (1990, 350).

1750" (1989) is essentially a prequel to that "chef d'oeuvre." "Produced on my own to satisfy curiosity,"[26] as he says, the chapter details 200 years of silver (a commodity) flowing out of the New World into Europe, where it was coined into money; and from which it then flowed farther to India and China, where it entered hoards and so essentially returned to commodity status. The lesson Charlie takes from this experience is that no single theory of the balance of payments could possibly apply to all three of these areas, and, further, that what looks to modern eyes like a balance of payments disequilibrium can be and was in fact sustained not only in the short run but even in the long run. He offers this historical perspective, so he says, as a contribution to the then current anxiety about "dollars pouring out of the United States, circulating into and out of Europe, and ending up in the coffers of Japan and Taiwan."[27] Maybe it's more sustainable than people think?

Similarly, three chapters at the end of the book (chs. 11, 12, and 15) use his financial history of Europe as a frame for thinking about the current problems of Third World countries: "problem loans and bad debts, exchange-rate crises, [and] capital flight."[28] And two chapters in the middle of the book (chs. 9, 10) do the same for the current problems of a United States apparently in decline, more or less updating his comprehensive "US Foreign Economic Policy, 1776–1976" (Ch. 8). Chapters on the ratchet effect and the Panic of 1873 respond, so he says, to the US stock market collapses of October 19, 1987, and October 13, 1989, which is to say that they represent attempts to provide historical perspective on pressing current events.

One apparently new thing in the book is two forays into the history of economic thought: one on Adam Smith and another on Thomas Mun. The Smith essay, however, is largely an engagement instead with "Stephen Marglin's recent suggestion that the division of labour was

---

[26] Kindleberger (1990, ix).
[27] Kindleberger (1990, 37).
[28] Kindleberger (1990, 353). Here we also see Charlie doing his best to build on the work of a favorite student, Carlos Diaz-Alejandro, subsequent to his untimely death in 1985. Not included is Charlie's 1989 memorial essay, "From Graduate Student to Professional Peer: An Appreciation of Carlos F. Diaz-Alejandro" which he would reprint in a later collection (1999, ch. 16).

practiced under capitalism less for efficiency than for lowering the return to labour,"[29] testing that suggestion against the available literature on the organization of production at the time Adam Smith wrote. And the Mun essay is essentially a spinoff from the "Spenders and Hoarders" project, interesting to Charlie because Mun wrote during the time of the Spanish silver flows in an attempt to make sense of what he was seeing in his role as director of the East India Company. Both chapters thus are properly works of economic history more than history of economic thought.

Charlie pitches the book to economics instructors looking for a "Bridge between Liberal Arts and Business Studies" (the subtitle of ch. 1), but that's not all. Says Charlie, in the final sentence of his concluding chapter: "Historical economics, I contend, can bridge the chasm between abstractions and facts, test theories against the course of events, and ensure the discard of models that are unuseful in illuminating concrete situations."[30] Here we recognize the creed that he had worked out in *Economic Response* (1978) and pursued thereafter in *Manias, Panics, and Crashes* and then ultimately *A Financial History of Western Europe*. Like that earlier book, *Historical Economics* is a work of evangelism, a collection of exemplars of comparative economic history intended to convert others to the true faith by showing concrete practice of it.

The last thing Charlie did before moving to Brookhaven was to put together a draft of his autobiography, which would be published as *The Life of an Economist* (1991). Encouraged by his friend David Warsh, columnist at *The Boston Globe*, he put it together in a blizzard of typing in only a month.[31] There were bits and pieces already available at hand: a published essay "The Life of an Economist" (1980c), the preface to *World in Depression*, an oral history taken down by the Truman Library, some reminiscences from the fiftieth reunion of his 1928 Kent School class, the "Interim Biography" he had written in an effort to get cleared, a long report on his eventful year in Atlanta, plus of course his FBI file, letters home during the war, and a lifetime of academic correspondence

---

[29] Kindleberger (1990, 109), Marglin (1974).
[30] Kindleberger (1990, 354).
[31] Personal communication, David Warsh.

and student files. But there was no time to dig through it all, much less the appetite (or perhaps capacity?) for self-reflection after a life of WASP reticence and self-deprecation. As a consequence, there is in the book none of the loving attention Charlie devotes to tracing the flow of silver, or the international transmission of the Panic of 1873. Instead, the book is merely what he calls a "professional biography": an account of what happened when, sprinkled with the occasional charming anecdote. The most personal part of it is the sequence of fourteen plates which alert the reader to the existence of a deeper story, but without actually telling that story.

Ken Galbraith, a lifelong friend who Charlie leaned on for the foreword to the book, tells us that it is "a book by a scholar for scholars," meaning more or less the (limited) audience of Charlie's presidential address "and its larger penumbra," not the best-seller audience for which Galbraith himself wrote. Not only does Charlie leave out much of the wartime drama, but also the academic drama: "Kindleberger is not a person who suffers fools gladly. But he suffers them in tolerant silence, and not less those with whom he is thrown into scholarly disagreement."[32] Maybe so, but I would point further to the role of Charlie's professed antiperfectionism. Probably that was the essential trait that enabled him to pound out a draft even as he shipped off to the archives all of the rich source material, most of it unused.

Charlie thus arrived at Brookhaven with the decks cleared, but still it took him a while to get settled. The untimely death of his son Richard's wife in 1990, leaving two young children, created additional family responsibility. Also, Brookhaven was new, and Charlie and Sarah were among its very first residents, so Charlie found himself getting involved in creating a community culture, not least by recruiting family (on Sarah's side, her siblings Francis and Jen) and professorial friends (on Charlie's side, his MIT colleague Bob Solow) to join them over the next years. Unlike many who make this kind of transition late in life, Charlie had ample experience in total institutions, harking back to boarding school and his summer shipboard adventures, so he knew what he was in for and adapted easily. It was not the endgame he had hoped for, but he made

---

[32] Galbraith (1991, x, xi).

the best of it, a lifelong habit of resilience, adaptation, and resolute optimism standing him in good stead.

As Charlie relaxed into the rhythms of his new life, gradually he began again to accept the occasional outside speaking engagement, some even involving international travel. A first toe in this water was the eightieth birthday celebration for him: a luncheon event at the Terrace Restaurant at Columbia University on October 12, 1990. Fifty of his closest associates had put together a book of their reminiscences, which they presented to him. Perhaps Paul Streeten captured the general mood the best: "Charlie had many honors bestowed on him. The one I would propose is that of the most lovable economist."[33]

Meanwhile, back at his new home, as a kind of occupational therapy, he filled his spare time with a vanity project that would eventually appear as his third Wheatsheaf book: *Mariners and Markets* (1992). The back-cover picture of himself in 1930 as deck boy on the SS *Bird City* tells us that he is revisiting his youth, and inside the covers we find again the loving attention, and the taste for the telling detail, that characterizes his best work. Mostly it is an account of the seaman's life in the age of sail, distinguishing the experience of whalers, fishermen, slavers, merchant marine, and Navies, comparing British, American, Dutch, and French accounts of that experience.

The way the book came about, apparently, is that Charlie was asked to review a book, *Markets in History*, edited by David W. Galenson, which consisted of six essays "joined by a belief in the efficiency of the market," the product of Chicago School true believers. The assertion in one of the essays that labor markets for seaman were efficient was too much for Charlie: "It is hard to believe in the efficiency of labor markets where recruits for the separate merchant vessel and whaling fleets were drawn from all over the world, largely from the urban lower classes or from the farm, often by the forceful methods of impress, pressgangs and shang-haiing, and experienced high rates of desertion."[34] But if labor markets for seamen weren't efficient, then what were they? Notwithstanding that his entire professional expertise was in international money, not at all in

[33] KPMD, Box 24, "Reminiscences of Charles P. Kindleberger."
[34] Kindleberger (1991b, 203, 205).

labor markets, Charlie's curiosity was piqued, and off he went. The book was the result.

For our purposes, the important thing is that the occupational therapy worked. When the little book was done, Charlie was ready to move on to a bigger one. Back in September 1990, shortly after the move to Brookhaven, he had attended at Harvard a conference to launch a new large-scale and long-term project on "The Vitality of Nations," sponsored by the Luxembourg Institute for European and International Studies under the directorship of Armand Clesse. As part of that project, in early 1993, so Charlie says, he started work on the book that would appear as *World Economic Primacy: 1500–1990* (1996), offering a partial draft for comment at another Harvard conference in May 1994.

To make sense of the book, it is helpful to read it in the context of two other books Charlie published at about the same time: *World Economy and National Finance in Historical Perspective* (1995) and *Centralization vs. Pluralism: A Historical Examination of Political-Economic Struggles and Swings within Some Leading Nations* (1996). The first, a collection of essays, is a kind "hors d'oeuvre," he says, for the main course, sketching themes that he would develop more fully in *Economic Primacy*. And the second is a kind of after-dinner sweet (my metaphor, not his), that mops up some unfinished business. It is these three books that would occupy his energies at the end of his career.

"Casual observation attests," so Charlie states as the opening gambit in *Economic Primacy*, "to the successive economic primacy of the Italian city-states, the Spanish-Portuguese empire, the Low Countries, Great Britain, and the United States, with failed challenges and impressive growth in France and Germany."[35] Accordingly, the core of the book is seven chapters, one on each of these instances, plus an eighth, "Japan in the Queue?," possibly a late addition. The first three of these and the last required new research, which took time, but the other four very much build on previous work. In a departure from his previous practice, Charlie treats all eight of the cases in a common analytical framework, which he outlines in chapters 2 and 3 and reprises in the conclusion.

---

[35] Kindleberger (1996a, 37).

Charlie's method is economy history, but his goal is now comparative political economy.

For Charlie, the whole point of the exercise was to provide historical perspective on the present condition of the world system. By the time he was writing, his hope that Plaza might serve as a pivot point for restoration of US leadership had been disappointed by events. As opposed to 1971, the problem now was not the willingness of the United States to lead but rather its capacity to do so, similar to Britain in 1931: "The real fear coming into prominence in the summer of 1991 is a return in the United States to quasi isolationism."[36] Prominent in Charlie's mind was the recently concluded Gulf War, so-called Operation Desert Storm, which had reversed the Iraqi invasion of Kuwait. The United States did most of the work, but then it passed the hat, asking Germany and Japan to pay for it: "The fact that the United States sought large monetary contributions from them is, in fact, one indication of US economic aging."[37]

There are basically two ideas in Charlie's "model" of economic primacy. First, there is the idea that nations undergo a kind of inherent life cycle, not unlike the ages of man, birth, growth and decline: "It is vitality and flexibility giving way to rigidity that determines the pattern."[38] And, second, there is the idea that the international system has a strong tendency to be organized hierarchically. Putting the two ideas together, Charlie suggests that the succession of primacy involves the interaction of these two tendencies as new countries in their prime surpass older countries in decline, only in time to be surpassed themselves.

If Desert Storm had suggested that the United States was aging, subsequent events confirmed the diagnosis: "The social cohesion that operated at the time, say, of the Marshall Plan, has evaporated, at least temporarily. Attitudes are rigid, uncompromising, sclerotic";[39] "By 1990,

---

[36] Kindleberger (1995, 108).
[37] Kindleberger (1995, 105).
[38] Kindleberger (1996a, 36). He nods to Mancur Olson (1982) as one who had similar ideas, but his own thinking along these lines clearly predates, as seen, for example, in his essay "The Aging Economy" (Kindleberger 1990, ch. 9). Similarly, he nods to the ubiquity of the "S- or Gompertz or logistic curve" (1996a, 15; 1999, 121). I read both of these as instances of Charlie looking for allies, as he had done previously with his embrace of Minsky.
[39] Kindleberger (1996a, 185).

discipline and readiness to sacrifice for a concerted purpose had been lost for more than a decade."[40] American decline, Charlie came to believe, was simply a fact, a consequence of aging, and so probably impossible to reverse by any politically possible policy intervention.

The central question posed by the historical record was therefore the question of succession. And here there was bad news, as it appeared that the most obvious candidates, Germany and Japan, were at most seeking dominance in their own backyards, Europe and Asia respectively, not at the level of the world as a whole.[41] Even more, after the events of 1989, Germany's focus was inevitably absorbed with the challenge of reunification with East Germany, putting off the wider European unification project.[42] And meanwhile in Japan, the bursting of the real estate and stock market bubble in 1991 had led to a shift in attitudes: "Rather than push for world-market share and even primacy, working like robots and becoming an economic giant, perhaps the time has come, some political and business leaders think, to turn to domestic problems."[43]

The question of succession thus remaining open, the next relevant question was how to bridge the time gap between US leadership and whatever comes next. For this, Charlie put his faith in "muddling through." International lender of last resort can perhaps be assured because it is operated by the leading central banks through the swap network, but provision of other public goods will likely be more problematic: "For the years immediately ahead, it would appear we have to rely on all the methods of producing public goods, trilateralism, regional-bloc building, international organizations, and perhaps especially regimes . . . I am a wobbly – not firm – believer in proceeding as the way lies open, muddling through, unwritten constitutions";[44] "I happen not to be a prophet or the son of a prophet, but I predict muddle."[45]

Those reared on the Bible may recognize the initial clause in this last quotation as coming from Amos 7:14. In the original, the passage

---

[40] Kindleberger (1996a, 222).
[41] Kindleberger (1996a, 224).
[42] Kindleberger (1996a, 169).
[43] Kindleberger (1996a, 208).
[44] Kindleberger (1995, 46–7).
[45] Kindleberger (1996a, 228).

continues "rather I was a shepherd and a tender of sycamore-fig trees." Charlie is thus identifying with Amos, called from humble beginnings to warn Israel of trouble ahead. As for the second clause, Charlie had reason to know from the experience of the 1970s that muddling through could work. Repeatedly he references the creation of the Eurocurrency markets and the central bank swap network as prime examples: "the two most far-reaching organizations of the postwar period grew like Topsy rather than springing full blown from the brow of an economist."[46] In Charlie's understanding, these institutions had been key to muddling through after Nixon's abdication. The international monetary system did not collapse then, so maybe it will be okay now as well?

The key thing for muddling through to work is to have some idea of the general direction you are trying to go so that you can recognize a possible path forward when it appears through the fog of Darwinian evolution. That's where historical perspective can help. Says Charlie: "I think I know more about desirable ultimate goals and outcomes than I do about the path or paths the world will follow in getting to them."[47] Obviously, muddle-through will be second best for provision of international public goods: "In due course a country will emerge from the muddle for a time as the primary world economic power."[48]

Having pointed to the importance of the Eurocurrency market and the central bank swap network as crucial for the successful muddle-through of the past, Charlie turns his attention to present developments in financial markets, which presumably will be crucial for successful muddle-through in the future. Most important, financial innovation is leading to the diminished importance of traditional financial intermediaries, which stand in between ultimate borrowers and lenders, offering each one the kind of financial asset/liability that it prefers. Instead, today, increasingly borrowers and lenders find one another directly and then fine-tune their preferred risk exposure using financial derivatives: "Banks and nonfinancial firms can find that pattern of liquidity that

---

[46] Kindleberger (1995, 63). See also p. 46, and Kindleberger (1969c, 14).
[47] Kindleberger (1995, 102).
[48] Kindleberger (1996a, 228).

suits them in terms of cash flows in and out through financial contracts that adjust the time profile of anticipated receipts and payments."[49]

Here, in the shifting balance between "Intermediation, Disintermediation, and Direct Trading," Charlie points to a general pattern of history that we can see in all markets, a pattern significant enough to qualify as a possible fifth "economic law" to be added to the four he had explored in his 1980 lectures *Economic Laws and Economic History*. For present purposes, the important point is that financial innovation was creating new channels for capital flow. Maybe these will provide the bridge we need until a new leader emerges? For now, to the extent that these new mechanisms work well, there is less need for a leader to manage capital flows directly.[50] Significantly, Charlie's paper on these matters was prepared for a festschrift in honor of Hyman P. Minsky. Not for the first time, Charlie's impulse was to lean against the prejudice of his audience.

Even more, Charlie would go on to suggest that the problem now had become one of the government stepping in too often and too much as lender of last resort, even when there is no real threat to the system as a whole, so defeating the necessary discipline of the market:

> Many high-minded principles suffer from entropy or decay over time, and the lender of last resort may be one of them . . . Rather than move to having government take over the financial system, including banking, I would prefer to try to stuff the genie back into the bottle, reduce the last-resort function to a weapon of rare and occasional use.[51]

Significantly, this follow-up was presented at City University Business School, where the audience would have been exactly those Charlie thought were becoming too accustomed to government bailout of their bad decisions.

This is of course a very suggestive line of thinking, but it seems to have been beyond Charlie's ability to develop it much further, given the highly technical nature of modern finance. One indication of this is his

---

[49] Kindleberger (1995, 141).
[50] Kindleberger (1995, ch. 10, 11).
[51] Kindleberger (1995, 147, 160).

repeated puzzlement in respect of why foreign lenders to US firms (and government) do not insist on lending in their own currency rather than dollars.[52] The answer, as we know today, is that lenders can and do hedge exchange risk in FX swap markets and that the central bank swap network in effect operates as backstop to those private FX markets. The larger point is that, while the United States may well have become unable to lead, the global dollar system not only survived but even expanded, with central bank cooperation serving as the key mechanism to put a floor underneath the muddle.[53]

A central theme running throughout *Economic Primacy* is the tension between centralization and pluralism. In good times, decentralization is best, while in crisis times centralization is essential. As Charlie would later put it: "On shipboard, the captain may stay below in his cabin in smooth sailing, but must come back on deck or to the bridge to assume responsibility in storm or in navigating tricky passages."[54] At the level of the international system, the problem is that institutional lag makes it difficult to switch from one mode to another in time. This same problem of course exists at the level of individual countries as well, so maybe we can learn something by looking at the historical experience of individual countries first? That's the goal of Charlie's brief follow-up book, which I have termed an after-dinner sweet. As in *Economic Primacy*, Charlie begins *Centralization versus Pluralism* with an analytical frame (chapter 2: "Theory"), and then proceeds to examine the experience of multiple individual countries, concluding that, at the level of the nation-state, "changing mentalities and institutions back and forth may not be possible, or at least not probable."[55] It goes without saying that the problem is even less amenable to solution at the international level. For lack of a captain, muddle-through is the only way forward.

It will not have escaped the reader's attention that, even as he was focused on the problem of US aging, Charlie was grappling with his own

---

[52] Kindleberger (1995, 41; 1996b, 187).
[53] Mehrling (2015).
[54] Kindleberger (1999, 23).
[55] Kindleberger (1996b, 88). See Kindleberger (1974b) for an earlier attempt to use the historical experience of individual nation-states to shed light on the possible dynamics at work in the international realm.

personal problem of aging. He might have been talking about himself when he wrote "The older a country becomes, the more it is interested in the past, rather than the future, and in art, scholarship, and literature rather than trade and industry."[56] Indeed, one source of energy for bringing the *Primacy* project to conclusion was likely its substantial therapeutic element for him. Charlie felt himself to be in decline and was concerned about his own succession. Several times in his life, Charlie had felt that he was writing his last substantive book. This time he knew it. For *Economic Primacy*, he relied heavily on the scholarly network assembled by Clesse to feed him with raw intelligence, as he indicates in the Acknowledgments to the book.[57] Going forward, however, he would have nothing but his own much-reduced library.

Writing had always been occupational therapy for him, however, so he could not very well stop. Instead, after *Economic Primacy*, he just scaled back his ambition. The main thing seems to have been periodic updating of *Manias, Panics, and Crashes*, with new editions coming out in 1996 and 2000. His 1999 collection *Essays in History: Financial, Economic, Personal* contains only three essays written later than 1995, and Charlie explicitly tells the reader that the book is "another exercise in tidying up more or less recent work for the benefit of my literary executor." Similarly, his 2000 collection *Comparative Political Economy: A Retrospective* is merely a collection of his greatest hits of a lifetime.

For our purposes, *Essays in History* is the more interesting of these efforts, in particular two chapters of personal history. Here we see him reading what others had been writing about the conduct of World War II and about the making of the Marshall Plan, and responding to them based on his own memory of events. To some extent, this is an exercise in setting the record straight, insisting for example on the important role played by his boss William Clayton in formulating the Marshall Plan. But the overall tone is more one of Charlie reliving what were for him his glory days, in effect swapping stories with others who lived through the same, even if their experience was only vicarious through archival research.

---

[56] Kindleberger (1996a, 31).
[57] Kindleberger (1996a, ix).

The only substantial post-1995 research paper included in the collection is a twenty-page essay: "Economic and Financial Crises and Transformation in Sixteenth Century Europe." Charlie tells us how that paper came to be written: "I called the project 'Operation Penelope', hoping to weave by day and unravel by night – though I had no suitors – until the Reaper came to collect. Sadly, I finished it . . . "[58] He would find other such projects to keep him busy: a planned book titled "Theory and Experience in Economics," which he abandoned after two chapters, and another on "Salt," which he completed but which was rejected for publication in 2001.

Against the background of all this scribbling, decline continued. Sarah passed away on February 26, 1997, but the "family circle" assembled at Brookhaven remained and continued to provide daily support. Increasing deafness led to increasing isolation, for which Charlie compensated by maintaining a wide correspondence with old friends and new, whom he welcomed whenever they dropped by for visits. I was one of those new friends, reaching out to him for information on Alvin Hansen when writing my first book and continuing periodically to correspond and visit thereafter, with no idea then that I would eventually be writing the present book. Finally, the Reaper did come to collect: July 7, 2003.

As body declined, reputation actually increased. Maybe not so much among economists, notwithstanding the valiant defense by people such as Barry Eichengreen and Ed Kane; a collection of reminiscences by former students published in the *Atlantic Economic Journal* (2005) mostly praise Charlie's inspirational teaching. Economic historians appreciated him a bit more, primarily as a synthesizer of work by others, but nonetheless "one of the founders of the modern school of financial history that studies financial systems as elaborate networks rather than focusing only on one or two components of that network."[59] Most of all, it was the new field of international political economy, a subfield of political science, that claimed him as a founder of so-called hegemonic stability theory.[60]

---

[58] Kindleberger (1996b, 2).
[59] Eichengreen (1997), Kane (2005), Jones (2005), Findlay (2005), Fischer (2005), Bhagwati (2005), Sylla (2005, 32).
[60] Kirshner et al. (1997), Cohen (2008, ch. 3).

It should be observed that each of these academic communities touched only one part of the Kindleberger corpus, the part that intersected with their own specific disciplinary focus. The result is that today there are multiple Kindlebergers in the literature, none of them doing full justice to the man. Similarly, outside academia, Kindleberger is mostly remembered as the author of a single book, the hardy perennial *Manias, Panics, and Crashes*, yet another partial Kindleberger. Charlie himself contributed to the impression of multiple Kindlebergers when he selfdeprecatingly "accused" (his word) himself of having a "grasshopper mind," jumping from one thing to another.[61]

My own view of the biographical truth, as elaborated in the pages preceding, is more or less exactly the opposite. There are deep constants that run throughout Charlie's life: a sense of curiosity about the world around him that fueled repeated exhaustive investigations to find the truth of the matter, largely by digging through reports that others had written and using these pieces to construct a picture of the whole. He was, as I have said, essentially an intelligence analyst, and it is this constant that is at the core of his remarkable "ability to transform" – the quality that he always insisted was the essential difference between developed economies and underdeveloped ones. His insistence on cross-checking reports from multiple sources, multiple eras, and written in multiple languages reflects the determination of an intelligence analyst to use all the information available, sorting through for the needle in the haystack, the telling detail that will make all the pieces fall into place.

Call it comparative economic history, as he did in *Economic Response*, or comparative political economy, as he did in his *Retrospective*, but that's just Charlie's way of drawing the attention of a specific target audience. Charlie was never content just to satisfy his own curiosity. He wanted to tell others so that they could use this new knowledge – indeed, he felt a positive duty to do so, even (or perhaps especially) when the truth he had to tell was uncomfortable or unwelcome.

The world, so Charlie insists, needs "strong leadership, best when it is disguised,"[62] lest it be resented and resisted. Charlie's own disguise was in

---

[61] Kindleberger (1999, 1).
[62] Kindleberger (1996a, 227).

plain sight. As a self-proclaimed "literary" economist, he posed no threat to the "theorists." He was just a country gentleman with a history hobby in addition to beekeeping, a devoted teacher who had no interest in collecting disciples, a team player at MIT no matter his disagreements, and a man of principle rather than worldly ambition. No one resented or resisted Charlie, even when he was telling them something unwelcome, because he always made it seem like he was just having a bit of fun, doing his bit to keep the dinner party conversation lively. A constant in the reminiscences of his students is that initially they thought he was a terrible teacher, but looking back they realize that they learned more in his class than in any other. That's leadership, well disguised.

Bibliography

MANUSCRIPT COLLECTIONS

KPMD   = Charles P. Kindleberger Papers, MIT Library, Department of Distinctive Collections
KPTL   = Charles P. Kindleberger Papers, Harry S. Truman Library

ARTICLES AND BOOKS

Agmon, Tamir and Charles P. Kindleberger, eds. 1977. *Multinationals from Small Countries.* Cambridge, MA: The MIT Press.

Alacevich, Michele, Pier Francesco Asso, and Sevastiano Nerozzi. 2015. "Harvard Meets the Crisis: The Monetary Theory and Policy of Lauchlin B. Currie, Jacob Viner, John H. Williams, and Harry D. White." *Journal of the History of Economic Thought* 37 No. 3 (September): 387–410.

Alexander, Sidney S. 1952. "Effects of a Devaluation on a Trade Balance." *Staff Papers (International Monetary Fund)* 2 (April): 263–278.

Angell, James W. 1922. "International Trade Under Inconvertible Paper." *Quarterly Journal of Economics* 36 No. 3 (May): 359–412. https://doi.org/10.2307/188603.

Angell, James W. 1925. "The Effects of International Payments in the Past"; "The Debts and American Finance." Chapters 5 and 6 in *The Inter-Ally Debts and the United States,* pages 138–228. New York: National Industrial Conference Board.

Angell, James W. 1926. *The Theory of International Prices: History, Criticism and Restatement.* Cambridge, MA: Harvard University Press.

Angell, James W. 1929. *The Recovery of Germany.* New Haven, CT: Yale University Press.

Angell, James W. 1931. "America's Role in the International Economic Situation." *Proceedings of the Academy of Political Science* 14 No. 2 (January): 70–80.

Angell, James W. 1932. Report of Committee of Economists on Intergovernmental Debts. Available at https://clio.columbia.edu/catalog/SCSB-689117.

Angell, James W. 1933a. *Financial Foreign Policy of the United States.* New York: Council on Foreign Relations.

Angell, James W. 1933b. *The Program for the World Economic Conference, The Experts' Agenda and other Documents*. Boston, MA: World Peace Foundation.

Angell, James W. 1936a. "Equilibrium in International Payments: The United States 1919–1935." Pages 13–25 in *Explorations in Economics: Notes and Essays contributed in honor of F. W. Taussig*. New York: McGraw-Hill.

Angell, James W. 1936b. *The Behavior of Money: Exploratory Studies*. New York: McGraw-Hill.

Angell, James W. 1941. *Investment and Business Cycles*. New York: McGraw-Hill.

Arnold, Thurman W. 1937. *The Folklore of Capitalism*. New Haven, CT: Yale University Press.

Arnon, Arie and Warren Young. 2002. *The Open Economy Macromodel: Past, Present, and Future*. Boston, MA: Springer.

Askari, Hossein and Franco Modigliani. 1972. "The International Payments System: Past, Present, and Future." *Sloan Management Review* 13 No. 3 (Spring): 1–16.

Asso, Pier Francesco and Luca Fiorito. 2009. "A Scholar in Action in Interwar America: John H. Williams on Trade Theory and Bretton Woods." Pages 180–242 in *American Power and Policy*, edited by Robert Leeson. London: Palgrave Macmillan.

Auboin, Roger. 1955. "The Bank for International Settlements, 1930–1955." *Essays in International Finance* No. 22 (May). Princeton University. Available at https://ies.princeton.edu/research/historicalpublications/.

Babington-Smith, Constance. 1987. *Air Spy: The Story of Photo Intelligence in World War II*. New York: Harper and Row.

Bank for International Settlements. 1940. *Tenth Annual Report*. Basel: BIS.

Bator, Francis M. 1968. "The Political Economics of International Money." *Foreign Affairs* 47 No. 1 (October): 51–67.

Bernes, Thomas, Paul Jenkins, Perry Mehrling, and Daniel Neilson. 2014. *China's Engagement With an Evolving International Monetary System: A Payments Approach*. Waterloo, Ontario, and New York: Center for International Governance Innovation and Institute for New Economic Thinking.

Bhagwati, Jagdish. 2005. "Remembering Charlie." *Atlantic Economic Journal* 33: 27–28.

Bhagwati, Jagdish and H. G. Johnson. 1960. "Notes on Some Controversies in the Theory of International Trade." *Economic Journal* 70 No. 277 (March): 74–93.

Bhagwati, Jagdish and H. G. Johnson. 1961. "Notes on Some Controversies in the Theory of International Trade." *Economic Journal* 71 No. 282 (June): 427–430.

Bhagwati, Jagdish N., Ronald W. Jones, Robert A. Mundell, and Jaroslav Vanek. 1971. *Trade, Balance of Payments, and Growth. Papers in International Economics in Honor of Charles P. Kindleberger*. Amsterdam: North-Holland.

Bird, Kai. 1992. *The Chairman: John J. McCloy and the Making of the American Establishment*. New York: Simon and Schuster.

Bissell, Richard M. 1996. *Reflections of a Cold Warrior: From Yalta to the Bay of Pigs*. New Haven, CT: Yale University Press.

Blackmer, Donald L. M. 2002. *The MIT Center for International Studies: The Founding Years 1951–1969*. Cambridge, MA: MIT Center for International Studies.

Bloomfield, Arthur I. 1949. "Induced Investment, Overcomplete Adjustment, and Chronic Dollar Shortage." *American Economic Review* 39 No. 5 (September): 970–974.

Bloomfield, Arthur I. 1950. *Capital Imports and the American Balance of Payments, 1934–39: A Study in Abnormal International Capital Transfers.* Chicago, IL: University of Chicago Press.

Bloomfield, Arthur I. 1952. "Review of *The Dollar Shortage*, by C. P. Kindleberger." *Review of Economics and Statistics* 32 No. 4: 189–190.

Bloomfield, Arthur I. 1969. "Recent Trends in International Economics." *The Annals of the American Academy of Political and Social Science* 386 (November): 148–167. https://doi.org/10.1177/000271626938600114.

Boughton, James H. 2003. "On the Origins of the Fleming-Mundell Model." *IMF Staff Papers* 50 No. 1: 1–9.

Boughton, James M. and Roger J. Sandilands. 2003. "Politics and the Attack on FDR's Economists: From the Grand Alliance to the Cold War." *Intelligence and National Security* 18 No. 3 (June): 73–99.

Cairncross, Alec. 1985. "Economics in Theory and Practice." *American Economic Review* 75 No. 2 (May): 1–14.

Cairncross, Alec. 1986. *The Price of War, British Policy on German Reparations, 1941–1949.* Oxford: Basil Blackwell.

Cherrier, Beatrice. 2014. "Toward a History of Economics at MIT, 1940–72." Pages 15–44 in E. Roy Weintraub (ed.), *MIT and the Transformation of American Economics.* Durham, NC: Duke University Press.

Chipman, John S. and Charles P. Kindleberger. 1980. *Flexible Exchange Rates and the Balance of Payments: Essays in Memory of Egon Sohmen.* Amsterdam: North-Holland.

Clarke, Stephen V. O. 1967. *Central Bank Cooperation, 1924–31.* New York: Federal Reserve Bank of New York.

Clarke, Stephen V. O. 1973. *The Reconstruction of the International Monetary System: The Attempts of 1922 and 1933.* Princeton Studies in International Finance, No. 33. Princeton, NJ: Princeton University. Available at https://ies.princeton.edu/research/historicalpublications/.

Clarke, Stephen V. O. 1977a. "The Influence of Economists on the Tripartite Agreement of September 1936." *European Economic Review* 10: 375–389.

Clarke, Stephen V. O. 1977b. *Exchange-Rate Stabilization in the Mid-1930s: Negotiating the Tripartite Agreement.* Princeton Studies in International Finance, No. 41. Princeton, NJ: Princeton University. Available at https://ies.princeton.edu/research/historicalpublications/.

Clavin, Patricia. 1996. *The Failure of Economic Diplomacy: Britain, Germany, France and the United States, 1931–1936.* New York: St. Martin's Press.

Clavin, Patricia. 2013. *Securing the World Economy: The Reinvention of the League of Nations, 1920–1946.* Oxford: Oxford University Press.

Clay, Lucius. 1950. *Decision in Germany.* Garden City, NY: Doubleday and Co.

Cohen, Benjamin J. 2008. *International Political Economy: An Intellectual History.* Princeton, NJ: Princeton University Press.

Colm, Gerhard, Joseph M. Dodge, and Raymond W. Goldsmith. 1955. "A Plan for the Liquidation of War Finance and the Financial Rehabilitation of Germany." *Zeitschrift fur die gesamte Staatswissenschaft* 111: 204–243.

Connell, Carol M. 2013. *Reforming the World Monetary System: Fritz Machlup and the Bellagio Group*. London: Pickering and Chatto.

Coombs, Charles A. 1963. "Treasury and Federal Reserve Foreign Exchange Operations." *Federal Reserve Bulletin* (September): 1216–23.

Coombs, Charles A. 1976. *The Arena of International Finance*. New York: John Wiley and Sons.

DeCecco, Marcello. 1974. *Money and Empire: The International Gold Standard, 1890–1914*. Oxford: Basil Blackwell.

DeLong, J. Bradford and Barry Eichengreen. 2013. "Foreword" to *40th Anniversary edition of The World in Depression, 1929–1939*, by Charles P. Kindleberger. Berkeley, CA: University of California Press.

Denison, Edward F. 1967. *Why Growth Rates Differ: Postwar Experience in Nine Western Countries*. Washington, DC: Brookings Institution.

Department of State. 1946. *United States Economic Policy toward Germany*. European Series 15. Washington, DC: US Government Printing Office.

Department of State. 1947. *Occupation of Germany, Policy and Progress: 1945–1946*. European Series 23. Washington, DC: US Government Printing Office.

Despres, Emile. 1938. Review of *International Short-Term Capital Movements* by Charles Poor Kindleberger. *Journal of the American Statistical Association* 33, No. 201 (March): 296–298.

Despres, Emile. 1973. *International Economic Reform, Collected Papers of Emile Despres*, edited by Gerald M. Meier. New York: Oxford.

Despres, Emile, Charles Kindleberger, and Walter Salant. 1966. "The Dollar and World Liquidity: A Minority View." *Economist* 218, No. 6389 (February 5). Reprinted as pages 42–52 in Charles P. Kindleberger, 1981. *International Money: A Collection of Essays*. Boston, MA: Allen and Unwin (Ch. 4) and pages 207–218 in Charles P. Kindleberger, 2000. *Comparative Political Economy: A Retrospective*. Cambridge MA: MIT Press (Ch. 9).

De Vries, Margaret Garritsen. 1987. *Balance of Payments Adjustment, 1945 to 1986. The IMF Experience*. Washington, DC: International Monetary Fund.

Dornbusch, Rudiger. 1976. "Exchange Rate Expectations and Monetary Policy." *Journal of International Economics* 6: 231–44.

Dornbusch, Rudiger. 1980. *Open Economy Macroeconomics*. New York: Basic Books.

Edey, Maitland. 1983. "Some recollections of Kent in the 1920s." *Kent Quarterly* (Winter): 14–26.

Eichengreen, Barry. 1997. "Reflections on Financial Instability and the Need for an International Lender of Last Resort." Pages 340–343 in Jonathan Kirschner, Peter A. Gourevitch, and Barry Eichengreen. 1997. "Crossing Disciplines and Charting New Paths: The Influence of Charles Kindleberger on International Relations." *Mershon International Studies Review* 41 No. 2 (November): 333–345.

Einzig, Paul. 1937. *The Theory of Forward Exchange*. London: Macmillan.

Enke, Stephen and Virgil Salera. 1947. *International Economics*. New York: Prentice Hall.

Enright, Rosemary and Sue Maden. 2010. *Jamestown, A History of Narragansett Bay's Island Town*. Charlestown, SC: The History Press.

Enright, Rosemary and Sue Maden. 2014. *Legendary Locals of Jamestown*. Charlestown, SC: Arcadia Press.

Enright, Rosemary and Sue Maden. 2016. *Historic Tales of Jamestown*. Charlestown, SC: The History Press.

Ferguson, Thomas and Peter Temin. 2003. "Made in Germany: The German Currency Crisis of July 1931." *Research in Economic History* 21, 1–53.

Findlay, Ronald. 2005. "Kindleberger: Economics and History." *Atlantic Economic Journal* 33: 19–21.

Fischer, Stanley. 2005. "Charlie Kindleberger." *Atlantic Economic Journal* 33: 23–26.

Flandreau, Marc, Carl-Ludwig Holtfrerich, and Harold James, eds. 2003. *International Financial History in the Twentieth Century, System and Anarchy*. New York: Cambridge University Press.

Fleming, J. Marcus. 1962. "Domestic Financial Policies under Fixed and under Floating Exchange Rates." *Staff Papers* 9 No. 3 (November): 369–380.

Fleming, J. Marcus and Robert A. Mundell. 1964. "Official Intervention on the Forward Exchange Market: A Simplified Analysis." *Staff Papers* 11 No. 1 (March): 1–19.

French, John C. 1944. "Tribute to Louis Wardlaw Miles." *ELH [English Literary History]* 11 No. 1 (March): v–vi.

Frenkel, Jacob A. and Harry G. Johnson. 1976. *The Monetary Approach to the Balance of Payments*. London: Allen and Unwin.

Friedman, Milton. 1946. "Lange on Price Flexibility and Employment: A Methodological Criticism." *American Economic Review* 36 No. 4: 613–631.

Friedman, Milton. 1948. "A Monetary and Fiscal Framework for Economic Stability." *American Economic Review* 38 No. 3: 245–264.

Friedman, Milton. 1953. "The Case for Flexible Exchange Rates." Pages 157–203 in *Essays in Positive Economics*. Chicago, IL: University of Chicago Press.

Friedman, Milton, ed. 1956. *Studies in the Quantity Theory of Money*. Chicago, IL: University of Chicago Press.

Friedman, Milton. 1959. *A Program for Monetary Stability*. New York: Fordham University Press.

Friedman, Milton. 1969. "Round Table on Exchange Rate Policy." *American Economic Review* 59 No. 2 (May): 364–366.

Friedman, Milton. 1970. "Discussion." Pages 109–119 in *The International Adjustment Mechanism: Proceedings of the Monetary Conference [October 1969]*. Federal Reserve Bank of Boston Conference Series, No. 2.

Friedman, Milton and Robert Roosa. 1967. *The Balance of Payments: Free Versus Fixed Exchange Rates*. Washington, DC: American Enterprise Institute.

Friedman, Milton and Anna Schwartz. 1963. *A Monetary History of the United States, 1867–1960*. Princeton, NJ: Princeton University Press.

Friend, Tad. 2009. *Cheerful Money: Me, My Family, and the Last Days of Wasp Splendor*. Boston, MA: Little, Brown and Company.

Galbraith, Kenneth. 1991. "Foreword." Pages x–xii in Charles P. Kindleberger, 1991. *The Life of an Economist: An Autobiography*. Cambridge, MA: Basil Blackwell.

Gerschenkron, Alexander. 1962. *Economic Backwardness in Historical Perspective: A Book of Essays*. Cambridge, MA: Belknap Press.

Giraud, Yann. 2014. "Negotiating the 'Middle-of-the-Road' Position: Paul Samuelson, MIT, and the Politics of Textbook Writing, 1945–55." Pages

134–152 in E. Roy Weintraub (ed.), *MIT and the Transformation of American Economics.* Durham NC: Duke University Press.

Gottlieb, Manuel. 1956/1957. "Failure of Quadripartite Monetary Reform 1945–1947." *FinanzArchiv* 17 H. 3: 398–417.

Gross, Stephen G. 2017. "Gold, Debt and the Quest for Monetary Order: The Nazi Campaign to Integrate Europe in 1940." *Contemporary European History* 26 No. 2: 287–309.

Halm, George N. 1970. *Approaches to Greater Flexibility of Exchange Rates: The Burgenstock Papers.* Princeton, NJ: Princeton University Press.

Hammes, David. 2001. "Locating Federal Reserve Districts and Headquarters Cities." Federal Reserve Bank of Minneapolis, *The Region* (September). Available at www.minneapolisfed.org/article/2001/locating-federal-reserve-districts-and-headquarters-cities.

Hansen, Alvin H. 1939. "Economic Progress and Declining Population Growth." *American Economic Review* 29 No. 1 (March): 1–15.

Hansen, Alvin H. 1965. *The Dollar and the International System.* New York: McGraw-Hill.

Hansen, Alvin H. and C. P. Kindleberger. 1942a. "The Economic Tasks of the Postwar World." *Foreign Affairs* 20 No. 3 (April): 466–476.

Hansen, Alvin H. and C. P. Kindleberger. 1942b. *International Development Loans.* Planning Pamphlet #15 (September). Washington, DC: National Planning Association.

Hawtrey, Ralph. 1927. Review of *The Theory of International Prices* by James W. Angell. *Economic Journal* 37 No. 148 (December): 597–599.

Herrick, Bruce H. 1966. *Urban Migration and Economic Development in Chile.* Cambridge, MA: MIT Press.

Hoffman, Stanley, Charles P. Kindleberger, Lawrence Wylie, Jesse R. Pitts, Jean-Baptiste Duroselle, and Francois Goguel. 1963. *In Search of France.* Cambridge MA: Harvard University Press.

Hymer, Stephen. 1976. *The International Operations of National Firms: A Study of Direct Foreign Investment.* Cambridge, MA: The MIT Press.

International Monetary Fund. 1977. *The Monetary Approach to the Balance of Payments.* Washington, DC: IMF.

Jacobsson, Erin E. 1979. *A Life for Sound Money, Per Jacobsson, His Biography.* Oxford: Clarendon Press.

James, Harold. 2012. "The Multiple Contexts of Bretton Woods." *Oxford Review of Economic Policy* 28 No. 3: 411–430.

Johnson, Harry G. 1973. "The Problems of Central Bankers." *Economic Notes,* Monte dei Paschi di Siena 2 No. 3 (September–December).

Johnson, Harry G. 1981. "Networks of Economists: Their role in international monetary reforms." Pages 79–90 in *Knowledge and Power in a Global Society,* edited by William M. Evan. Beverly Hills, CA: Sage.

Johnson, Harry G. and Alexander K. Swoboda, eds. 1973. *Economics of Common Currencies: Proceedings of 1970 Madrid Conference on Optimum Currency Areas.* Cambridge, MA: Harvard University Press.

Jones, Joseph Marion. 1955. *The Fifteen Weeks (February 21–June 5, 1947).* New York: Harcourt Brace.

Jones, Ronald W. 2005. "Remembering Charlie Kindleberger." *Atlantic Economic Journal* 33: 15–17.

Kane, Edward J. 2005. "Charles Kindleberger: An Impressionist in a Minimalist World." *Atlantic Economic Journal* 33: 35–42.

Kaplan, Jacob J and Gunther Schleiminger. 1989. *The European Payments Union, Financial Diplomacy in the 1950s.* Oxford: Clarendon Press.

Katz, Barry M. 1989. *Foreign Intelligence: Research and Analysis in the Office of Strategic Services, 1942–1945.* Cambridge, MA: Harvard University Press.

Keohane, Robert. 1984. *After Hegemony: Cooperation and Discord in the World Political Economy.* Princeton, NJ: Princeton University Press.

Keynes, John Maynard. 1919. *The Economic Consequences of the Peace.* London: Macmillan.

Keynes, John Maynard. 1933. "National Self-Sufficiency." *The Yale Review* 22 No. 4 (June): 755–769.

Keynes, John Maynard. 1936. *The General Theory of Employment, Interest, and Money.* London: Macmillan.

Killian, James Rhyne. 1985. *The Education of a College President: A Memoir.* Cambridge, MA: MIT Press.

Kindleberger, Charles P. 1934. "Competitive Currency Depreciation between Denmark and New Zealand." *Harvard Business Review* 12 No. 4 (July): 416–427.

Kindleberger, Charles P. 1936. "Review of Iverson, Nurkse, and Malpas." *Political Science Quarterly* 51 No. 4 (December): 607–610.

Kindleberger, Charles P. 1937a. "Flexibility of Demand in International Trade Theory." *Quarterly Journal of Economics* 51 No. 2 (February): 352–361.

Kindleberger, Charles P. 1937b. *International Short-Term Capital Movements.* New York: Columbia University Press.

Kindleberger, Charles P. 1939. "Speculation and Forward Exchange." *Journal of Political Economy* 47 No. 2 (April): 163–181. Reprinted as pages 271–289 in Charles P. Kindleberger, 1966. *Europe and the Dollar.* Cambridge, MA: MIT Press.

Kindleberger, Charles P. 1941. *Britain's Trade in the Post-War World. Planning Pamphlet #9 (December).* Washington, DC: National Planning Association.

Kindleberger, Charles P. 1943a. "Planning for Foreign Investment." *American Economic Review* 33 No. 1, Part 2, Supplement (March): 347–354.

Kindleberger, Charles P. 1943b. "International Monetary Stabilization." Pages 375–395 in *Postwar Economic Problems,* edited by Seymour E. Harris. New York: McGraw-Hill.

Kindleberger, Charles P. 1949a. "The Foreign-Trade Multiplier, The Propensity to Import and Balance-of-Payments Equilibrium." *American Economic Review* 39 No. 2 (March): 491–494; "Rejoinder." *American Economic Review* 39 No. 5 (September): 975.

Kindleberger, Charles P. 1949b. "Review of *A Charter for World Trade* by Clair Wilcox." *The Review of Economics and Statistics* 31 No. 3 (August): 241–242.

Kindleberger, Charles P. 1950. *The Dollar Shortage.* Cambridge, MA: MIT Press.

Kindleberger, Charles P. 1951a. "Bretton Woods Reappraised." *International Organization* 5 No. 1 (February): 32–47.

Kindleberger, Charles P. 1951b. "Group Behavior and International Trade." *Journal of Political Economy* 59 (February): 30–47. Reprinted as pp. 19–38 in Kindleberger, Charles P. 1978a. *Economic Response, Comparative Studies in Trade, Finance and Growth.* Cambridge, MA: Harvard University Press; and pp. 51–72 in Kindleberger, Charles P. 2000a. *Comparative Political Economy: A Retrospective.* Cambridge, MA: MIT Press.

Kindleberger, Charles P. 1952a. "Review of Monetary Problems of an Export Economy: Cuban Experience–1914–1947 by Henry Christopher Wallich." *The Review of Economics and Statistics,* 34 No. 1 (February): 94–95.

Kindleberger, Charles P. 1952b. "Review of *The Economy of Turkey: An Analysis and Recommendations for a Development Program* by International Bank for Reconstruction and Development: *The Economic Development of Guatemala* by International Bank for Reconstruction and Development: *Report on Cuba* by International Bank for Reconstruction and Development." *The Review of Economics and Statistics* 34 No. 4 (November): 391–394.

Kindleberger, Charles P. 1953. *International Economics.* Homewood, IL: Richard D. Irwin. Revised edition, 1958.

Kindleberger, Charles P. 1955a. "Economists in International Organizations." *International Organization* 9 No. 3 (August): 338–352.

Kindleberger, Charles P. 1955b. "Review of *Trade, Aid, or What?* by Willard L. Thorp." *The Review of Economics and Statistics* 37 No. 4 (November): 437–438.

Kindleberger, Charles P. 1956. *The Terms of Trade: A European Case Study.* Cambridge, MA: Harvard University Press.

Kindleberger, Charles P. 1957a. "The Objectives of United States Economic Assistance Programs," a study prepared at the request of the Special Committee to Study the Foreign Aid Program, United States Senate, by the CIS, MIT (January). 85th Congress, 1st Session.

Kindleberger, Charles P. 1957b. "Partial vs. General Equilibrium in International Trade." *Indian Journal of Economics* 38 No. 148 (July): 31–39.

Kindleberger, Charles P. 1958a. *International Economics.* Revised Edition. Homewood, IL: Richard D. Irwin.

Kindleberger, Charles P. 1958b. *Economic Development.* New York: McGraw-Hill.

Kindleberger, Charles P. 1959. "United States Economic Foreign Policy: Research Requirements for 1965." *World Politics* 11 No. 4 (July): 588–614.

Kindleberger, Charles P. 1961. "La fin du role dominant des Etats Unis et l'Avenir d'une politique economique mondiale." *Cahiers de l'Institut de Science Economique Appliquee,* No. 113 (May): 91–105.

Kindleberger, Charles P. 1962. *Foreign Trade and the National Economy.* New Haven, CT: Yale University Press.

Kindleberger, Charles P. 1963a. "The Postwar Resurgence of the French Economy." In Hoffman, Stanley, Charles P. Kindleberger, Lawrence Wylie, Jesse R. Pitts, Jean-Baptiste Duroselle, and Francois Goguel. 1963. *In Search of France.* Cambridge MA: Harvard University Press. [Reprinted as pages 166–201 in Charles P. Kindleberger, 1990. *Historical Economics: Art or Science?* Berkeley, CA: University of California Press.]

Kindleberger, Charles P. 1963b. "Review of *Economic Backwardness in Historical Perspective: A Book of Essays* by Alexander Gerschenkron." *The Journal of Economic History* 23 No. 3 (Sept.): 360–362.

Kindleberger, Charles P. 1964. *Economic Growth in France and Britain, 1851–1950.* Cambridge, MA: Harvard University Press.

Kindleberger, Charles P. 1965a. "Trends in International Economics." In *The Annals of the American Academy of Political and Social Science* 358 (March): 170–179.

Kindleberger, Charles P. 1965b. "The United States Balance of Payments in the Nineteenth Century: a review article." *Explorations in Entrepreneurial History* 3 No. 1 (Fall): 50–55.

Kindleberger, Charles P. 1965c. "The United States Balance of Payments in the Nineteenth Century, A Review Article." *Explorations in Entrepreneurial History* 3 No. 1: 50–55.

Kindleberger, Charles P. 1966. *Europe and the Dollar.* Cambridge, MA: MIT Press.

Kindleberger, Charles P. 1967a. "The International Firm and the International Capital Market." *Southern Economic Journal* 34 No. 2 (October): 223–230.

Kindleberger, Charles P. 1967b. *Europe's Postwar Growth: The Role of Labor Supply.* Cambridge, MA: Harvard University Press.

Kindleberger, Charles P. 1969a. *American Business Abroad: Six Lectures on Direct Investment.* New Haven, CT: Yale University Press.

Kindleberger, Charles P. 1969b. "Measuring Equilibrium in the Balance of Payments." *Journal of Political Economy* 77 No. 6 (November): 873–891.

Kindleberger, Charles P. 1969c. "The Eurodollar and the internationalization of United States monetary policy." *Banca Nazionale del Lavoro Quarterly Review* (March): 3–15. Reprinted as pages 100–110 in Kindleberger (1981a).

Kindleberger, Charles P. 1970a. *Power and Money: The Economics of International Politics and the Politics of International Economics.* New York: Basic Books.

Kindleberger, Charles P. 1970b. "The Dollar System." *New England Economic Review* (Sept./Oct): 3–9.

Kindleberger, Charles P., ed. 1970c. *The International Corporation.* Cambridge, MA: The MIT Press.

Kindleberger, Charles P. 1971. "Review of Mundell and Swoboda, *Monetary Problems of the International Economy*." *Journal of International Economics* 1 No. 1 (February): 127–131.

Kindleberger, Charles P. 1973. *The World in Depression, 1929–1939.* Berkeley, CA: University of California Press.

Kindleberger, Charles P. 1974a. "The Great Transformation by Karl Polanyi." *Daedalus* (Winter): 45–53.

Kindleberger, Charles P. 1974b. "The Formation of Financial Centers: A Study in Comparative Economic History." *Princeton Studies in International Finance* No. 36. Princeton, NJ: Princeton University Press.

Kindleberger, Charles P. 1976a. "*Review of On Economics and Society*, by Harry G. Johnson." *The Journal of Business* 49 No. 2 (April): 270–272.

Kindleberger, Charles P. 1976b. "Review of *A World Divided: The Less Developed Countries in the International Economy*, edited by G. K. Helleiner." *Journal of Development Economics* 3: 299–305.

Kindleberger, Charles P. 1977a. "Review of *The End of French Predominance in Europe: The Financial Crisis and the Adoption of the Dawes Plan* by Stephen A. Schuker." *The Journal of Economic History* 37 No. 3 (September): 843–845.

Kindleberger, Charles P. 1977b. "Internationalist and Nationalist Models in the Analysis of the Brain Drain: Progress and Unsolved Problems." *Minerva* 15 No. 3/4: 553–561.

Kindleberger, Charles P. 1977c. "Review of *The Arena of International Finance*, by Charles A. Coombs." *Journal of Portfolio Management* 3 No. 3 (Spring): 73–74.

Kindleberger, Charles P. 1977d. "In Memoriam Egon Sohmen 1930–1977." *Journal of International Economics* 7: 307–308.

Kindleberger, Charles P. 1978a. *Economic Response, Comparative Studies in Trade, Finance and Growth*. Cambridge, MA: Harvard University Press.

Kindleberger, Charles P. 1978b. *Manias, Panics, and Crashes: A History of Financial Crises*. New York: Basic Books.

Kindleberger, Charles P. 1978c. "The OECD and the Third World." Pages 105–121 in *From Marshall Plan to Global Interdependence*. Paris: OECD.

Kindleberger, Charles P. 1978d. "World War II Strategy." Review of Zuckerman (1978). *Encounter* [London] 51, No. 5 (November): 39–41.

Kindleberger, Charles P. 1980a. "Review of *Money in International Exchange: The Convertible Currency System* by Ronald I. McKinnon." *Journal of Political Economy* 88 No. 4 (August): 819–822.

Kindleberger, Charles P. 1980b. "Myths and Realities of Forward-Exchange Markets." Pages 127–38 in *Flexible Exchange Rates and the Balance of Payments*, edited by John S. Chipman and Charles P. Kindleberger. Amsterdam: North-Holland.

Kindleberger, Charles P. 1980c. "The Life of an Economist." *Banca Nazionale del Lavoro Quarterly Review* 134 (September): 231–245.

Kindleberger, Charles P. 1981a. *International Money: A Collection of Essays*. Boston, MA: Allen and Unwin.

Kindleberger, Charles P. 1981b. "Review of *The Great Depression Revisited*, by Karl Brunner." *Journal of Economic Literature* 19 No. 4 (December): 1585–1586.

Kindleberger, Charles P. 1982. "Assets and Liabilities of International Economics: The Postwar Bankruptcy of Theory and Policy." Pages 47–64 in *Experiences and Problems of the International Monetary System, 1972–1982*. Special Issue of *Economic Notes*. Siena, Italy: Monte dei Paschi di Siena.

Kindleberger, Charles P. 1984a. *A Financial History of Western Europe*. London: Allen and Unwin.

Kindleberger, Charles P. 1984b. *Multinational Excursions*. Cambridge, MA: MIT Press.

Kindleberger, Charles P. 1984c. "The Dollar Yesterday, Today, and Tomorrow." *Banca Nazionale del Lavoro Quarterly Review* No. 155 (December): 295–308.

Kindleberger, Charles P. 1985a. "International Public Goods without International Government." *American Economic Review* 76 No. 1: 1–13.

Kindleberger, Charles P. 1985b. "The Functioning of Financial Centers: Britain in the Nineteenth Century, the United States since 1945." Pages 7–32 in "International Financial Markets and Capital Movements, A Symposium in Honor of Arthur I. Bloomfield." *Essays in International Finance* No 157

(September). Princeton, NJ: International Finance Section, Department of Economics, Princeton University.

Kindleberger, Charles P. 1985c. *Keynesianism vs. Monetarism, and Other Essays in Financial History.* Boston, MA: Allen and Unwin.

Kindleberger, Charles P. 1986a. *The World in Depression, 1929–1939.* Revised and enlarged edition. Berkeley, CA: University of California Press.

Kindleberger, Charles P. 1986b. "My Working Philosophy." *The American Economist* 30 No. 1 (Spring): 13–20.

Kindleberger, Charles P. 1987a. *International Capital Movements (The Marshall Lectures).* New York: Cambridge University Press.

Kindleberger, Charles P. 1987b. *Marshall Plan Days.* Boston, MA: Allen & Unwin.

Kindleberger, Charles P. 1987c. "Gunnar Myrdal, 1898–1987." *Scandinavian Journal of Economics* 89 No. 4 (December): 393–403.

Kindleberger, Charles P. 1987d. "Henry George's Protection or Free Trade." Williams College Research Paper No. 102 (May).

Kindleberger, Charles P. 1988a. *The International Economic Order: Essays on Financial Crisis and International Public Goods.* Cambridge, MA: The MIT Press.

Kindleberger, Charles P. 1988b. "Review of 'Balance of Payments Adjustment, 1945 to 1986: The IMF Experience,' by Margaret Garritsen de Vries." *American Journal of International Law* 82 No. 4 (October): 895–898.

Kindleberger, Charles P. 1989a. *Economics Laws and Economic History.* New York: Cambridge University Press.

Kindleberger, Charles P. 1989b. *The German Economy, 1945–1947: Charles P. Kindleberger's Letters from the Field.* London: Meckler.

Kindleberger, Charles P. 1989c. "How Ideas Spread Among Economists: Examples from International Economics." Pages 43–59 in *The Spread of Economic Ideas,* edited by David C. Colander and A. W. Coats. New York: Cambridge University Press.

Kindleberger, Charles P. 1990. *Historical Economics: Art or Science?* Berkeley, CA: University of California Press.

Kindleberger, Charles P. 1991a. *The Life of an Economist: An Autobiography.* Cambridge, MA: Basil Blackwell.

Kindleberger, Charles P. 1991b. "Review of *Markets in History,* edited by David W. Galenson." *Weltwirtschaftliches Archiv,* Vol. 127, No. 1: 203–206.

Kindleberger, Charles P. 1992. *Mariners and Markets.* New York: New York University Press.

Kindleberger, Charles P. 1993. *A Financial History of Western Europe.* 2nd ed. New York: Oxford University Press.

Kindleberger, Charles P. 1995. *The World Economy and National Finance in Historical Perspective.* Ann Arbor, MI: University of Michigan Press.

Kindleberger, Charles P. 1996a. *World Economic Primacy: 1500–1990.* New York: Oxford University Press.

Kindleberger, Charles P. 1996b. *Centralization versus Pluralism: A Historical Examination of Political-Economic Struggles and Swings within Some Leading Nations.* Copenhagen: Handelshojskolens Forlag.

Kindleberger, Charles P. 1997. "In the Halls of the Capitol: A Memoir." *Foreign Affairs* 76 No. 3 (May–June): 185–190.

Kindleberger, Charles P. 1999. *Essays in History: Financial, Economic, Personal.* Ann Arbor, MI: University of Michigan Press.

Kindleberger, Charles P. 2000a. *Comparative Political Economy: A Retrospective.* Cambridge, MA: MIT Press.

Kindleberger, Charles P. 2000b. "A New Bi-Polarity?" Pages 3–20 in *The Euro as a Stabilizer in the International Economic System,* edited by Robert Mundell and Armand Clesse. Norwell, MA: Kluwer Academic Publishers.

Kindleberger, Charles P. 2013 [1973]. *The World in Depression, 1929–1939.* 40th Anniversary edition. Berkeley, CA: University of California Press.

Kindleberger, Charles P. and David B. Audretsch. 1983. *The Multinational Corporation in the 1980s.* Cambridge, MA: The MIT Press.

Kindleberger, Charles P. and Jean-Pierre Laffargue, eds. 1982. *Financial Crises: Theory, History and Policy.* Cambridge: Cambridge University Press.

Kindleberger, Charles P and F. Taylor Ostrander. 2003. "The 1948 Monetary Reform in Western Germany." Pages 169–195 in Marc, Flandreau, Carl-Ludwig Holtfrerich, and Harold James, eds., *International Financial History in the Twentieth Century, System and Anarchy.* New York: Cambridge University Press.

Kindleberger, Charles P. and Andrew Shonfield. 1971. *North American and Western European Economic Policies.* London: Macmillan.

Kindleberger, Charles P. and G. O. Trenchard. 1935. "Bank Credit and Business Demands." *Barron's* 15 No. 30 (July 29): 6.

Kirschner, Jonathan, Peter A. Gourevitch, and Barry Eichengreen. 1997. "Crossing Disciplines and Charting New Paths: The Influence of Charles Kindleberger on International Relations." *Mershon International Studies Review* 41 No. 2 (November): 333–345.

Lamfalussy, Alexandre. 1985. "The Changing Environment of Central Bank Policy." *American Economic Review* 75 No. 2 (May): 409–414.

Lary, Hal B. 1963. *Problems of the United States as World Trader and Banker.* New York: NBER.

Leffler, Melvyn P. 1996. "The Struggle for Germany and the Origins of the Cold War." Occasional Paper No. 16. Washington, DC: German Historical Institute.

Lewis, W. Arthur. 1954. "Economic Development with Unlimited Supplies of Labour." *The Manchester School* 22 No. 2 (May): 139–191.

Lindert, Peter H. 1969. *Key Currencies and Gold, 1900–1913.* Princeton Studies in International Finance No. 24. Princeton, NJ: Princeton University.

McCauley, Robert. 2020. "The Global Domain of the Dollar: Eight Questions." *Atlantic Economic Journal* 48 No. 4 (December): 421–429.

Machlup, Fritz. 1964. *International Monetary Arrangements: The Problem of Choice; Report on the Deliberations of an International Study Group of 32 Economists.* Princeton, NJ: International Finance Section, Princeton University.

Maes, Ivo. 2013. "On the Origins of the Triffin Dilemma." *European Journal of the History of Economic Thought* 20 No. 6: 1222–50.

Maes, Ivo and Ilaria Pasotti. 2016. "The European Payments Union and the Origins of Triffin's Regional Approach Towards International Monetary Integration." National Bank of Belgium Working Paper No. 301 (September).

Maes, Ivo and Ilaria Pasotti. 2021. *Robert Triffin: A Life.* New York: Oxford University Press.

Marglin, Stephen A. 1974. "What Do Bosses Do, The Origins and Functions of Hierarchy in Capitalist Production." *Review of Radical Political Economics* Vol. 6 No. 2 (July): 60–112.

Meardon, Stephen. 2014. "On Kindleberger and Hegemony: From Berlin to MIT and Back." Pages 351–374 E. Roy Weintraub (ed.), *MIT and the Transformation of American Economics.* Durham NC: Duke University Press.

Mehrling, Perry G. 1997. *The Money Interest and the Public Interest: American Monetary Thought 1920–1970.* Cambridge, MA: Harvard University Press.

Mehrling, Perry G. 1999. "The Vision of Hyman P. Minsky." *Journal of Economic Behavior and Organization* 39 No. 2: 129–158.

Mehrling, Perry. 2005. *Fischer Black and The Revolutionary Idea of Finance.* Hoboken, NJ: John Wiley and Sons.

Mehrling, Perry. 2011. *The New Lombard Street: How the Fed Became the Dealer of Last Resort.* Princeton, NJ: Princeton Press.

Mehrling, Perry. 2013. "Essential Hybridity: A Money View of FX." *Journal of Comparative Economics* 41 No. 2 (May): 355–363.

Mehrling, Perry. 2014. "MIT and Money." Pages 177–197 in E. Roy Weintraub (ed.), *MIT and the Transformation of American Economics.* Durham NC: Duke University Press.

Mehrling, Perry. 2015. "Discipline and Elasticity in the Global Swap Network." *International Journal of Political Economy* 44 No. 4 (October): 311–324.

Mehrling, Perry G. 2017. "Financialization and its Discontents." *Finance and Society* 3 No. 1: 1–10.

Miles, Louis Wardlaw. 1930. *The Tender Realist and Other Essays.* New York: Henry Holt.

Millikan, Max F. and W. W. Rostow. 1957. *A Proposal: Key to an Effective Foreign Policy.* New York: Harper and Brothers.

Milne, David. 2008. *America's Rasputin, Walt Rostow and the Vietnam War.* New York: Hill and Wang.

Minsky, Hyman. 1976. Review of *Did Monetary Forces Cause the Great Depression?* by Peter Temin. *Challenge* 19 No. 4 (Sept/Oct): 44–46.

Minsky, Hyman P. 1982. "The Financial Instability Hypothesis: Capitalist Processes and the Behavior of the Economy." Pages 13–39 in Charles P. Kindleberger and Jean-Pierre Laffargue, eds. 1982. *Financial Crises: Theory, History and Policy.* Cambridge: Cambridge University Press.

Minsky, Hyman P. 1984. "Banking and Industry Between the Two Wars: The United States." *Journal of Economic History* 13 No. 2: 235–272.

Mitchell, Wesley Clair. 1967. *Types of Economic Theory: From Mercantilism to Institutionalism.* New York: A. M. Kelley.

Modigliani, Franco. 1944. "Liquidity Preference and the Theory of Interest and Money." *Econometrica* 12 No. 1: 45–88.

Modigliani, Franco. 1963. "The Monetary Mechanism and Its Interaction with Real Phenomena." *Review of Economics and Statistics* 45 (1, pt. 2, suppl.): 79–107.

Modigliani, Franco. 1973. "International Capital Movements, Fixed Parities, and Monetary and Fiscal Policies." Pages 239–253 in Jagdish Bhagwati and

Richard Eckaus, eds. *Development and Planning, Essays in honour of Paul Rosenstein Rodan*. London: Allen and Unwin.

Modigliani, Franco and Hossein Askari. 1971. "The Reform of the International Payments System." *Essays in International Finance* no. 89. Princeton, NJ: International Finance Section, Economics Department.

Modigliani, Franco and Hossein Askari. 1973. "The International Transfer of Capital and the Propagation of Domestic Disturbances Under Alternative Payment Systems." *Banca Nazionale del Lavoro Quarterly Review* No. 107 (December): 3–19.

Modigliani, Franco and Peter Kenen. 1966. "A Suggestion for Solving the International Liquidity Problem." Banca Nazionale del Lavoro *Quarterly Review* no. 76 (March): 3–17.

Moggridge, Donald E. 2008. *Harry Johnson: A Life in Economics*. New York: Cambridge University Press.

Moulton, Harold. 1918. "Commercial Banking and Capital Formation." *Journal of Political Economy* 26 Nos. 5, 6, 7, 9: 484–508, 638–663, 705–731, 849–881.

Mundell, Robert A. 1961. "The International Disequilibrium System." *Kyklos* 14 No. 2: 154–172.

Mundell, Robert A. 1961. "A Theory of Optimum Currency Areas." *American Economic Review* 51 (November): 509–517.

Mundell, Robert A. 1963. "Capital Mobility and Stabilization Policy under Fixed and Flexible Exchange Rates." *The Canadian Journal of Economics and Political Science* 29 No. 4 (November): 475–485.

Mundell, Robert A. 1968. *International Economics*. New York: Macmillan.

Mundell, Robert A. 1969. "Toward a Better International Monetary System." *Journal of Money, Credit and Banking* 1 No. 3 Conference of University Professors (August): 625–648.

Mundell, Robert A. 1971. *Monetary Theory, Inflation, Interest, and Growth in the World Economy*. Pacific Palisades, CA: Goodyear Publishing Co.

Mundell, Robert A. 1973. "A Plan for a European Currency." Pages 143–173 in Harry G. Johnson, and Alexander K. Swoboda, eds., *Economics of Common Currencies: Proceedings of 1970 Madrid Conference on Optimum Currency Areas*. Cambridge, MA: Harvard University Press.

Mundell, Robert A. and Armand Clesse, eds. 2000. *The Euro as a Stabilizer in the International Economic System*. Norwell, MA: Kluwer Academic Publishers.

Mundell, Robert A. and Alexander K. Swoboda. 1969. *Monetary Problems of the International Economy*. Chicago, IL: University of Chicago Press.

Neilson, Daniel H. 2019. *Minsky*. Cambridge: Polity Press.

Olson, Mancur. 1982. *The Rise and Decline of Nations: Economic Growth, Stagflation and Social Rigidities*. New Haven, CT: Yale University Press.

Ostrander, F. Taylor. 2009. "My Wonderful Summer of Study in Geneva." Pages 45–52 in M. Johnson and W. J. Samuels, eds., *Documents from Glenn Johnson and F. Taylor Ostrander* (*Research in the History of Economic Thought and Methodology*, Vol. 27 Part 3), Bingley: Emerald Group Publishing Limited. https://doi.org/10.1108/S0743-41 54(2009)000027C006.

Parker, William N. 1986. *Economic History and the Modern Economist*. New York: Basil Blackwell.

Polak, Jacques J. 1957. "Monetary Analysis of Income Formation and Payments Problems." *Staff Papers* 6 (November): 1–50. Reprinted in Jacques J. Polak, 1994. *Economic Theory and Financial Policy: The Selected Essays of Jacques J. Polak.* Brookfield, VT: Edward Elgar (II:39–88).

Polak, Jacques J. 1994. *Economic Theory and Financial Policy: The Selected Essays of Jacques J. Polak.* Brookfield, VT: Edward Elgar.

Polak, Jacques J. 2002. "The Two Monetary Approaches to the Balance of Payments." Pages 19–41 in Arie Arnon and Warren Young, eds., *The Open Economy Macromodel: Past, Present, and Future.* Boston, MA: Springer. [Reprinted as pages 227–248 in Jacques J. Polak, 2005. *Economic Theory and Financial Policy, Selected Essays of Jacques J. Polak 1994–2004,* edited by James M. Boughton. Armonk, NY: M. E. Sharpe.]

Polak, Jacques J. 2005. *Economic Theory and Financial Policy, Selected Essays of Jacques J. Polak 1994–2004,* edited by James M. Boughton. Armonk, NY: M. E. Sharpe.

Rey, Helene. 2018. "Dilemma not Trilemma: The Global Financial Cycle and Monetary Policy Independence." Working Paper 21162. Cambridge MA: National Bureau of Economic Research.

Rostow, Walt W. 1952. *The Dynamics of Soviet Society.* Cambridge: Technology Press of MIT.

Rostow, Walt W. 1954. *The Prospects for Communist China.* Cambridge: Technology Press of MIT.

Rostow, Walt W. 1960. *The Stages of Economic Growth: A Non-Communist Manifesto.* Cambridge: Cambridge University Press.

Rostow, Walt W. 1978. *The World Economy: Theory and Prospect.* London: Macmillan.

Rostow, Walt W. 1981a. *The Division of Europe after World War II: 1946.* Austin, TX: University of Texas Press.

Rostow, Walt W. 1981b. *Pre-Invasion Bombing Strategy: General Eisenhower's Decision of March 25, 1944.* Austin, TX: University of Texas Press.

Rostow, Walt W. 1992. "Waging Economic Warfare from London." *Studies in Intelligence* 35 No. 5: 73–79.

Rutherford, Malcolm. 2011. *The Institutionalist Movement in American Economics, 1918–1947: Science and Social Control.* Cambridge and New York: Cambridge University Press.

Salmond, John A. 1990. *The Conscience of a Lawyer, Clifford J. Durr and American Civil Liberties, 1899–1975.* Tuscaloosa, AL: University of Alabama Press.

Schenk, Catherine R. 2020. "Central Bank Cooperation and US Dollar Liquidity: What Can We Learn from the Past?" *Per Jacobsson Lecture.* Basel: Bank for International Settlements.

Schwartz, Anna J. 1975. "Review of *The World in Depression, 1929–1939,* by Charles P. Kindleberger." *Journal of Political Economy* 83 No. 1: 231–237.

Smit, Carel Jan. 1934. "The Pre-War Gold Standard." *Proceedings of the Academy of Political Science* 16 No. 1 (April): 53–56.

Sohmen, Egon. 1957. "Demand Elasticities and the Foreign-exchange Market." *Journal of Political Economy* 65 No. 5 (October): 431–436.

Sohmen, Egon. 1961a. *Flexible Exchange Rates: Theory and Controversy.* Chicago, IL: University of Chicago Press.

Sohmen, Egon. 1961b. "Notes on Some Controversies in the Theory of International Trade: A Comment." *Economic Journal* 71 No. 282 (June): 423–426.

Sohmen, Egon. 1969. *Flexible Exchange Rates*. Revised edition. Chicago, IL: University of Chicago Press.

Solow, Robert M. 1957. "Technical Change and the Aggregate Production Function." *Review of Economics and Statistics* 39 (August): 312–320.

Sproul, Allan. 1956. "Reflections of a Central Banker." *FRBNY Quarterly Review*, 21–28. Available at www.newyorkfed.org/medialibrary/media/research/quar terly_review/75th/75article5.pdf.

Sylla, Richard. 2005. "Charles P. Kindleberger: Reluctant Yet Seminal Historian." *Atlantic Economic Journal* 33: 29–33.

Temin, Peter. 1976. *Did Monetary Forces Cause the Great Depression?* New York: Norton.

Temin, Peter. 1989. *Lessons from the Great Depression*. Cambridge, MA: MIT Press.

Temin, Peter. 2002. "The Golden Age of European Growth Reconsidered." *European Review of Economic History* 6: 3–22.

Toniolo, Gianni. 2005. *Central Bank Cooperation at the Bank for International Settlements, 1930–1973*. New York: Cambridge University Press.

Tooze, Adam. 2007. *The Wages of Destruction, The Making and Breaking of the Nazi Economy*. New York: Praeger.

Triffin, Robert. 1957. *Europe and the Money Muddle: From Bilateralism to Near-Convertibility, 1947–1956*. New Haven, CT: Yale University Press.

Triffin, Robert. 1960. *Gold and the Dollar Crisis: The Future of Convertibility*. New Haven, CT: Yale University Press.

Vane, Howard R. and Chris Mulhearn. 2006. "Interview with Robert A. Mundell." *Journal of Economic Perspectives* 20 No. 4 (Fall): 89–110.

Vilar, Pierre. 1976. *A History of Gold and Money, 1450–1920*. London: New Left Books.

Viner, Jacob. 1924. *Canada's Balance of International Indebtedness, 1900–1913*. Cambridge, MA: Harvard University Press.

Weintraub, E. Roy, ed. 2014. *MIT and the Transformation of American Economics*. Durham, NC: Duke University Press.

White, Harry D. 1933. *The French International Accounts, 1880–1913*. Cambridge, MA: Harvard University Press.

Whitham, Charlie. 2016. *Post-War Business Planners in the United States, 1939–1945: The Rise of the Corporate Moderates*. London: Bloomsbury Publishing.

Williams, John H. 1929. "The Theory of International Trade Reconsidered." *Economic Journal* 39 No. 2 (June): 195–209.

Williams, John H. 1934. "The World's Monetary Dilemma – Internal versus External Stability." *Proceedings of the Academy of Political Science* 16 No. 1 (April): 62–68. Reprinted as pages 191–198 in John H. Williams, 1944. *Postwar Monetary Plans and Other Essays*. New York: Knopf.

Williams, John H. 1937. "The Adequacy of Existing Currency Mechanisms under Varying Circumstances." *American Economic Review* 27 No. 1, Supplement (March): 151–168. Reprinted as pages 199–227 in John H. Williams, 1944. *Postwar Monetary Plans and Other Essays*. New York: Knopf.

Williams, John H. 1944. *Postwar Monetary Plans and Other Essays*. New York: Knopf.

Williams, John H. 1947. *Postwar Monetary Plans and Other Essays*. Third ed., revised and enlarged. New York: Knopf.

Williamson, Jeffrey G. 1978. "Review of *Economic Response*, by Charles P. Kindleberger." *Journal of Economic History* 38: 788–789.

Willis, Henry Parker. 1923. *The Federal Reserve System: Legislation, Organization and Operation.* New York: Ronald Press.

Willis, Henry Parker and John M. Chapman. 1934. *The Banking Situation. American Post-War Problems and Developments.* New York: Columbia University Press.

Willis, Henry Parker and John M. Chapman. 1935. *The Economics of Inflation, The Basis of Contemporary Monetary Policy.* New York: Columbia University Press.

Winks, Robin W. 1987. *Cloak and Gown: Scholars in the Secret War, 1937–1961.* New York: Morrow; 2nd ed.: 1996. New Haven, CT: Yale University Press.

Young, Allyn A. 1921a. "Commercial Policy in German, Austrian, Hungarian, and Bulgarian Treaties." Pages 61–84, Vol. V, Chap. 1, pt. 3, in *A History of the Peace Conference,* ed. by H. W. V. Temperley. London: Institute of International Affairs.

Young, Allyn A. 1921b. "The Economic Settlement." Pages 291–318 in *What Really Happened at Paris,* ed. by Edward M. House and Charles Seymour. New York: Scribner's.

Young, Allyn A. 1924. "War Debts, External and Internal." *Foreign Affairs* 2 no. 3 (March 15): 397–409.

Young, Allyn A. and H. Van V. Fay. 1927. "The International Economic Conference." *World Peace Foundation Pamphlets* 10 No. 4: 361–411.

Young, Warren and William Darity, Jr. 2004. "IS-LM-BP: An Inquest." *History of Political Economy* 36: 127–164.

Zuckerman, Solly. 1978. *From Apes to Warlords.* New York: Harper & Row.

Index

Printed in the United States
by Baker & Taylor Publisher Services